Seizing Life's
SECOND
CHANCES

Activating Your Inner
Survival Mechanisms for
Conquering Life's Fears

Paul Vigyikan
M.A., M.S.W.

Paul Vigyikan

11-7-90

STILLPOINT

STILLPOINT PUBLISHING

Books that explore the expanding frontiers
of human consciousness
For a free catalog or ordering information write

Stillpoint Publishing, Box 640, Walpole, NH 03608 USA
or call
1-800-847-4014 TOLL-FREE *(Continental US, except NH)*
1-603-756-9281 *(Foreign and NH)*

Grateful acknowledgement is made to Viking Penguin for permission to reprint the poem "Vitality" by D. H. Lawrence,
from *The Complete Poems of D. H. Lawrence,*
Vivian de Sola Pinto and Warren Roberts, editors
(New York: Penguin Books, 1971).

This book is manufactured in the United States of America.
Cover design by Bellwether Peers.
Text design by Karen Savary.

Published by Stillpoint Publishing International, Inc.,
Box 640, Meetinghouse Road, Walpole, NH 03608.

Library of Congress Catalog Card Number: 90-70421

Vigyikan, Paul
Seizing Life's Second Chances
ISBN 0-913299-66-9

This book is printed on acid-free 100% recycled paper
to save trees and preserve earth's ecology.

1 3 5 7 9 8 6 4 2

To my wife, Nancy, and to my
children, Dean and Laurie—
survivors who have made this world
a better place.

Contents

Preface

ALTHOUGH I WAS OBLIVIOUS to it at the time, the inspiration for this book came nearly thirty years ago when, as a young college junior, I found myself in the restful study of Dr. Alfred W. Price, then rector of old St. Stephen's Church in Philadelphia. He was a man large in stature and spiritual presence, and he said something to me that I will remember forever. "Paul," he said, "if you can change your thinking, you can change your position in life."

Something happened on that day in Philadelphia, something that would ultimately change the course of my life. Perhaps it was the dawning of maturity or self-awareness. Whatever it was, it turned me around forcefully and sent me in a direction the opposite from the one in which I had been heading.

I did change my thinking. *I had to.* If I had not done so, then I would surely have been a dead man . . . if not physically, then clearly in spirit. I could not have survived the continuing depletion of life energy that, for all those years before meeting Dr. Price, had been so integral to my daily regimen.

Is this a book about overcoming depression? Yes. I hope, however, it is more than that. Many books deal with depression. Is this a book about overcoming fear? Again, yes. But I hope it is more than that, too. You can readily obtain many fine books and articles dealing with fear. You can consult a therapist or attend workshops.

The reason I wrote this book was to illustrate, as clearly and simply as I know how, the *survival mechanisms* inherent in each of us, mechanisms that ultimately drive us toward our goals and dreams and do so, sometimes, despite our most valiant attempts to thwart them.

Many theories attempt to explain why people get sick and even why they remain sick. But I have found few theories that explain, in simple terms, how we can become and *stay well emotionally*. The concept of survival mechanisms represents an attempt to bridge the gap.

This book clearly defines and illustrates these survival mechanisms as I have come to observe them in my own life and in the lives of the hundreds of clients I have been privileged to know and value over the years. I believe that each of us is on a continuum of maturity, or self-worth, or whatever we choose to call it. As we go through life's journey, we move either up the scale or down. We rarely remain stationary. If we did, we would die. Those of us who move up the scale become increasingly productive and happy. Those who have the misfortune of moving down the scale become increasingly nonproductive and unhappy. The choice, I believe, is ultimately ours to make. *No one else can choose for us!* I also believe that the degree to which we discover and develop our survival mechanisms will determine the degree to which we will progress.

Many thousands of us live, work, and play in an emotional twilight zone. Neither sane nor crazy, alive nor dead, these vast throngs suffer from a mental syndrome known as borderline personality disorder.

Although the condition varies greatly in severity, the problem of borderline personality disorder is so widespread that it affects every household in the country. During my past seventeen years as a practicing psychotherapist, I have worked with and studied more than six hundred families in which at least one member suffered from this disorder. Data collected from my research has yielded conclusions that I believe are applicable to the general population.

From these findings I have formulated what I believe to be a new theory of human emotional survival. Specifically, individuals suffering from a borderline personality disorder have developed coping strategies to support (unconsciously) ten survival mechanisms that keep them alive emotionally. Although this is not a book about borderline personality disorder, it will show how the survival mechanisms I have observed in borderline cases can be used to enhance the lives of those of us who perceive ourselves as normal.

It is my belief that these ten mechanisms are present in everyone, not just persons with a borderline personality disorder. Overall, however, they remain undiscovered by the average person. This realization stirred within me the fire to teach people an effective method of recognizing, developing, and using the ten survival mechanisms already present in each of us. These mechanisms counteract negative emotions, thoughts, and actions by enhancing and sustaining four basic life elements, which I have identified as self-image, inner strength, personal control, and life meaning or life purpose. I will show you how to find not only inspiration but also courage, not merely platitudes but a road map for personal survival in an emotional ice age.

As I write these lines, I am nearing my fiftieth birthday. When I was twenty-five, I never consciously thought I would live this long. I never *consciously* thought that. But somewhere deep within me a silent voice was speaking the sounds of survival. Although I didn't know it then, that voice was stronger than I. It was stronger than my parents, stronger than my family, stronger even than the bully who rubbed my face in the mud as a child.

I will forever be thankful that I did one thing right. I listened to that voice! I listened because I somehow knew it spoke of life . . . of survival. I believe each of us possesses such a voice deep within the structure of our unconscious minds. If we heed it, this voice will lead us out of the darkest valleys imaginable. It will lead us into sunlight and such power that even our most terrifying demons will despair and leave us.

Acknowledgments

Wʀɪᴛɪɴɢ ᴀɴᴅ ᴘᴜʙʟɪsʜɪɴɢ a book is truly a lesson in humility. Without the help and cooperation of significant individuals, no book would go beyond the head of its author. Indeed, this book would still be lying in a heap of scattered notes were it not for the kindness and expertise of key persons. Although I cannot name all of them, there are those whose contributions were indispensable. First and foremost among them is my wife, Nancy, whose encouragement, patience, and undying belief in the project enabled me to see it through. Special thanks go to my publisher, Meredith Young-Sowers of Stillpoint International, for her ever-helpful suggestions and insights and for the vision that turned the dream into reality. I wish to thank Dorothy Seymour, Senior Editor at Stillpoint, whose incisive editing took the fuzzy edges off the manuscript and made it sing. Thanks also to Pat Kozma for her support and expert typing skills.

I reserve a special place of gratitude for the survivors—those individuals whose lives have been strengthened through suffering and in whom music shall forever ring.

Author's Note

THROUGHOUT THIS BOOK I have used numerous case vignettes to breathe life into the survival mechanisms theory. In each case I have made changes in order to preserve the confidentiality of any one person, couple, or family. These changes do not detract from the ultimate purpose of the case material. After nearly twenty years' experience as a professional therapist, I have found that predictable patterns of interaction and personality dynamics are part of the human condition. So if the reader thinks he or she recognizes any one case, that perception will be incorrect. What is recognized is the common pattern or dynamic that is part of the fabric of humanness.

There is no duty we so much
Underrate as the duty to be happy.
—ROBERT LOUIS STEVENSON

Introduction

I LOVE THIS BOOK ! It represents all that I am, all that I have been, and perhaps all that I will be. It is a book about emotional survival, and I wrote it to help you, the reader, to seize upon life's "second chances," to survive and prosper.

To me, emotional survival offers a far greater challenge in our present world than merely surviving physically. What makes this so, I believe, are a number of factors—many of them hidden—ranging from the increased speed of our civilization and technological advances to the threat of nuclear catastrophe.

The hurried pace of daily living combined with the computer-age "information explosion" has created such system overload as to burden the average person to the breaking point and beyond. Most of us are so stressed out with ever-mounting "things-to-do" (and diminishing time in which to do them) that our lives have become a treadmill from which there appears no escape.

For millions of Americans life has become so tension-filled that even an occasional pause to chat with a friend is fraught with anxiety because of the time limitations built into our daily schedules. Whenever we inquire casually as to someone's well-being, for example, rarely do we wait for the answer. If we waited and carefully listened to the seemingly innocuous reply, "Oh, I'm surviving," we might hear an ominous ring. Beneath the mirthful response a plea may be sounding, a yearning for something more.

My purpose is to show others a way to find that "something more." I want to help them achieve fulfillment by utilizing hidden resources they already have within them.

These resources, while hidden from most people, can be immediately discovered and made accessible. Not everyone finds them, however. Indeed, even as most search the dark caverns of their unconscious and probe endlessly into the past for answers to life's mysteries, only a small band of souls find a simple yet effective way to lead happy and prosperous lives.

Who are these people, and where do they come from? Superficially, they are no different from you and me. And they come virtually from all walks of life. What distinguishes them, however, is their zealous dedication to using those obvious and readily available resources that the rest of us tend to ignore or, at best, take for granted. They not only use those resources, they have learned the secret of gaining *conscious control* over them.

The inevitable byproduct of their efforts is a measure of personal happiness and prosperity the like of which the rest of us can only imagine. We could, if we tried, claim such happiness as our own.

In order to achieve this control, I believe it is necessary to become aware of specific, untapped mechanisms lying within easy reach. These mechanisms are already present within each of us, waiting to go to work for our benefit. I have chosen to call them the survival mechanisms.

Someone once said, "It's not what you have that counts, it's how you *use* what you have." Demonstrating how to strengthen and use these readily available survival mechanisms is what this book is all about. The degree to which we are able to achieve this end will, in my opinion, determine our life outcome.

You undoubtedly have heard the expression attributed to Yogi Berra: "If you don't know where you're going, you'll probably wind up somewhere else." I don't think even Yogi realized the profound truth of those words, but their value to dreamers and goal-setters is likely to remain for generations to come.

As a psychotherapist working with sad, lonely, and beaten people, I have learned that the vast majority of us miss the essential ingredient of personal happiness because we don't know where we're going. As a result, we wind up somewhere else. We do this simply because we have deluded ourselves into believing that giving up is easier than pressing on. We are somehow more prepared to accept the highway of defeat than the rocky trail to victory. Perhaps this human tendency is what caused the poet to lament, "The tragedy of life is not that we die, but that we die with our music still within us."

In the ensuing pages, you will read about the survival mechanisms that you and I have had within us practically from the moment we were born. Your increased awareness of them will bring a new happiness and vitality into your life.

In support of what I have to say regarding the survival mechanisms concept, I have cited several authors who I believe are on the right track when it comes to understanding the human condition. Some of their ideas, concepts, and theories have been incorporated into the body of this work. To me, they represent the refined gold of self-help authors. They have found a way of removing all the impurities of the quick-fix theories and have forged a strategy for living with substance. They understand survival and what it takes to achieve it while still remaining truly human.

I

*Are You Prospering
or Merely Surviving?*

1

Emotional Survival

Survival Mechanisms and the Four Basic Life Elements

Ten emotional survival mechanisms are, I believe, unique to the human species. They are *love, work, play, friendship, creativity, recognition, new experience, perception, spiritual belief,* and *positive mental attitude.* These survival mechanisms are, of course, instantly recognizable to virtually everyone. I have discovered, however, that although everyone may be familiar with them, few people understand the mechanisms sufficiently to be able to use them for advancing personal happiness to its fullest potential. During the course of this book, I will show exactly how these basic, everyday mechanisms are underutilized by the average person and how you can put them to work in your own life.

The mechanisms do not operate randomly. They have a definite, clear-cut purpose. Human beings are infinitely complex organisms with many needs and desires. The strength of these needs and desires dictates that, during the course of human evolution, the human system had to devise survival mechanisms to meet them.

While researching the essential components of our ten

emotional survival mechanisms, I theorized that, in addition to generating personal happiness, these mechanisms had a more specific life-sustaining task. After careful study of their function in the daily lives of more than six hundred families over seventeen years, I defined four specific elements of human organization that the survival mechanisms, individually and collectively, sustained and strengthened. I believe that these four aspects of life are absolutely vital to maintaining a person's emotional health and, ultimately, his or her survival. These four basic life elements are *self-image, inner strength, personal control,* and *life meaning.*

Further research on the ten survival mechanisms and four basic life elements revealed an unmistakable interrelationship and interdependency between them: the degree to which the survival mechanisms sustained the four basic life elements determined the level of an individual's personal happiness and prosperity. This realization drove home to me exactly how important the survival mechanisms are. I theorized that, without their *own* strength, the mechanisms would be poorly equipped to sustain, on even a minimal basis, the four basic life elements. And without the life elements operating much the way the pistons of a car do to keep it going, an individual's chances for personal happiness, prosperity, and emotional survival are practically zero.

In those cases where the survival mechanisms were particularly weak or nonexistent, the four basic life elements atrophied and in some instances died. When this occurred, the person, too, may just as well have died physically, because mentally, he or she was already dead.

One case that underscored this fact to me was that of a thirty-two-year-old mother of three young children. Despite several opportunities to return to school, she chose instead to remain at home and on welfare. When I asked her why she made this decision, I expected her to use her children as the reason. Instead, her answer was more startling: "I'd rather be with my soaps." When I asked her if watching soaps all day, *every* day, wasn't at least as boring as going back to school, she shrugged, smiled lazily, and stared off into space. Her work survival mechanism was dead. When it died, it took to the grave not one but all four of her basic life elements.

It is not my intention to imply that all welfare recipients are lazy or ineffectual: that would be absurd. Countless individuals on welfare are "locked into the system" and for years have been desperately seeking a way out. They need our encouragement and praise. The issue here, however, is one of *choice*. When we choose failure over success, despite opportunities, we choose the death of our four basic life elements. In such cases, personal happiness and prosperity are impossible.

Common Themes

While listening to clients over the years, I detected common emotional themes, both positive and negative, that kept recurring within the context of the four basic life elements. The major themes I noted were anger/forgiveness, sadness/joy, apathy/hope, loneliness/involvement, powerlessness/capability, guilt/self-acceptance, meaninglessness/purpose, suspicion/trust, despair/hope, failure/success, self-doubt/self-confidence, disorganization/order, fear/faith, and life/death.

By paying careful attention to these themes and their frequency, I determined not only the specific life element to which they were directed, but also, and more important, the relative *strength and/or weakness* of that particular basic life element. A person making negative statements about how sad or depressed he was, for example, usually did so within the context of the way he felt as a *person*. In other words, as the sadness theme kept repeating itself, over and over, I found that I could determine the individual's self-image merely by listening to the frequency of the sadness theme. Chronically sad people generally have poor self-images. In addition, these themes normally have a pattern or cycle associated with them—that is, the lower the self-image, the more frequent the sadness theme, and the more frequent the sadness theme, the lower the self-image. Self-doubters, people who are guilt-ridden, or those who feel powerless, invariably suffer from problems of both self-image and inner strength, for the same reasons: negative themes reinforced by negative statements.

Conversely, individuals who feel self-assured and have healthy levels of conscience usually have good self-images and feelings of inner strength. These people invariably have positive themes running through their lives, reinforced by positive statements. Instead of the sadness theme, for example, they express joy reinforced by statements reflecting that condition. Instead of powerlessness, they express the theme of capability.

Since the most frequently recurring themes in my clients' lives seemed to be negative rather than positive, and since I could readily observe the results of this in the relative strength and/or weakness of their four basic life elements, I began to question exactly what it was that *sustained* them in their daily struggle for survival.

What, for example, enabled them to get up in the morning when all they had to greet the new day was apathy and despair? How could they perform even the most rudimentary of tasks—finding their shoes, cooking dinner—when feelings of powerlessness and failure haunted them? How could they hold down a job or even begin to cope with the demands of a family when disorganization had been the theme of their lives? In other words, what was it that *sustained* their four basic life elements? What was it that enabled them to find even minimal happiness?

Needless to say, with so many negatives occurring—sometimes in rapid succession and in virtually endless combinations—one has to question how even the best among us could survive, let alone find happiness. For, despite seemingly insurmountable odds, these individuals, with bloodied but unbowed heads, plodded forward. I decided that, in order for them to survive on even an elementary basis, these people had some kind of *internal support system* to keep them from literally falling apart. I further concluded that, considering the enormity and compounding nature of their life condition, such a support system would have to be very basic and fundamental in meeting the emotional needs of the individual. Anything less would be destined to fail.

What actually constituted that support system, I found, were the ten emotional survival mechanisms. For, although my clients' lives displayed recurring negative themes *most* of the time and at concentrated levels, they were able to survive and at times even prosper, despite dehumanizing problems.

They achieved this herculean task, I believe, by spontaneously calling upon one or several of the survival mechanisms to eliminate, or reduce, the negative themes sufficiently to permit, at least on a minimal basis, survival of the four basic life elements. Once they attained this objective, they could move ahead and be reasonably happy. It was almost as if the survival mechanisms were white blood cells attacking the cancer of the negative themes in order to defend the body.

If these ten survival mechanisms are present in the lives of my clients, they must also be present in the life of the average person. Indeed, practically all of us have negative themes running through our lives at least some of the time. Fortunately, these negative themes are rarely equal to those suffered by the victims of emotional or mental disturbance.

If the survival mechanisms can sustain people who otherwise surely would perish and even keep them reasonably happy, I wondered, what, then, could they achieve for those of us who may be fairly normal? Moreover, what might they achieve for us if, instead of passively awaiting their spontaneous assistance, we would *consciously* call upon them to enhance our lives? With these questions, I began to acquire not only respect for the survival mechanisms but awe at their potential and real power in sustaining human life, sometimes in the midst of debilitating circumstances.

Not in all cases did my clients survive. In fact, I could

cite many cases in which people died not only emotionally but sometimes physically. Truly, if these people had one major character flaw, it was their gross inability to *sustain* themselves over any given length of time. Many of them had been so ravaged by life circumstances and chronic anxiety that they frequently reminded me of miniature wind-up toys.

Into the office they would come, all hurried, out of breath, fearful, defensive, and most of all weakened by both inner and outer forces over which they seemed to have little control. They came asking me to pick them up, prop them up, wind them up, and then send them on their way to nowhere. Soon however, their little internal springs would either weaken or break, and the entire mechanism would grind to a stop.

Considering the difficulties inherent in day-to-day survival, it is understandable that homo sapiens would need and subsequently evolve the kind of internal support system provided by the ten survival mechanisms. In short, we have learned the art of *adaptation*. I believe that each of us needs the ten survival mechanisms in order to change into positive themes the negative ones running constantly through our lives. The more negative themes we have, the weaker our four basic life elements will be. The weaker the basic life elements, the more we need the survival mechanisms to buttress them. As we become more adept at changing the negative themes into positive ones, we are more effective at nurturing and sustaining the four basic life elements—our source of personal happiness and prosperity.

Freud and the Mechanisms of Defense

Sigmund Freud's brilliance lay in his discovery of what, until then, had been a great unknown entity: the unconscious mind. He pointed out that much of what motivated our conscious waking hours lay in that great reservoir of information, memories, fantasies, and dreams he called the unconscious. Freud proved to his skeptics that there was an unconscious mind by analyzing dreams, slips of the tongue and pen, and actions people took that, if consciously thought out, they would not take. He termed this technique *psychoanalysis.*[1]

Almost as well known as Freud's discovery of the unconscious mind are his *mechanisms of defense,* a concept further developed by his daughter Anna.[2] Both Sigmund and Anna believed the ego, or the self, to be a vulnerable psychic entity requiring protection from anxieties generated from within as well as outside the person. In order to protect itself, they theorized, the ego developed defense mechanisms that operated *unconsciously* to ward off any perceived threat or danger. If the particular defense mechanism operated properly, the ego felt secure. In other words, the person's anxiety level lowered. If the defense mechanism failed to work or malfunctioned in some way, anxiety rose correspondingly. The Freuds thus theorized that the primary purpose of ego defense mechanisms was to keep a person's anxiety at a tolerable level.

Although Sigmund's and Anna's basic premise is sound, it implies that, in order for the self to survive, it must be on the *defensive;* thus the phrase *ego defense mechanisms.* But the Freuds also theorized that while such defense mechanisms may protect the self, they may also sustain a negative behavior and/or thought process that is causing the person great unhappiness: for example, the alcoholic may deny he has a drinking problem and project blame onto his spouse or employer. Denial and projection are key defense mechanisms as defined by the Freuds. So although the person's anxiety level may be lowered by the use of these defenses, he remains essentially unhappy because his life doesn't change. He remains an alcoholic. His relationship with his spouse or employer continues along a negative path.

While defense mechanisms may aid the self to reduce anxiety, they are *negative* in that they serve to produce a defensive posture within the person. A football team that is constantly on the defense will never win a game simply because it has no *offense*. According to Freudian theory, we have evolved carefully-developed defenses but have failed to develop the same kind of offenses, or *positive* life forces, that would propel us *forward* instead of merely keeping us at the status quo—or worse, sending us backward.

Freud neglected to develop a theory about those survival mechanisms that are positive and, as such, may be viewed as *offensive* rather than defensive in nature. Unlike Freud's defense mechanisms, which are by definition unconscious, these "offense mechanisms" are totally *conscious*. This is an important distinction, because it means we have *control* over what happens to us. Indeed, things don't happen *to* us. We *make* them happen! For better or worse, we *do* control our destinies. We are the captains of our souls. The degree to which we can believe this will determine not only our capacity for survival but also how far we can expect to go in life. To merely survive is not enough. Wild animals can do that. But to survive and *prosper* . . . that should be our ultimate goal.

One client said to me recently, "I just want to make it through the night." "What then?" I asked. He hesitated for a moment and then replied, "Make it through another night, I guess." That's not prospering. That's not happiness. That's surviving. Each of us deserves more out of life than merely surviving on a day-to-day basis. To achieve more we must have the courage to go on the offense. We must learn not only to protect ourselves from real or perceived dangers but also to go after whatever in life is truly meaningful to us. Thus, as we learn to hone and develop our survival mechanisms, they become *offense mechanisms* that enable us to survive *and* prosper. Most of all, we learn how to achieve genuine happiness.

The Offense Mechanisms Way of Thinking

The Freuds discovered a specified number of defense mechanisms and gave them precise names, such as denial, projection, sublimation, introjection, repression, and regression.[3] They clearly and carefully described how each of the defenses worked and the conditions under which they went into action. Each analyst would attempt to help his or her patient gain insight into what the patient's conflicts were (that is, to make the unconscious conscious) in the hope of dislodging and eradicating them. Sometimes an analyst's technique worked and sometimes it didn't. Frequently, patients would acquire significant insight, but their behavior remained unchanged. Patients might understand *why* they had a problem but remain quite unhappy.

I believe that merely knowing *why* a problem exists is not enough to correct it. *Action* must be taken. In addition, the person experiencing the problem must assume responsibility for the action. To leave this to someone else merely perpetuates the problem and frequently makes it worse. Thus, in order to do something, we must take an *offensive posture* toward whatever it is that troubles us. We must develop *offense mechanisms*. This posture represents more than merely becoming a more assertive person. It represents, instead, a change in thinking and attitude.

A number of years ago a very handsome young man was sitting in my office. He had experienced several upsetting events, including difficulties in both his marriage and job. I listened quietly as he poured out his story. Suddenly, and with great urgency in his voice, he exclaimed, "Aren't you going to *do* something?" "What would you have me do?" I responded. "I don't know, but *do something!*" he shouted back. I thought, "What a strange request . . . for *me* to do something, when it is *you* who is experiencing the problem."

Unfortunately, most of us tend to think the way this young man had been thinking. We go along in life never tending to the important issues until they become urgent. Then we tend to them. As we do so, however, other important issues have also become *urgent*. We are then forced to deal with them. This pattern keeps repeating itself so that most of us never do address the really important issues, because by the time we get to them others have also become urgent.

How does this negative pattern get set into motion? I believe it happens as a result of our not having offense mechanisms in place to prevent urgent situations from arising. Thus, when we fail to act, we are acted upon. When we fail to decide, others decide for us. When we are forever on the defense, we have neither time nor energy for offense. The young man in this example wanted *me* to act for him. He wanted *me* to decide for him. He was on the defense, not the offense. He maintained a negative rather than a positive mental posture.

Most of us have been programmed to think negatively. My mother used to have a favorite saying that went something like this: "Paul, it is always better to be afraid than to become suddenly frightened." Think about that statement for a moment. It had far more impact when she said it in her native Hungarian, but even the English translation is startling! This was clear *defensive* programming at its best . . . or worst.

Offensive thinking requires eradicating defensive thought patterns. To do this involves a conscious, consistent, and unyielding effort. As we acquire skill at breaking or unlearning negative, defensive thought patterns and replacing them with positive, offensive ones, the process becomes easier and easier. The key is to get started. Remember, "Beginning is half done."

What It Takes to Be a Survivor

Many years ago I spoke with a brilliant first violinist of a major symphony orchestra. We were both attending the same university. I was taking course work in graduate school while he was working toward an undergraduate degree in economics. I was curious as to why he would be studying economics when he already had his degree in fine arts from a leading conservatory and a chair with one of the top five orchestras in the world.

When I inquired about this, he merely smiled, waved the fingers of his left hand, and said, "What if something happens to one of these?" I have often thought of that man and what he said. It was only many years later that I truly *heard* what he meant! He wasn't about to sit around worrying about what might happen to his fingers and career if some tragic accident should befall him. Instead, he assumed an offensive posture. He determined that he would not only survive in the event of tragedy, he would also *prosper.* I'm certain he wasn't consciously thinking about using his survival mechanisms, but use them he did, in a conscious decision. He was an offensive thinker and doer. A survivor!

Each of us has, already within us, survival mechanisms ready and willing to work for our benefit. We need only become aware of them and develop them to their full potential. I view these mechanisms much in the same light as did the Freuds with their mechanisms of defense, but while their mechanisms were more directed toward warding off anxiety, mine are designed more to enhance the self . . . to fulfill human potential rather than merely maintaining the status quo.

What makes the survival mechanisms theory unique is its accessibility to each of us . . . *continuously.* We don't have to wade through our unconscious to find them. We have conscious control over them. All we need to do is become aware of which survival mechanisms need strengthening and then go directly to their assistance. As these mechanisms are enhanced, they in turn strengthen the four basic life elements over which they exert influence.

How Viktor Frankl Used Creativity to Survive

In his beautifully written book, *Man's Search for Meaning,* the Viennese psychiatrist Viktor Frankl describes his ordeal in the Nazi death camps of Auschwitz and Dachau.[4]

He explains how he and a handful of compatriots were able to survive and *prosper* under horrendous conditions while others perished. Frankl attributes his survival to the fact that he and his co-inmates found *meaning* to their lives while those who died gave up. He cites various factors that enable one to find meaning in life, such as a loved one waiting back home, a job to get back to, or a manuscript needing publication.

According to Frankl, whatever the person in a death camp chose as his or her objective was, in fact, a "will to meaning"—a survival mechanism at work. With the exception of one sister, Frankl's entire family was murdered by the Nazis. He had only one meaningful thing left in his life: a manuscript about his clinical ideas that he wished to have published. After the Nazis seized and destroyed his manuscript, he labored endlessly to reconstruct its contents on scraps of paper for publication when he was liberated.[5] His creativity survival mechanism was at work!

How We Can Consciously Control Our Destinies

I am convinced, beyond doubt, that within each of us there exist survival mechanisms that, when consciously activated, will come forward enabling us to cope successfully with any situation life may thrust in our direction. I believe there is a corresponding survival mechanism for every defense mechanism . . . for every negative a positive. The defense mechanisms, however, are naturally occurring, unconscious phenomena. Not so with the survival mechanisms. We must work consciously at developing and strengthening them. Once we have done so, they will perform for us as smoothly, effortlessly, and automatically as any of our defense mechanisms.

The survival mechanisms are universal, even though we may never have thought of them as survival mechanisms. Each of them is present in us and has been there right along. Moreover, each of them can be used, consciously, to enhance our lives and fortunes.

A tragic price is paid by those who live life solely from a defensive posture. One of every two marriages ends in divorce. Parents and children, instead of being partners, are estranged from each other. Huge chunks of the work force would prefer doing something other than what they're doing. Although we are a nation of more than 250 million people, legions of us are plagued by loneliness. And in the richest land on earth, we have grinding poverty. Even among those of us fortunate enough to earn a regular paycheck, many struggle just to keep our heads above the financial waterline.

So what's wrong? I believe much of the answer lies in our attitude toward life and ourselves. The great psychiatrist, Karl Menninger, said, "Attitudes are more important than facts."[6] I believe that. I recently quoted Dr. Menninger's statement to a young woman in her early thirties. She smiled patronizingly and went on to tell me how much she disliked herself. She couldn't make the connection between her low self-image and the fact that her life was not working. Instead, she hung on, with dogged determination, to her old negative, defensive outlook. She had paid a great price for her misery and wasn't about to give it up!

Attitude *is* more important than fact. If you doubt that, just spend fifteen minutes in the back wards of a state mental hospital. A brief tour there will tell you more quickly and eloquently than I ever could exactly how important a role attitude plays in our lives and fortunes. So I ask you now to believe that you *can* change, that you will discover the survival mechanisms that are within you.

As you discover these survival mechanisms and begin to strengthen them, applying them to your life on a daily basis, you will find yourself becoming a more positive and successful person. You will find yourself creating your own destiny.

NOTES

1. Sigmund Freud, *A General Introduction to Psychoanalysis* (New York: Washington Square Press, 1935).

2. Anna Freud, *The Ego and the Mechanisms of Defense* (New York: International Universities Press, 1966).

3. *Ibid.*, pp. 42-53.

4. Viktor E. Frankl, *Man's Search for Meaning* (Boston: Beacon Press, 1962).

5. *Ibid.*, p. 106.

6. Robert Schuller, *The Be-Happy Attitudes* (Waco: Word Books, 1985), p. 13.

2

The Four Basic Life Elements

WHAT IS THE PURPOSE of the emotional survival mechanisms? Friendship is a survival mechanism, but what does friendship do to *cause* survival? Why is love so important? So-called "lower forms" of life don't seem to need love to the same degree that humans do. What is love doing for us that it doesn't need to do for chimpanzees?

Gradually, the answer came in work with my clients. Common, repetitive themes echo from client to client until they seem to form a gigantic chorus singing, in unison, the same melody, about loneliness and defeat, about sadness and meaninglessness. The most frequently recurring themes are anger, mistrust, failure, self-doubt, fear, powerlessness, depression, and despair. Ultimately, I came to hear the themes not as separate and distinct, but rather as part of a larger chorus of human suffering and need.

When I began to listen and hear on a deeper level, it was like observing a starving person begging for food or a blind man who had lost his way. Something was missing from the lives of these people. Some great abyss had opened up between them and their quest for a normal life.

The question of what it was kept burning inside of me.

Why, I wondered, were these people so rage-filled? So needy? So defeated? Why the self-doubt and sense of failure? What did these people hunger for? Why were they emotionally starving to death? Why did they choose to live in an emotional twilight zone?

Even when, in some cases, these people received the best psychological and psychiatric help, they seemed destined to perish. They were somehow too weak to absorb the life-saving nourishment. They were like starvation victims: desperately in need, but too far gone for help. Some, however, despite enormous odds, were helped. They were the survivors. What made the difference?

The difference seemed to lie in the degree to which they were able to cope and adapt to whatever life dished out. And that coping capacity appeared to be rooted in four specific aspects of their consciousness, or, as I have come to call them, the four basic life elements. As you recall, these are self-image, inner strength, personal control, and life meaning.

These four basic elements are not static, motionless structures to be observed in a vacuum. Rather, they are dynamic forces within each of us. Some people have developed them to a high level, while others have neglected them. Some of us may have one or two elements well-developed, but the others have atrophied or are near death.

I believe that the extent to which our four basic life elements are developed will determine the degree of our personal happiness in this life. For most of us, our central concern is *to be happy*. Unfortunately, we often forget that happiness is a byproduct of they way we live our lives rather than a goal in itself.

Basic Life Element #1: Self-Image

The self-image of an individual determines his or her success in life. No matter who we are, what we do, or where we've been, our self-image is there. It's our constant companion. If our self-image is poor, we will think, say, and do the things that reinforce that negative quality. If a man desires a better job and his self-image is poor, for example, he will tend to talk himself out of the better job in order to bring his vocation into conformity with his self-image. He will *do* the things that correspond to what he says about himself. His dilemma then becomes a cyclical self-fulfilling prophesy.

Exactly what is the self-image? The self-image, essentially, is who and what we *really* are, after all the outside trappings have been stripped away. It is the sum total of all our hopes, dreams, beliefs, and values tied up in a human package that inside our heads is labeled "ME." It is, in essence, *how we see ourselves* as a result of the lifetime recording of the video camera we call our brains.

The self-image, however, is really *more* than this. It is more of a *dynamic force* than a thing. When we possess a positive self-image, we have the profound satisfaction of knowing who we are. We know that we know. We can accept and love ourselves easily and unconditionally. We can free ourselves from the bondage of fear and self-doubt. We have the courage to stay up when we honestly believe it would be easier to be down. A positive self-image is the silent voice inside us that whispers, "I am somebody!" even when stones are being thrown at us.

Unfortunately, most people, by the time they reach mid-adolescence, have a negative self-image. Some researchers believe that from sixty to sixty-five percent of the people struggle with some kind of self-image problem at some point in their lives.

I believe that the self-image is connected directly to the concept of *perception*, one of the survival mechanisms discussed in this book. Self-perception, or the way we see ourselves, is frequently tied to the way we think we're being perceived by others. It can perhaps best be illustrated by the little verse, "I'm not who I think I am; I'm not who you think I am; I am who I think you think I am."

To illustrate how perception, especially as it relates to self-image, plays a crucial role in their lives, I frequently ask my clients to engage in a form of mental imagery. I turn out the lights in my office and pull the blinds (please don't get any erroneous ideas!). I then ask if the room is dark or light. If they say, "It is dark," as they usually do, I simply turn on the light and say, "No, it is light." If they say, "It is light" (a response that, of course, contradicts reality), I simply leave the light off.

Our perception of reality and of ourselves is determined by *the one who controls the switch*. If we remain at the controls of our minds, our reality, along with our self-image, will be whatever we choose. Our fears, guilt, self-doubt, and anger (though perhaps never totally eliminated) can, as with the darkness, certainly be overcome.

One can scarcely pick up a self-help book without finding some reference to the concept of self-image or self-esteem. Despite its popularity and the variety of definitions given to it, the self-image remains an elusive entity.

As mentioned earlier, the self-image is basically the psychological and emotional "core" or nucleus of the way we see ourselves. So, it is closely related to and part of the ego, or self—a concept I will develop more fully later on.

The terms "low self-image" and "high self-image" usually describe the manner in which a person views or perceives himself or herself within the broader context of sociocultural, religious, political, economic, and other environmental circumstances. Frequently, the terms are used erroneously. When, for example, we hear people described in such phrases as, "He's got a lot of ego" (the person is self-centered) or "She's got a lot of brass" (she's got "nerve"), we tend to think that the person being referred to is somehow "gutsy," daring, brave, or courageous. We believe that person must have high self-esteem. Actually, however, people with "brass" or "ego" quite frequently *do not* possess the qualities of ego strength to which I refer here. In fact, a person described as having "brass" or lots of "ego" is likely to be someone seriously *lacking* those characteristics!

This point was recently demonstrated to me vividly when an irate client called my secretary complaining bitterly about trying in vain to arrange an appointment. The secretary calmly tried to explain that we were heavily booked and that an appointment would be granted as soon as possible. After an additional tirade of words and vindictive remarks, the man hung up abruptly. The secretary told me that the man would probably call back and ask to speak directly with me, warning me to expect an earful!

Later that day he did call back, and I awaited the barrage of angry words. Predictably, they never did materialize. In fact, the man was so meek, so self-effacing, that I wondered if he was the same person who, just two hours earlier, had terrorized the hapless secretary. Instead of the lion, he was more "the mouse who roared."

Each of us, at one time or another, has encountered someone like this caller. Such people have a loud bark but very little bite. They frequently come across as "brassy" and projecting a lot of "ego." In truth, it's usually just the opposite. Their egos or self-images are generally weak and vulnerable, somewhat like Smaug's underbelly in Tolkien's classic, *The Hobbit*. When confronted with reality, these people will often crumble. Instead of courage, what we frequently see is cowardice masked by false bravado.

A person with a positive, solid self-image needs put forth no false front. Who he or she is speaks for itself. Instead of loud phoniness, what usually comes across is a quiet, firm, consistent resolve that, as adapted from in the immortal words of Fritz Perls, says:

> I am I,
> And you are you,
> I'm not in this world
> to live up to your
> expectations.
> And you're not in this world to
> live up to mine.
> I is I,
> And you is you.
> Amen[1]

Basic Life Element #2: Inner Strength

> Look well into thyself; there is a
> source of strength which will
> always spring up if thou will
> always look there;
> —*Marcus Aurelius*

Several years ago, Michael Korda wrote a book on power focusing on setting up the outward trappings of power, or on "one-upmanship" in business and social settings.[2] Robert Ringer's bestseller, *Winning Through Intimidation*,[3] also focuses on strategic maneuvering that places one person in a position of power or planned control over another.

The kind of power I deal with here refers more to an inner bastion of courage or *nerve* that enables a person to move forward, sometimes in the face of overwhelming opposition or adversity. That is the reason I call this second basic life element inner strength rather than personal power.

What It Means to be Mentally Tough

Inner strength can be defined as a form of mental toughness with which the individual faces life's challenges. It represents a mind-set that says: "I'm going to keep on keeping on . . . no matter what!" Inner strength is the *power of will.*

Many of my clients have demonstrated mental toughness, sometimes in the most extreme circumstances. Bill, for example, came from a broken home and had lived to see his two older brothers shot and killed—one in a botched hold-up attempt, the other in a domestic triangle. Bill's father had served time in a state prison for arson, and his mother, a prostitute, deserted the family when he was only twelve years old.

By the time Bill reached his sixteenth birthday, he had already been in two residential treatment centers for punching his teacher, truancy, and stealing. He was an angry, defiant youngster who felt deceived by the establishment. He wasn't about to cooperate with anyone who wanted him to change his ways.

Bill somehow managed to join the armed forces. After completing basic training, he began developing severe migraine headaches so debilitating that he three times attempted suicide. The suicide attempts landed Bill in two psychiatric hospitals, where he was diagnosed schizophrenic and a danger to himself and others. Following his discharge from psychiatric care, Bill lived for several months in a convalescent home. Eventually, he made it back home, miraculously still in one piece.

When he was twenty-five Bill met an attractive young woman whom, after a brief courtship, he married. About six months into the marriage, his new bride discovered she had terminal cancer. Within a year she was dead.

Clearly, any of these circumstances would have devastated the strongest among us. Bill, however, just kept right on going. He was like some kind of magical machine: impervious to the onslaught of the misfortune that seemed endlessly to haunt him.

At the age of thirty-eight, a time when most of us have fewer aspirations to change our way of life, Bill decided to return to school. He had several years earlier received his high school equivalency diploma and had been earning his living as a welder. Now he felt he could do more. He believed that the spears and arrows fate had thrust into him had some purpose . . . some *meaning* that, until now, had remained hidden.

Bill was accepted into a local community college, where he eventually earned his associate's degree. He then went on to earn his bachelor's degree in psychology. Because of his academic success and natural rapport with delinquent youth, Bill obtained a scholarship to graduate school, where he earned a master's degree in social work. Today, just shy of his fiftieth birthday, Bill is a supervisor in a youth detention facility, a survivor teaching others to survive. He is a man who, in the words of Robert Schuller, "turned his scars into stars."[4] He has that *inner strength,* that "mental toughness" that separates winners from los-ers . . . the survivors from those who give up.

Recently I asked Bill what got him through the bat-tlefield his life had been. He thought for a moment and then, smiling, said, "I never really saw the world as a bad place . . . only a place where bad things sometimes hap-pen." His answer hit me like a rock. *Perception*, I thought. It's not *what* we see that matters, it's *how* we see it.

Bill's ability to perceive his circumstances positively, optimistically, was a matter of choice. Who could have faulted him if he had remained angry and vengeful? The survival mechanism of perception, which he chose *con-sciously*, strengthened him emotionally. The way he per-ceived life gave him victory when others would have crumbled in defeat. It gave him courage when self-doubt and fear were about to overtake him.

Having inner strength means having a "hang-in-there" mentality. It means we persevere when it would be easier to give up and give in. We have only to look around us to see this quality in action: the mother who loses her only child to cancer but can smile through her mind-numbing grief; the marriage that is on the brink of divorce, but the partners won't quit; the office manager who is about to kill himself but finds his children give him a reason to live; the teenager ostracized by his peers for not trying crack who finds the courage to seek new friend-ships.

This is the stuff of which inner strength is made. It's an indefinable quality that shouts: "Mind over matter . . . positive over negative . . . victory over defeat!"

William Glasser, in his book, *Positive Addiction*,[5] dif-ferentiates between positive and negative addiction. He points out that when we become positively addicted to anything, such as running or meditating, we gain mental strength. Conversely, whenever we become negatively ad-dicted, such as to gambling or alcohol, we lose strength to our addiction.

This concept is relevant to the basic life element I call inner strength. In essence, it says that we need to develop

and enhance any positive activity and discourage or eliminate any negative activity. When we do this, we make
available to ourselves the vast reservoir of energy already
within us and, more important, we free our brains to be
the creative instruments they were designed to be.

Basic Life Element #3: Personal Control

There are many Bills in this world. Some of them are
eleven years old, some of them seventy-five. Unlike Bill,
what most have in common is a lack of *personal control*
over their own destinies. This deficiency extends beyond
the boundaries of the normal, everyday routines of work,
marriage, social life, and family relationships. It extends
to the subtle yet more powerful dimensions of thoughts,
feelings, hopes, and dreams.

What Personal Control is Not

Whenever we hear the word "control," we tend to
visualize tight, rigid, unyielding actions or constraints we
place on others. Or we may suspect the reverse—rigid and
unyielding actions directed *toward us* by some person, institution, or force.

This is *not* the type of control to which I refer here.
Personal control, as I use the term, refers to the act of
taking charge of our lives in a manner that reflects our
true human potential.

Some of the most glaring human suffering occurs
when a person feels "out of control." Depression, loneliness, anger, loss, fear, powerlessness, poverty, unabating
frustration—all are symptoms of loss of control. Whenever
these demons take charge of our lives, we are running from
life and the fulfillment of our human potential.

As I noted earlier, all of the four basic life elements
are closely interconnected and mutually interdependent.
Thus personal control is closely aligned with self-image.
If our self-image is poor, our personal control is also likely

to suffer. That is because a low self-image will dictate that our choices in life be inadequate to meet even our most basic needs. When we choose improperly, we invariably lose control, and our true human potential is compromised.

Every day I see this sad but consistent phenomenon occurring in the lives of those undergoing psychotherapy. The beaten, bedraggled faces march by in a never-ending parade of human misery. They remind one of holocaust victims walking the final steps to the gas chambers.

This is the place where dreams end . . . where the final battle is fought. Here, only the memories of broken promises, lost opportunities, interrupted projects, and shattered ideals remain. All else is gone.

Why? Why do capable, good, kind, generous people come to such an ignominious end? The answer, of course, is multidimensional. I believe that these souls have never truly learned how to utilize the ten survival mechanisms. This failure has in turn resulted in the gradual atrophy and death of the four basic life elements. Fortunately, there are those who have, either by conscious decision or unconsciously, learned the secret of survival. Many have never read a book, much less *this* book. They have, however, almost instinctively, realized what their emotional needs are and developed the corresponding survival mechanisms to meet them.

Losers have lost personal control. Winners have found it. Regrettably, losers could be winners if they would choose success over failure. Personal choice is an option available to each of us. We tend, however, to deny this if we have a poor self-image. If we refuse to see ourselves as successful, we surely will not reach out and accept any victory.

Four major factors affect our ability to control our lives and destinies: our feelings, our thoughts, our words, and our actions. *At the deepest level, everything begins with a feeling. Feelings lead to thoughts. Thoughts lead to words. Words lead to actions. Actions become habits, and habits form a way of life.*

Feelings

Sadness, joy, guilt, anger, passion, depression, compassion, elation, love, fear—all represent parts of the spectrum of our feelings. Are these feelings merely random, or is there some rational explanation for them? There is an explanation, but it is not always *rational.*

Our feelings come from the deepest level of our mental apparatus. And try as we may, we cannot always consciously control our deepest passions, fears, and disappointments, as evidenced in the following examples.

After being passed by as the vice-presidential running mate to Michael Dukakis, the Reverend Jesse Jackson glared into the television cameras and stated to reporters that he was "not angry," that he was "too controlled" to be angry. And in the frantic aftermath of the Reagan assassination attempt, a bewildered Alexander Haig kept protesting, "I'm in charge, I'm in charge!"

In moments of stress—when our survival is threatened—our emotions, more often than our thoughts, take command over us. This happens because our primitive, instinctual survival system is activated for our defense. Conversely, this survival system is also activated when we feel pleasurable sensations, as in love-making or artistic expression.

We must, however, gain control over our feeling/emotional selves through our thinking selves. Indeed, if we are to achieve real happiness, we must learn the value of one of our greatest assets: our thoughts.

Thoughts

Our thoughts essentially represent who we are, so we are literally a product of our thoughts. Out-of-control thoughts mean we, too, are out of control. Allowing other people, circumstances, or events to influence our thoughts against our better judgment means we give up personal control to those people and circumstances.

Thoughts should be regarded with the same value as

the greatest treasure. The Bible states, "As a man thinketh in his heart, so is he." If we are to preserve one of our greatest assets, *our thoughts*, we must take that statement literally.

Words

What we say is what we get. Someone once said, "We are hung by the tongue." It is remarkable how mere words, used sometimes unthinkingly, can exert such a powerful command over us.

Recently, a middle-aged man came to me for help on a way to save his crumbling marriage. As many clients do, he was searching frantically for a "quick-fix" solution to a long-standing problem. His wife, who had accompanied him to the session, sat next to him with a look of utter disgust. It was obvious that she didn't want to be there. Soon, the three of us were able to agree on a diagnosis of "poor communication" as a central problem in the marriage.

It was only toward the end of the session, however, that a far more important issue emerged. I had noticed earlier that this man had a rather disturbing habit of tacking the expression "I guess" onto the end of practically every sentence. He would say: "Our marriage was good at one time . . . I guess;" or, "I have a pretty good job . . . I guess;" or, "Our kids don't give us much of a problem . . . I guess." After a while it became exasperating for me to keep hearing that tentative, doubt-filled, noncommittal statement. He was "second-guessing" his entire life!

His wife sat there, fuming and staring in the opposite direction. I could readily see why his marriage was in trouble. Between his tentativeness, his wife's frustration, and their mutual communication problems, it was miraculous the marriage had endured at all!

"Tom," I told him, "every time you tack on 'I guess' at the end of a statement, you automatically negate its value." "Oh," he said, dismissing my observation, "that's just a habit. I've always done that, ever since I was a kid."

Indeed he had! And the results of that habit showed up in virtually every aspect of his life, not just his marriage.

Actions

Actions or deeds also carry with them great emotional weight. Goethe wisely stated, "Only *begin* and then the mind grows heated; only *begin* and the task will be completed." When we do something, when we begin a project, soon we find ourselves committed to the task. We should therefore pay great heed to those actions we undertake.

Habitual actions soon lead to habitual thoughts ... which tend to reinforce those actions. The actions in turn reinforce the thoughts, thus leading to a *pattern of living*—positive or negative, depending on the original thoughts.

Remember, first comes the feeling, then the thought, then the words, then the action. We can, if we truly decide to, control all four. Why is control so important? Because if we don't control our circumstances, *they* will control us.

Basic Life Element #4: Life Meaning

What does it mean to be happy in this life? Strengthening and sustaining the four basic life elements through the survival mechanisms we all have obtains for us that personal happiness after which we all strive.

Viktor Frankl and others concluded that meaning in life is the central factor in achieving personal happiness. A number of studies dealing with suicidal patients have proved that people will go so far as to choose death over life when meaning is absent from their existence.

Just recently a ten-year-old boy sitting in my office threatened to kill himself because life held no meaning for him. When I asked him to explain, he replied, "My mother doesn't want me, I don't want to live with my father, and I don't want to be any place else."

For the average ten-year-old, options and the breadth

of one's thinking are, of course, quite limited. This youngster had run out of possibilities for achieving personal happiness and meaning. I asked him if he could think of *anything* else that might bring him happiness. He thought for a moment and then, as a smile started to form on his face, he said, "A puppy!" "What would you do with a puppy?" I asked. "Take care of it. I'd really take care of it and feed it and take it for walks and love it!" The words came out in a joyous staccato. His gloom had lifted, at least momentarily, and life had come back into his voice. Just the thought of his very own puppy had brought a sense of meaning back into his young life. At least for now, he would choose life over death.

In the introduction to this book, I emphasized the importance of the survival mechanisms as a means of strengthening the four basic life elements. For many people, strengthening the element of life meaning is most critical.

Viktor Frankl emphasizes that most forms of therapy stress "meaning through therapy," whereas he instead places importance on "therapy through meaning." Frankl's distinction is important. People go to therapists for one major reason: *to become happier.* The degree to which they find happiness is connected directly with the degree to which they find personal meaning in their lives. That meaning can come in any number of ways, from a happier marriage to a better, more meaningful job or, in some cases, even a warm puppy.

Personal happiness, on a deeper level, is always correlated with a sense of meaning or life purpose. Sometimes meaning is revealed on a grand scale, such as becoming a missionary in a far-off land. Sometimes it manifests itself in seemingly insignificant ways, as when we run an errand for a friend. Meaning may come from a planned and purposeful venture or a more spontaneous, even jolting confrontation. Whatever the case, we all seem to need meaning in our lives, even when we are forced to derive it from tragedy.

Neither I nor any of us who saw the event will ever forget the morning of January 28, 1986, when the *Chal-*

lenger space shuttle exploded in the cold blue sky over the Atlantic Ocean. My nerves froze as my mind tried to block out the awful reality of the television pictures that refused to lie.

Those of us seeing the *Challenger* disintegrate before our very eyes felt some part of ourselves lost out there with the seven astronauts. For weeks after the disaster I read every word of newspaper coverage, listened to and watched every radio and television news broadcast. I couldn't get the image of that fireball out of my mind . . . *nor did I want to.*

My preoccupation with the *Challenger* disaster even now, I realize, is not unique. As I write these lines, a memorial plaque is being unveiled at Arlington National Cemetery honoring the five men and two women who paid the ultimate price.

We choose to pay tribute to our heroes, to those who sacrifice their all. In cases of great tragedy, such as the *Challenger* disaster, our minds won't allow us to forget. We have to keep playing the pictures over and over again in our minds in order to master our own trauma.

Why Our Minds Won't Let Us Forget

There is another reason we don't forget "unforgettable" events. We don't *want* to. We choose to remember, even when there is great pain in remembering . . . perhaps especially when there is great pain. For in remembering, we create meaning. If you listened carefully to newscasters' accounts after *Challenger*'s demise, you could hear them comparing its mission with that of Christopher Columbus, Sir Francis Drake, Vasco da Gama, Magellan, and others, many of whom died on their voyages of discovery.

The overriding message in these comparisons was that, as a result of the bravery of these men and women, our society and civilization advance. They did not die in vain. There was meaning in their death. And we should not despair, because our heroes have taught us great lessons in courage. It is important that we not forget such lessons.

Santayana said, "The person who does not learn from history is condemned to repeat it." The human mind is so capable of forgetting even the most heinous events that we seem to constantly need reminders. This is why, I believe, the Jewish people *want* to remember the holocaust. They want to remember the "six million." They want the memory of that unspeakable time in history to remain alive and well, forever etched in human consciousness. Only in so doing can true meaning come from their battle cry, "Never again, never again!"

Ultimately, then, our main objective is to achieve a personal and lasting happiness. The degree to which we achieve this end, within the context of unconditional regard for our fellow human survivors, is related directly to the degree to which we have found a sense of meaning in our lives. When we find meaning, and when we derive it within the broader context of human betterment, we are blessed with happiness that is reserved for a chosen few.

NOTES

1. Fritz Perls, *The Gestalt Approach & Eye Witness to Therapy* (New York: Bantam Books, 1973), pp. 141-142.

2. Michael Korda, *Power! How to Get It, How to Use It* (New York: Ballantine Books, 1975).

3. Robert J. Ringer, *Winning Through Intimidation* (Greenwich: Fawcett Publications, 1974).

4. Robert H. Schuller, *Peace of Mind Through Possibility Thinking* (Garden City: Doubleday & Co., 1977), p. 62.

5. William Glasser, *Positive Addiction* (New York: Harper & Row, 1976), pp. 62-91.

3

The Grist of Life: Surviving and *Prospering*

PROBABLY FEW OF US have thought of love or friendship or creativity as mechanisms for survival. These concepts are usually just words in our vocabulary depicting stages or conditions in our lives and associated with vague mental images.

As I worked with clients over the years, and as my awareness of the human condition increased, I began to realize that these concepts are more than mere words or images: they are the grist of life itself. New experience, positive mental attitude, and perception are not idle concepts floating around. They are, instead, neglected mechanisms, survival mechanisms, waiting to be discovered and used. Discovering the deeper meaning and validity of these concepts was for me like finding gold after the last vein had been mined. Just when people were taking them for granted, their new meaning and impact was being driven home to me with revolutionary force.

The more I spoke with people, the more I became involved in their lives—clients and non-clients—and the more I listened carefully to what they said, the more convinced I became that to survive and be happy they used ten common mechanisms that I have identified and defined in this book as survival mechanisms. These clients adopted the mechanisms to strengthen the four basic life elements: self-image, inner strength, personal control, and life meaning. If we fail to use these mechanisms, they will, in the course of time, atrophy and die, and if they die, so will the four basic life elements. Yet if we use and strengthen these mechanisms, they will serve to make our lives happy and prosperous.

To strengthen the survival mechanisms, we must discover and use strategies that we find are best suited to do the job; I'll elaborate on these strategies later. For now, remember, it is impossible to "over-strengthen" the survival mechanisms—you can't have too much self-esteem, inner strength, control, or meaning in your life.

Mutual Interdependence of Survival Mechanisms with the Four Basic Life Elements

Although we use some or all the survival mechanisms to strengthen our four basic life elements and some or all the strategies to strengthen the mechanisms, most of us tend to do so randomly—that is, we don't *consciously* and *deliberately* set out to strengthen either the mechanisms or the strategies. And we often fail to realize the degree to which the mechanisms and the basic life elements are intimately interconnected and interdependent.

This phenomenon struck me recently as I waited in a garage while my car was being serviced (one of my least favorite activities). A scruffy-looking mechanic stood idly behind the counter when a well-dressed, intelligent-looking young woman came into the waiting area. The two of them greeted each other as if they were friends.

Since they were only a few feet from where I was sitting, I couldn't help overhearing their conversation. "I saw your picture in the paper recently," the young woman said excitedly.

"Really?" the mechanic responded with a smile and instant animation.

"Yes, you were directing a play or something," responded the young woman.

Suddenly, the mechanic seemed to be transformed right in front of my eyes! His greasy, grimy work clothes appeared to be replaced, as if by magic, with a spanking-clean, razor-creased black tuxedo. His face, now beaming, seemed to glow as if by some inner light. His hands, just moments before lifeless and dingy, were now alive with gestures. One could almost see the baton of a symphony conductor clasped between his fingers. "Yes, yes ... I ... Well ... You see ... this is what I do in my spare time!" he stammered, trying to punch out the excited words. By now the mechanic was oblivious to his surroundings, his job, and the telephone, which was jingling insistently.

This fellow, who moments before looked like something past its prime, was now transformed into a totally alive, vibrant human being. My first thoughts as I observed this metamorphosis were: This young woman's saying that she saw his picture reminds this person he has *meaning* in his life: he's not just a "grease monkey." She's also triggered his sense of *self-esteem*.

I then began to look for the survival mechanisms that were at work here. Let's see, I thought. *Creativity*, definitely creativity's at work. What else? *Play*. For sure play is at work too. Anything else? Hm . . . . Oh—how could I miss it? *Recognition!* He practically grinned his face off when she told him she saw his picture in the paper.

I then began thinking about this fellow a little more seriously. I'll bet he doesn't have the slightest inkling of just how important creativity or play or recognition are to him, I surmised—at least, not consciously. I'll bet he's never even dreamed of those things as mechanisms for survival, much less thought of them as vehicles for strengthening the meaning and self-image elements of his life.

I couldn't help imagining what this mechanic's life could be like if he consciously and deliberately set out to do more directing, to be even more creative, so that he would achieve even more recognition. I could tell by his beaming reaction that whatever kind of directing he did (I never did find out), it was *play* to him. What would his self-image be like, I wondered, if he played even more?

The young woman took care of her business and left. The mechanic, still looking somewhat radiant, went about his duties, disappearing into an adjoining garage where tires were being changed. After a short time he emerged and was, once again, standing behind the counter where I first saw him. Another startling change! Gone was the beaming, glowing face. The grubby, grease-caked clothes were back, and instead of the conductor's baton, he lifelessly clutched a crescent wrench in his hand. It was almost as if he had aged ten years right in front of me.

I thought about that mechanic when I went to bed that night. I thought about him a lot.

Courage

Thoreau wisely observed that "The mass of men lead lives of quiet desperation."[1] With speed and technology outstripping our ability to keep pace, we all seem to be plagued with varying degrees of fear and self-doubt. These two demons have singlehandedly destroyed more dreams and dreamers than all others combined. And together, they have managed to destroy our humanness.

Each of us needs to dream and believe in someone or something. When that belief and dream are shattered, fear and self-doubt enter and become the guardians of our minds. To succeed in life we must learn to replace disbelief and fear with courage. We are not blessed automatically with courage, however; we achieve it by hard work and struggle. As we gradually overcome our disbelief and fear and gain courage, our survival mechanisms begin to work for us. Self-doubt is replaced with confidence, fear with faith.

A fourteen-year-old girl living in a foster home heard

of the death of her grandmother, whom she dearly loved. As an expression of her grief, she sent a modest bouquet of flowers to the funeral home. Her father, from whom she had been estranged for several years, returned the wilting flowers to her with a terse note saying that he had already sent flowers on behalf of the family and that she had no business sending others on her own.

This young teenager was hurt profoundly by her father's reaction, yet somehow she managed to survive. And I recall thinking at the time: After you've done your best and have had the world spit in your face . . . to have it trample your spirit until you can't even feel the mind-numbing pain any more, and you decide you can still go on, then you will have gained courage, and with it *strength*. The strength will be that of one unafraid, because there is simply nothing left that the world can do to you. And to be unafraid is to grow in ever-widening circles of courage and tenacity, to meet any challenge, to defeat any foe.

Who Survives?

Over the years I have worked thousands of therapy hours with hundreds of clients encompassing a wide cross-section of humanity. Some were desperate souls who literally existed on a day-to-day basis. Others did fairly well as long as their stress level remained low and they continued in therapy. A few fortunate cases needed just a little nudge in the right direction. Despite their differences in age, cultural background, religious affiliation, and socioeconomic status, they all showed one common talent: ability to *survive*.

Some survived merely on a physical basis while remaining mentally and emotionally dead. The vast majority, however, managed to find life and hope by developing little techniques or strategies to sustain themselves during the rough times. Some consciously thought up these strategies; others developed them unconsciously. These survival strategies, as I have come to call them, came in various forms, such as becoming engrossed in a hobby, taking an interest in the arts, becoming involved in various causes or civic responsibilities, developing interpersonal interests, and becoming more deeply involved in work-related projects or with their families. Many of these people had multi-faceted, debilitating problems that would leave anyone broken in spirit, and yet they carried on. Day in and day out they arose from their beds and somehow accomplished the task of living, albeit on a marginal level. But *survive* they did!

One poor woman had recently been divorced. Her oldest child had died tragically in a fire, and she had just received news of a cancer in her breast. As I attempted to comprehend the enormity of her situation, I heard her utter the words, "I just keep going. I'll pick up my crocheting and try not to think about it." I didn't pay much attention to that seemingly innocent statement at the time, but later I came to realize she was telling me that her survival mechanisms of work and creativity were doing their job. And to know that this was true, I wouldn't have had to look any further than the beautiful table covering on which my arm had been resting.

As I came to understand these people, I discovered that not only did they develop specific survival strategies to cope with life's otherwise insurmountable problems, these strategies were not necessarily random in nature. To the contrary, they frequently seemed to be chosen consciously to enhance a specific survival mechanism designed to enable the individual to survive emotionally.

The ten emotional survival mechanisms I've listed are the ones that seem to be used most frequently in most people as they go about the task of daily living. Undoubtedly, there are others that could readily be identified, but the ten on which I have focused seem to be the more common ones.

On the following pages you will read about the ten survival mechanisms that I believe are universal. Under each mechanism I have noted certain strategies we use to implement or strengthen that particular mechanism. These strategies are also, in my opinion, universal. The strategies I have noted do not represent an exhaustive list; they merely represent those strategies most people seem to use most frequently to successfully enhance and sustain a related mechanism. If you choose, I am certain you can develop and implement many strategies on your own that apply more specifically to your own life.

Two Simple Steps to a Happier Life

I cannot overstate the importance of developing and practicing the survival strategies to strengthen your survival mechanisms. If you do this, you will dramatically increase personal happiness and prosperity. In order to achieve this, you must follow these two steps:

1. Decide which survival mechanisms are *most* critical for your survival. Do this by using the Survival Mechanism Inventory, explained in the next section.
2. Practice the survival strategies listed under each mechanism you have selected as most important to you, in order to strengthen that specific survival mechanism.

Notice afterward that your four basic life elements are strengthened *automatically* as a result of working on the survival strategies. As you work on successful completion of these steps, you will achieve personal happiness and prosperity.

A Final Note

Although the survival mechanisms are present in everyone, not all of the mechanisms are developed to the same extent in everybody. While one person may have the work survival mechanism developed to a high level, for example, his or her love survival mechanism may be quite undeveloped. It is therefore necessary to increase your awareness of each mechanism and the degree to which it is developed or underdeveloped in you. As you learn to do this, you will know on which mechanisms to focus your attention so you can develop the basic life elements that are in greatest need. A balanced approach to strengthening the survival mechanisms leads, in turn, to a balanced life.

Although all survival mechanisms need not be strengthened *simultaneously,* you must enhance all ten in order to properly sustain the four basic life elements and thus achieve optimum personal happiness and prosperity. In addition, remember that all ten survival mechanisms directly affect each of the four basic life elements—although not to the same degree. In another section below I list the four basic life elements in *descending* order of the degree to which they are affected by the specific survival mechanism under which they occur.

So once you have determined the relative strength or weakness of a particular survival mechanism, simply check to see which basic life elements are most critically affected by that specific mechanism. You will then know exactly which basic life element you are expending your energies on.

Under the survival mechanism of love, for example, you will find all four of the basic elements listed. This means that, as you strengthen your love mechanism through the strategies suggested, all four of the basic elements of your emotional life will also be automatically strengthened. You will notice, however, that the first element listed is self-image. This means simply that self-image is the element in *most* critical need of development and the one receiving most attention at that time. Listed second is life meaning, then inner strength, and last personal control. This order of listing does not imply that any life element has priority over, or greater importance than, the others. It means simply that, for the love mechanism, self-image is the element affected most critically.

By deciding which survival mechanisms need your greatest attention, you will *simultaneously and automatically* accomplish the task of strengthening those basic elements of your emotional life that are weakest and of which you may have little, if any, conscious awareness. Focus on the relative strength or weakness of a particular survival mechanism rather than on the four life elements themselves, because determining the strength or weakness of the survival mechanisms is always simpler. Most of us, for example, might have difficulty *honestly* determining the level of our inner strength (who among us wishes to acknowledge personal weakness?), but we could probably answer truthfully whether we love or are loved adequately.

To assist you in this task, use the Survival Mechanism Inventory for each mechanism. You'll find it at the end of each chapter's discussion of that specific mechanism.

Each Survival Mechanism Inventory lists ten statements for which you are asked to make a judgment from among five choices: SA—Strongly Approve; A—Approve; U—Undecided; D—Disapprove; and SD—Strongly Disapprove. Each choice has been given a numerical rating ranging from a high of 5 for Strongly Approve (SA) to a low of 1 for Strongly Disapprove (SD).

I urge you to take a moment to complete each Survival Mechanism Inventory as you go through the book. The resulting numerical score represents that specific survival mechanism's "Strength Quotient." The Inventory is not intended to represent a sophisticated measuring device of your attitudes or feelings toward a particular topic or issue. It will, however, assist you in determining your "Strength Quotient" for each survival mechanism.

Remember, the ultimate purpose in all of this is to strengthen the four basic life elements. The more accurate you are in identifying those survival mechanisms needing the most help and strengthening them through the survival strategies, the stronger your basic life elements become. The end result is increased personal happiness and prosperity.

Personal Choice

As you learn to increase your awareness of the relative strength or weakness of the survival mechanisms, you will be developing the strategies most likely to meet the needs of each one.

The survival mechanism of love, for example, would be strengthened by using the survival strategy of "kindness toward a stranger," or "reading an inspiring book," or "meditation," or any combination of these. I found, however, that with the hundreds of people with whom I have worked, the actual strategies used were not the important factor. Far more important was to have *the person using them* develop and implement the strategies. My merely telling someone to get inspired or feel creative by listening to a Bach Cantata would not be nearly as effective as that person discovering Bach and then *consciously choosing* to listen to his music. Conscious choice increases the mechanism of creativity and with it the basic life elements called self-image, inner strength, personal control, and life meaning.

The reader will note that some of the strategies are duplicated under several survival mechanisms. Meditation, for example, is listed under the love mechanism as well as under the mechanism of spiritual belief. The duplication means simply that the meditation strategy can be used to strengthen either mechanism, love or spiritual belief. Both mechanisms will in fact be strengthened simultaneously. You will choose which survival strategy to employ.

The element of personal choice is critical in improving your emotional life. Choosing is an integral part of life almost from the beginning. We choose to be a "good" or "bad" baby, depending on the way we perceive our environment is treating us. We choose our friends. We choose colleges and careers and mates and places to live. We choose a place to retire and, in many cases, the place and manner in which we die.

Survival mechanisms are present in all of us . . . all the time. We were born needing to receive and give love. We were born with a desire to work and create. We all yearn for new experiences and recognition. Without these we feel empty and unfulfilled. Where would we be without friendship and play and a positive mental attitude? Without these universal mechanisms to sustain us, we would be bored with life and ourselves. The degree to which we develop them is up to us. It is our choice to make. If we allow others to choose, we sell ourselves out. We commit to them our lives and destinies.

Positive versus Negative Strengthening of Survival Mechanisms

Freud's mechanisms of defense, mentioned earlier, can be strengthened with use. If, for example, you consistently use projection, displacement, denial, or any of the other defense mechanisms, those mechanisms will become firmly and *permanently* ingrained in your ego structure. That is because the defense mechanisms ward off and re-lieve anxiety. The more you use such defense mechanisms, the more this unconscious process will continue.

So even though you may obtain relief by using a spe-cific defense mechanism, you may inadvertently be sus-taining a dysfunctional life pattern. The alcoholic does this consistently: although denying his or her addiction helps by not having to face chronic pain and the loss of self-control, the alcoholic perpetuates the pain cycle by con-tinuing to fail in life. This "Catch 22" rarely, if ever, occurs to the alcoholic, however, because it is sustained by un-conscious and uncontrollable forces.

If we apply the principle of defense mechanisms to the idea of using offense mechanisms, we readily can see that strengthening a survival mechanism involves a risk. If, for example, a person uses the survival mechanism of new experience in a dysfunctional way—running from one affair to another, never finding a solid relationship, or jet-ting around the country following the horses, gambling away his or her last penny—such an individual is merely strengthening the mechanism of new experience in a neg-ative direction. If this continues, the mechanism of new experience becomes a vehicle for failure rather than for growth.

When people do this, they abuse the survival mechanisms by using them as escapes, and their survival potential is lost. So when a man flits from one destructive relationship to another, he is not *really* developing the mechanism of new experience, he is merely maintaining the status quo of a previously dysfunctional life pattern. When a woman becomes a workaholic, she's not *really* strengthening her survival mechanism of work, she's merely escaping from other pursuits that might otherwise prove growth-producing and life-enhancing.

We must recognize when we may be misusing our survival mechanisms. We have to gain awareness of the subtle difference between true, positive strengthening as opposed to frantic, negative strengthening that ultimately proves self-defeating. Here are some potential abuses of survival mechanisms:

LOVE
Becoming involved in a series of relationships that ultimately prove self-destructive, such as marrying a spouse who is a carbon copy of the last one, all the time protesting how "different" he or she is.

WORK
Using work as an escape—becoming a "workaholic" and then denying this when confronted by a spouse or best friend.

PLAY
Always playing—forever taking vacations from reality; chronic escapism in the name of relaxation.

CREATIVITY
Using our creative energies in self-defeating ways, such as using writing skills to poison others' minds, and using electronic aptitude to construct an explosive device designed to harm others.

RECOGNITION
Seeking status and notoriety in a narcissistic way; joining groups and organizations merely to artificially sustain one's low self-image.

PERCEPTION
Allowing one's normally sharp perceptive powers to be dulled or influenced by those who would distort them.

FRIENDSHIP
Forming friendships only to exploit them later; forming relationships that repeatedly prove to be self-destructive; using people under the guise of friendship.

NEW EXPERIENCE
Escapism! Leap-frogging from one experience or project to another; never completing anything; constantly creating "emotional noise" to block out one's pain.

SPIRITUAL BELIEF
Using spiritual belief as dogma—twisting spiritual ideas or thinking to accommodate one's own biases.

POSITIVE MENTAL ATTITUDE
Assuming a "Pollyanna" attitude toward life; keeping one's head firmly buried in emotional quicksand—refusing to see or accept reality; doing this while thinking one is "positive," but really deluding oneself about the truth.

Genuine happiness, then, is a by-product of the degree to which we strengthen the four basic life elements. The stronger these basic elements, the greater our happiness. The more we try to "buy" happiness, or make it a conscious goal, the more it will elude us. Focusing on enhancing the basic elements of our lives, however, and forgetting the goal of happiness, will produce the happiness we all seek. The paradox of this approach can best be resolved by adopting the philosophy of "more is less and less is more."

We cannot buy happiness any more than we can buy a positive self-image or life meaning. Going to the supermarket and asking the clerk for a half-pound of self-image or three-quarters of a pound of meaning could land one in the state hospital. We can, however, strengthen our basic life elements by using the simple, everyday strategies I discuss under each survival mechanism.

So, if "beginning is half done," we need something with which to begin. Something has to ignite the flame of personal happiness. The ten survival mechanisms are the "ignitors." They are the sparks that ignite the basic elements of our emotional lives, and as they burn they in turn further increase the strength of our survival mechanisms, thus perpetuating the positive interdependence cycle that makes life the joyous experience it was meant to be!

NOTES

1. Henry David Thoreau, *Walden* (Columbus, Ohio: Charles E. Merrill Publishing Co., 1969), p. 10.

II

Your Ten Survival Mechanisms and How They Work

4

Survival Mechanism #1: Love

That Love is all there is,
Is all we know of Love . . . .
—*Emily Dickinson*

IN THE SEVENTEEN YEARS I have worked as a therapist, I have never ceased to be amazed at the incredible power of human love. Perhaps nowhere have I observed its impact more visibly than in marriage. I will never forget the interchange between a husband and wife in my office many years ago. The wife turned to her husband and said, "Honey, I just don't think we're making it." The husband responded with, "Honey, as long as we're calling each other 'honey,' we're making it!"

Indeed, nowhere is the love survival mechanism exemplified more clearly than within the marital bond and the families generated from it. In fact, I have considered regarding the family itself as a survival mechanism because clients used it so frequently to sustain the four basic life elements. I decided, however, that love was a more

49

universal concept and that family should be included under it, rather than the reverse.

We were born needing to give and receive love. Our families, by definition, afford a natural breeding ground for love . . . and for fear. If we are fortunate enough to be born into loving and caring families, our love survival mechanism will flourish. If not, we instead learn fear and distrust. This kind of negative learning ultimately weakens our love survival mechanism and with it the four basic life elements.

Our families serve as havens to which we can retreat and find comfort, particularly when we are under great stress. Families are, in the final analysis, a source of strength when our own reserves have been depleted.

Countless clients have told me that, when emotional and physical collapse was imminent, "leaning" on their families—parents, brothers and sisters, aunts, uncles, cousins, and children—gave them the support they needed to get through.

Volumes have been written on the family, both nuclear and extended, and a great deal more could be said here. For our purposes, however, I stress only that the love of one's family is a great and mighty force when emotional survival is threatened. I doubt that any of us have failed to seek out its sanctuary when life's storm clouds approached.

Love. Such a magnificent word. Such a beautiful concept. It is the foundation of any meaningful relationship. Without its presence, even the best of intentions go astray. Love is a concept that means different things to different people. There is, of course, the love between a husband and wife. There is the special bonding love that exists between parent and child. Lasting friendships that endure even the most trying of times and circumstances are formed out of mutual love and respect. There is the love one has for one's work or avocation. We can love our spiritual beliefs. Some of us are deeply moved by music and other art forms and gain such joy from them that we are "in love" with them. Many people are in love with love and life itself.

Perhaps one of the purest forms of love is healthy self-love. This kind of love contrasts sharply with narcissistic love, which is neurotic and ultimately self-destructive. Healthy self-love is the truest hallmark of a selfless person. This apparent contradiction is negated when we realize that the ability to give freely to others is related directly to inner strength, one of the four basic life elements.

Someone who has the capacity to give to others is not fearful of losing self in the process of giving. In fact, it is the very act of giving to others that in turn affords a person a sense of joy and personal strength. As one gives, one also receives. The more a person gives, the more he or she receives. Because the person feels inherently good about himself or herself, that person chooses to give more and more in order to receive more and more. Selflessness is his or her most direct expression of self-love.

Unfortunately, not all expressions of love are loving. I sadly recall the case of the alcoholic father of three young children. One night he came home in a drunken rage and brutally battered the youngest son until his face was a bloody, broken mass. After all three children were removed from the home and placed in custodial settings, I interviewed the father, determined to find out why he had beaten the child. With tears streaming down his haggard face he exclaimed, "Paul, of all my children, I love Joey the most. I did it because I love him. I was trying to teach him what's right." This little boy so reminded the father of himself and his own self-hatred that, in his distorted thinking, he literally tried to beat that self-loathing out of himself by battering his innocent child. Freud referred to this kind of negative defense mechanism as *reaction formation.*

Learning to love is the greatest survival mechanism we possess when it comes to controlling our unwanted emotions. Love is the mighty tonic for dark passions that threaten to push their way into our lives and destroy our hope for happiness. When we discover and develop this mechanism, our lives soar. But to possess it we must learn to banish fear.

Dr. Gerald Jampolsky, a leading psychiatrist and author of *Love Is Letting Go of Fear*, put it this way: "There are only two emotions; one is Love and the other is fear."[1] To live a life filled with fear means to live a life devoid of love. Love and fear cannot coexist. We must learn the art of loving and of being loved. This is what gives power and beauty to life.

How, then, does one learn to love? What magic key turns the lock that binds our hearts and minds? How do we discover this greatest of all survival mechanisms? We need look no further than the morning sunrise for the answer to these questions. Each new day abounds with opportunities to demonstrate love for one another, for our fellow creatures, for our planet, and for ourselves. But how does one show love when one doesn't have it to show? What if love has been crushed from our lives?

Human beings are creatures of habit. If we treat them with disdain or contempt, they will respond accordingly. If, however, we treat them with love and honor, we will be rewarded with the same. Those of us who feel we cannot love need only surround ourselves with loving people. We will then learn what it means to be loved and to love in return.

Have you ever said "Good morning!" to the rising sun or to the wet dew covering the grass? Have you ever taken yourself high on a hill and inhaled the sweet perfume of clover and lilacs? Did you ever smile at someone just to shock that person? Do you know the feeling of speaking kindly to a total stranger? Have you ever done something to brighten someone's day . . . and not get found out? I highly recommend these simple, yet powerful, love survival strategies. They are all self-esteem builders.

Over the years I've noticed that those who can discover and develop the love survival mechanism prosper both personally and interpersonally. They start by simply seeking ways to give, both to others and to themselves. It doesn't matter how, or how much, as long as they give. This very simple act of giving, when practiced on a consistent basis, somehow engenders strength in them. The more strength they acquire, the more they are able to give, and the more they give, the greater their strength. After a while, this positive cycle replaces the negative one of self-doubt and fear.

It took me many years to learn this survival mechanism. I was introduced to it on a crisp fall day in Philadelphia nearly thirty years ago. My depression forced me into an encounter that changed my life forever. There, in old St. Stephen's Church, I met Dr. Alfred W. Price, the rector. He gave me a vision of brighter tomorrows. He showed me how to listen to that inner voice . . . to tap the survival mechanism of love. He was a kindly man, and I could feel the love emanating from him like healing waters. In the six months that followed he taught me about healing . . . about truth and, most important, about survival.

The importance of *personal choice* and the manner in which choices occur throughout life cannot be overstated. Indeed, the phenomenon of personal choice permeates all the survival mechanisms. We choose, for example, which mechanisms require strengthening, or the strategies to use in order to strengthen a particular mechanism. In none of the survival mechanisms does the element of choice play such a major role as it does in the mechanism of love.

Recently I experienced a humorous, yet startling incident involving an eight-year-old client. One day, when this child's mother came to visit him at the institution, instead of showing his usual happiness at the prospect of seeing her, he recoiled and exclaimed, "I don't want to see my mother. I don't want to love her today!" On any other day he could love his mother, but on this day, he *chose* not to. This youngster was using avoidance as a defense against being close to his mother. He was using it also as a strategy to *weaken* his love survival mechanism. As he continued to use this strategy, it became a pattern or habit. Unless he breaks it, his love survival mechanism will serve him less and less well throughout life, and soon his life pattern will become not love but indifference and fear.

All too often we use various mechanisms to ward off perceived anxiety and fear. These are the defense mechanisms of which I spoke earlier. They enable us to survive, but at a great price. Remember, the goal in life is to survive *and* prosper. As we learn to develop the strategies that will enhance and implement the survival mechanisms, not destroy them, we acquire personal strength and the power to gain control over our lives.

As I have indicated, each survival mechanism requires certain strategies in order to work for that individual. Please remember that the specific strategies I mention below are not the *only* ones that will implement or strengthen a particular survival mechanism. They are merely the ones that most people seem to use most frequently. You will undoubtedly think of others that will work as well, if not better, for you.

Love Survival Mechanism Strategies

Strategy #1: Music

Perhaps the most universal survival strategy to implement the love survival mechanism is the use of music. Music is indeed the universal language. It speaks to us from different cultures, ethnic groups, races, and religious beliefs. Although one piece of music can mean different things to different people, music can reach across national and ethnic boundaries and touch the hearts and minds of most of us in universal ways.

Many people don't or won't recognize music as an important survival strategy. This is unfortunate, since music can affect lives significantly. Several years ago I worked with a group of delinquent teenage boys. Most of them had been in trouble with the law from the time they were ten or twelve years old. Different therapists had, with little success, tried various conventional approaches to working with these hard-to-reach young people. I decided to take a different route and began utilizing music in my therapy sessions with them. This approach included singing, playing the guitar, and listening to the latest rock music on cassette tapes. After a while, the usual barriers broke down. I began to see smiles instead of frowns. Rather than sullen silence, communication developed. Instead of anti-social behavior, these boys exhibited more socialized, positive behavior. And remarkably, it wasn't drudgery, it was fun . . . for all of us!

Try a little experiment the next time you feel "down." Instead of fretting about what you did or didn't do during the course of your day, when you arrive home sit down and turn on your favorite music station. If you prefer, slip in a cassette tape, record, or compact disc. I highly recommend investing in a quality stereo. The peace of mind you will receive from it will make it worth its weight in gold! Use your stereo on a consistent basis. Condition yourself to the music, not the worries. This pattern should gradually develop your love survival mechanism to a high degree.

In addition to my work as a therapist, I have always been interested in and held a deep love for music, especially vocal music. Opera has been one of my favorite forms of musical expression. Even as a youngster, I can recall the thrill of listening to the Texaco Metropolitan Opera Broadcasts . . . live from New York City! As Milton Cross, then the announcer for the Met broadcasts, came on the air to describe the opera to be broadcast that Saturday afternoon, my worries and anxieties would begin to melt away. A kindly, relaxed, and *loving* sensation came over me. It was miraculous! I didn't realize it, but my love survival mechanism was being strengthened, and the strategy I used was listening to music. It has been a love affair ever since!

Today's youth are deeply affected by various musical groups and by the music these groups write and perform. The many forms of music that attract them range from reggae to heavy metal. Even as I write this, new forms are evolving. The name of the musical style is unimportant. The extent to which the music *speaks* to these young people *is* important. It is vital to keep this in mind when you do *your* listening. If the music speaks to you, then it will do its best work in developing your love survival mechanism. If you feel uplifted as you listen, and if it is love that you feel, the music is speaking to you. Healing is taking place.

Strategy #2: Reading

Readers are leaders. Someone once told me, "Paul, what you will be ten years from today will depend largely on two factors: the books you read and the people you associate with." Over the years, I have discovered profound truth in that statement. Most of us fail to realize the tremendous power of the written word. What we read can affect our lives in many ways. Many people, for example, will read a gruesome mystery novel right before bedtime and then wonder why they have nightmares. Others will read in a magazine that all of humanity is going to die in a nuclear holocaust and believe every word simply because the person writing the article is a self-proclaimed "expert." We can become depressed as a result of what others think. In this way we allow others to control our moods, attitudes, and thoughts.

When I first met Dr. Price, I wasn't fully prepared for the power with which his ideas and concepts would affect my life. I was quite a troubled and disillusioned young man when, to my great fortune, he introduced me to *silent meditation,* a concept more fully developed below under the subhead of Meditation Strategy. Dr. Price's influence on me emphasizes the way simple words, *taken seriously to heart,* can completely alter one's mood and life outlook.

Upon entering Dr. Price's study on that brisk November day, I was impressed immediately with the atmosphere of calm and serenity. Even though I had never been there before, I felt safe and at home. Only years later did I realize that, in addition to this man's great spirituality, it was my own *expectation* that "something good was about to happen" that produced a sense of wonder and healing within me.

After asking a few simple questions and giving me a brief discourse on his ideas about healing and mental health, Dr. Price handed me a few pamphlets that he had prepared. He instructed me to read three phrases from them quietly to myself three times daily: in the morning, at noontime, and just before retiring. Each phrase was to be read over and over, *without giving it any conscious thought,* for approximately fifteen minutes. He made a point of telling me to *relax* while I did this and *not to think about it.* I followed his directions to the letter. Here are the three phrases:

1. "THANK YOU, DEAR LORD, FOR YOUR PRESENCE WITH ME—ALWAYS."
2. "I AM ETERNAL LOVE WITHIN YOU: YOU HAVE NOTHING TO FEAR; MY GRACE IS SUFFICIENT FOR YOU."
3. "I AM WITH YOU ALWAYS" (Pause, then repeat over and over), "I THANK YOU DEAR LORD, THAT YOUR WILL FOR ME IS HEALING AND WHOLENESS AND PEACE."

Those three simple phrases saved my life! They replaced my fear with love.

I use this illustration to emphasize the importance of what we read. It doesn't matter if the phrases are from the Judeo-Christian ethic or Hindu or Moslem. What matters is that they matter to *you.* If you approach what you read *expectantly,* whether it is positive or negative, it will affect you. The information will be absorbed and become a part of your emotional and psychological self. If the words are soothing and comforting and have a healing quality and texture, they will enhance your love survival mechanism. If not, the opposite will occur. Remember the computer axiom: GIGO—*garbage in, garbage out!* If you put only "garbage" into your computer, that's all you'll be able to get out of it. This is also true with your reading. Read the great books by contemporary authors. Names like Robert Schuller, Norman Vincent Peale, Denis Waitley, Norman Cousins, William Glasser, and Og Mandino should be in your vocabulary. What you read *will* make a difference in your life.

Strategy #3: Speaking

The great psychologist Albert Ellis pointed out the importance of choosing carefully what we say, either to others or ourselves . . . *especially ourselves!* Dr. Ellis called these self-expressions "self-sentences" and emphasized their profound impact on us, often when we least expect it.[2] Self-sentences have an especially high relevance to the love survival mechanism. As you recall, our ability to give love is related directly to our capacity for healthy self-love or self-esteem. And if, as Freud suggested, emotional health is correlated positively with our ability to love and work, then it behooves us to develop the love survival mechanism to its highest degree.

Dr. Ellis has drawn sharp attention to the impact self-sentences can have, especially when they are repeated over and over—as with the three phrases Dr. Price gave me to help lift my depression. What Dr. Price did for me illustrated the benefits of *positive* self-sentences. Understandably, then, negative self-sentences can produce correspondingly negative results.

The spring of 1961 brings back bittersweet memories for me. Although I was graduating from college that year and many family members would be there to share in my happiness, one very important person would be absent: my father. He died of a stroke that spring just a few short weeks before my graduation. I will never forget those sad days. But equally unforgettable was what happened at my father's wake.

As I stood next to my father's coffin with my grieving brother, John, suddenly and without explanation John exclaimed, "Dad lived to be sixty-five. That gives me another twenty-five years." I remember thinking what an incredible statement that was for him to make. I forgot that remark until years later when, as I stood next to my brother's coffin, his words again rang in my unbelieving ears. John died, as he had programmed himself to do, just a few months short of the twenty-fifth anniversary of my father's death.

This story represents only one illustration of the power of mental programming. Countless others could be cited. We do program our minds and emotions as a result of the sentences we speak to ourselves. And the programming goes on whether we are awake or asleep. Once we set the process in motion, it continues on automatic pilot.

Negative self-sentences are among the most devastating of all hindrances to developing the love survival mechanism. And, of course, behind these negative self-sentences are irrational ways of seeing ourselves and the world. To change these beliefs and make them more rational and positive should be our goal. As we learn to do this more effectively, our love survival mechanism increases in strength and power. This change translates into greater self-esteem and personal happiness. "Beware, beware!" cautioned the Hindu mystic. "What goes forth from you will come back to you." Speak the language of love . . . and watch love grow in your life!

Strategy #4: Meditation

Meditation is one of the surest ways of strengthening the love survival mechanism. It is a survival strategy readily accessible to everyone. You don't have to take a prolonged course in meditation or go to India to learn how to use it effectively. In addition, meditation does not necessarily have to occur in any prescribed or contrived fashion. Although I offer a brief overview of the meditative process in the chapter on the spiritual belief survival mechanism, many excellent books cover the subject of meditation so well that it would be pointless to reiterate here what has been said elsewhere by many others. If you want suggestions, see the bibliography for several excellent references. You can learn the "how to" of meditation from such books. Meditation is an outstanding example of a survival strategy to strengthen your love survival mechanism. It is accessible, and it works!

Dr. William Glasser, the brilliant psychiatrist and founder of Reality Therapy, states that one can become "positively addicted" to either meditation or running by engaging in those pursuits on a persistent basis. He sharply contrasts such positive "addictions" with the negative addiction normally associated with alcohol or drugs.[3]

What an exciting concept . . . to be addicted to something positive! As I mentioned earlier, the defense mechanisms as defined by Freud are essentially negative. The ten survival mechanisms are positive in that they produce both survival *and* prosperity.

Here is an example of this survival strategy in the story of a very beautiful young woman. A number of years ago she came to me all broken and bruised by her life experiences. She had been shattered both physically and mentally. Abused and violated as a child, she had emotionally crawled inside herself, where she silently suffered torments she could not reveal to the outside world. Her lifetime of anguish was matched only by the hopelessness with which she faced her future.

She eventually gained the courage to confide in me the horrors of sexual abuse she had sustained and the indifference of her family. Despite unspeakable atrocities, she had managed to survive. A number of survival mechanisms worked for her through the emotional darkness, most significantly the mechanism of love. So it was with joy that she welcomed the suggestion of meditation as a means of enhancing this mechanism. Love was the mechanism that had sustained her most, and it was about to be extinguished. Like flowing waters in the parched desert, the positive words used in meditation permeated her mind and spirit. As her love survival mechanism increased, so did her emotional and physical strength. Her self-esteem grew with each passing day as she was able to give to herself. This, of course, resulted in increased ability to give to others . . . a source of great joy to her.

It took a number of years for this dear soul to begin to see the light of a brighter tomorrow, but see it she did. The change was possible because she *persevered*. Despite the odds, she kept going. I cannot stress enough the importance of the word *perseverance*. It means, simply, that you "keep on keeping on," even when logic tells you to give up.

Whatever your current difficulty or heartache, try to advance yourself, to persevere, in *some way*, no matter how small it may seem. Keeping on is important, especially when nothing around you seems to be going right. It is vital to our love survival mechanism (and the other mechanisms as well) that, when our world seems to be crumbling, we see some progress . . . somewhere.

Strategy #5: Show Kindness toward a Stranger

Perhaps the greatest act of human kindness is for one human being to be willing to give up his or her life for another. The journals of war are filled with such examples. Every day we read in the newspapers and witness on television some dramatic demonstration of human kindness. The parents of a young child killed tragically in an automobile accident donate an organ of that child so another child, whom they have never seen, may live. A good samaritan gives a dollar to a youngster so he can take the subway home.

There was a dramatic moment in my own experience when I could easily have lost my life. I was ten years old, and my older brother, Joe, had just acquired his license to pilot single-engine aircraft. He was only twenty himself and in the beginning years of a Navy career. One day he asked my mother's permission to take my nephew and me for a ride. With great reluctance she agreed. As we taxied out toward the runway, a larger twin-engine plane suddenly appeared, heading directly toward us. Perhaps because of our plane's size, the pilot of the twin-engine plane did not see our tiny aircraft. With only seconds to spare, my brother flung the airplane door open and prepared to push my nephew and me out onto the tarmac! His thought, I learned later, was that we would run to safety while he either avoided a collision or faced the on-coming disaster alone. Fortunately, neither event occurred, because the other pilot *did* see us in time, and what could have turned into a catastrophe became only a "near hit" story.

Needless to say, my brother's act was clearly one of kindness, although in this case not to a stranger, but he told me many years later that he would have done exactly the same thing no matter who was in the plane! Such acts of kindness and heroism are not uncommon. But what about less dramatic actions directed toward strangers? We normally don't hear of these, but their impact is no less relevant, their motive no less pure.

The love survival mechanism thrives on the strategy of kindness. Each time we give something in kindness to a stranger, we grow. We prosper when we enable someone else to prosper. When our giving remains a well-kept secret, our spirits soar, and the stranger to whom we give becomes our eternal friend. What can we give? And to whom? Perhaps the best way I can explain this is through a little rhyme I wrote recently:

> We can give a smile to someone who has a frown.
> We can give compassion to someone who is down.
> We can give a cheery "hello" to the stranger on the
> street.
> We can give a tip of the hat to the policeman on the
> beat.
> But most of all we can give our love, the most
> precious gift we have, to the stranger in us all,
> and with kindness make him glad.

Basic Life Elements Affected by the Love Survival Mechanism

> First, self-image;
> second, life meaning;
> third, inner strength;
> and fourth, personal control.

NOTES

1. Gerald G. Jampolsky, *Love Is Letting Go of Fear* (New York: Bantam Books, 1979), p. 43.

2. Albert Ellis and Robert A. Harper, *A New Guide to Rational Living* (North Hollywood: Wilshire Book Co., 1975), pp. 202-220.

3. William Glasser, *Positive Addiction* (New York: Harper & Row, 1976), p. 47.

SURVIVAL MECHANISM INVENTORY # 1
LOVE

Inventory Statements	Rating Check Appropriate Box					
	SA 5	A 4	U 3	D 2	SD 1	Score
1. I can go to others when I hurt.						
2. Others can come to me when they hurt.						
3. The world appears to me as beautiful and friendly.						
4. The world seems a better place now than when I was eleven years old.						
5. I am able to cry upon hearing a sad or touching story.						
6. I am able to greet each day with hopeful anticipation.						
7. I would be willing to "loan out" my heart in support to someone who has broken his or hers.						
8. I am comfortable telling someone, "I love you."						
9. I am comfortable when someone tells me, "I love you."						
10. I like myself despite my shortcomings.						

SM Strength Quotient =

Key

SA - Strongly Approve
A - Approve
U - Undecided
D - Disapprove
SD - Strongly Disapprove

10 - 24 Weak
25 - 34 Average
35 - 50 Strong

5

Survival Mechanism #2: Work

Blessed is he who has found his work;
let him ask no other blessedness.
—*Thomas Carlyle*

RECENTLY, WHILE WHIZZING ALONG the highway, it occurred to me that all of us driving there were involved in some kind of mayhem, rushing about like frightened fish. And for what reason? I wondered. Most of us, of course, were heading for work. As such, we were engaged in the process of survival. But I had to believe that the survival went beyond the physical and economic. There also had to be an *emotional* component to it. People somehow had to find *meaning* and *purpose* in the mad rush.

Clearly, the meaning could not be found in the physical chaos of the speed and surge of traffic. It had to go beyond that . . . it had to have psychological roots. This awareness eventually led me to the development of the second survival mechanism: work.

Work is, perhaps, the single most important kind of endeavor outside our families to which we devote time and energy. We can safely estimate that fully one third of our lives will be spent in some kind of gainful work. Think about that for a moment. A third of our time will be spent working, whether for ourselves or someone else, for a paycheck.

Even more sobering, however, is that a large number of the people in the work force are *actively* unhappy with what they are doing. This, of course, says nothing about the throngs who may be dissatisfied but will not admit it or, worse, who *pretend* to like their jobs.

One wonders why people will work at unsatisfying jobs or with uninspired and uninspiring co-workers, or under conditions that are unfulfilling if not dehumanizing. And they will do so year after year until they are burned-out reminders of their former selves. Perhaps this is a major reason work is associated with pain and drudgery rather than happiness and personal satisfaction. Why is it that most people wait for Fridays to roll around? Why do people dread Monday mornings?

Perhaps one answer to these questions lies in the possibility that, despite all its shortcomings, work does hold *intrinsic* value and meaning for us. We may complain about them and, in some cases, curse them, but we somehow manage to "hang onto our jobs." Certainly, one of the factors behind this is our universal desire to survive physically by collecting a paycheck. But we could become "beach bums" or go on welfare if we so choose. We don't *have* to stick with any job or profession. No one is holding a loaded gun to our heads insisting that we do. So work must have some value for us in itself.

How, then, does work hold intrinsic value for us? To fully understand this, I believe it is necessary to differentiate *work* from a *job*. Personally, I believe many jobs are unnatural and dehumanizing experiences that rob people of their self-worth, freedom, and dignity. *Jobs*, not work, do that to people. Jobs produce a paycheck. Work produces self-esteem. Unfortunately, most of us confuse our jobs with the concept of work. We think we hate work whereas in reality we hate our jobs! Some people, of course, actually love their jobs as well as their work. I believe these individuals are rare. Many of us will claim to love our jobs, but we deny our true sentiments out of fear.

I spoke recently with a middle-aged man who had for the past fifteen years been working at the same job on an assembly line. He hated what he was doing but, despite holding a college degree, he felt powerless to change his circumstances. Besides hating his job, he also disliked his co-workers, whom he felt were incompetent and lazy. Although he was compensated for overtime work, he bitterly resented *having* to do it when he would rather have spent the time with his family. This unfortunate man's circumstances, of course, are not unique.

Imagine, for just a moment, the following scenario. You are twenty years old and acquire a job that may be beneath your true capabilities. You keep the job out of a need to pay your bills and perhaps "save for a rainy day." You are forced to perform tasks thrust upon you by someone who is a total stranger . . . a "boss" . . . and to carry out these tasks alongside other strangers . . . your "co-workers." Adding to this burden, you are expected to smile and be pleasant and take "constructive criticism" in stride and with humility. When additional tasks are heaped onto your already overwhelming work load, you must keep your complaints to a minimum, smile, and create ingenious ways to "get the job done."

If you are able to accomplish this herculean task, you are given recognition in a written form called a "job evaluation," which requires your signature even though you may disagree with it. Providing the evaluation is positive, you may then obtain a "raise" which, because of "cutbacks" and other factors within the organization and the economy, is not commensurate with cost of living increases. You are then left with the final task of accepting and explaining this phenomenon, in a palatable way, to your family.

Studies have shown that, by the time the average working person has reached age sixty-five, he or she has several times gone through the above sequence. It is difficult to imagine going through this process *once,* let alone repeatedly! And we wonder why people burn out or have "nervous breakdowns"!

Fortunately, not everyone burns out. Who are the lucky ones who escape this fate? I believe they are those who work primarily out of a deeper *psychological* need and whose work serves mainly as a vehicle for them to survive emotionally, not just physically and economically. Their work thus becomes, either consciously or unconsciously, a *survival mechanism* designed to promote *meaning* in their lives. I believe everyone is capable of utilizing work as a vehicle to promote meaning and thus psychological survival. In large measure, however, success depends on our ability and willingness to differentiate work from a job.

During the years I have practiced as a therapist, I have spoken with countless people regarding their personal hurts, fears, disappointments, and needs. With rare exception, every person whom I have counseled has expressed a need to find fulfillment in meaningful work of some kind. This desire could extend anywhere from very minimal work, a few hours per week, to full-time work and/or academic pursuits.

Regardless of the degree of work involved, one overriding factor has remained constant: these individuals were either searching for or had already found *meaning* in and through their work. Although they may not have liked their *jobs,* they found personal fulfillment and purpose through their work. And this phenomenon occurred despite severe obstacles or even personal tragedies. With work, they were making it. Without work, emotional survival was threatened, and they perceived that survival with the same degree of urgency as physical survival would be viewed by a victim of starvation.

Perhaps one of the most memorable cases I have treated over the years was that of a thirty-nine-year-old woman twice divorced and the mother of two teenagers. Her case illustrates not only the degree to which work puts meaning into our lives and thus serves as a survival mechanism but also the degree to which its *absence* robs us of that same meaning.

This woman's smile was broad and friendly. I sensed compassion and kindness in her. I also sensed an urgency and deep fear. I was heartened that, despite two failed marriages and trouble with her teenage daughter, she was able to trust the stranger asking her questions. She was suffering from severe rheumatoid arthritis and, although she did not know it then, a malignant tumor lurked in her brain. Her family had a long history of suffering and pain, but somehow she had managed to get through it all.

It was the "getting-through process" that interested me. How, despite all the anguish and guilt associated with loss, does one persevere? The answer came when she told me that it was important for her to *work*. She was a cleaning woman, but to her it wasn't just a job. It was a mission. Her eyes sparkled as she described, in great detail, how important her work was. After all, she cleaned a local church, and where and how could parishioners worship were it not for her? To her, that church was a cathedral and its parishioners kings and queens!

Eventually, however, time ran out. Despite surgery, the cancer had spread. But as she approached the end, she did so with glorious dignity and honor. To her, life had had great meaning. And what gave it such meaning, in addition to her family, was *work*. As I stood next to her coffin, I thought I detected the faint semblance of a smile. It made me think back to the first day we met, when I asked her what she did to keep herself going in order to cope with the sadness and pain. Her answer was quick and sure: Work. "I work, Paul. I don't know what I'd do without my work."

She died while relatively young. But despite the brevity of her life, I believe that without her work, her life would not have held the meaning it did . . . no matter how many the years. Possibly, had her illness not deprived her of her beloved work, she might even be alive today.

Perhaps it is difficult to grasp just how important work, as a survival mechanism, is until we have gone through a traumatic experience in which the absence of meaningful work leaves its mark indelibly upon us. If an individual is unemployed for an extensive period or is working at an unsatisfying job, he or she begins to lose self-esteem.

Many years ago, I encountered the misfortune of going through a prolonged period of unemployment. I had been involved in a number of private enterprises that had failed, and I was trying to get a "job" earning a regular paycheck. The weeks of job hunting, interviews, and waiting stretched into months. My anxieties about *ever* finding gainful employment mounted daily, and with them my sense of despair.

During this very bleak period in my life, I reread Viktor Frankl's *Man's Search for Meaning*. One of the passages that remained in my memory was one in which Dr. Frankl compared the utter futility and hopelessness of the condemned in Nazi prison camps with the sensations felt by persons experiencing prolonged unemployment.[1]

I recall thinking I would never again be able to support my family. Never again would I take a vacation or hold my head high among friends and loved ones. I would look in the mirror and see the face of failure. Day and night I was racked by my inability to come to terms with the enormous discrepancy I felt between where I was and where I thought I should be.

As the months dragged agonizingly by, as if in slow motion, I could feel myself slipping into a deep depression. All I could think of was, "Physician, heal thyself." My depression was matched only by the rage I felt toward myself and the rest of the world. It was difficult to believe that, no matter what I did, I could not find work. At one point, I was so convinced that my situation was permanent that I was actually preparing to die! I didn't know how I would die, but I somehow viewed death as the only solution to my predicament. At that time, actual death would have been far superior to the living death that courted me daily.

Life had no meaning . . . no purpose. How could I have

fallen to such depths? How could I be in such an outra-
geous position? In my mind, there was no answer . . . no
resolution. I was prepared for death!

Then, one day, the phone rang. It had the sound of
angels singing! I knew, instinctively, that this was the end
of suffering. I knew someone was calling with the offer of
a job interview that would lead to work. And so it was!
Soon thereafter, I accepted a position in a nearby clinic
and began to live again.

I have often thought of that frightening experience. It
taught me a valuable lesson. From it I learned the meaning
and value of work. Physical survival is only half the story.
The other, and perhaps more important, half is surviving
psychologically. Although I was not consciously aware of
it at the time, I was waging a war of psychological survival
as much as one to pay the mortgage.

Why is the survival mechanism of work such an important force in our lives? First of all, work is the basic
vehicle for providing goods and services for ourselves and
our family. This is the central social function of work and,
as such, it serves as a mechanism for physical survival.
On a deeper psychological level, however, this mechanism
is rooted in our need for *self-validation*. It is more profoundly connected to our yearning for what Dr. Roderic
Gorney terms "psychic intimacy" with work, as opposed
to "psychic alienation."[2] We work, essentially, to find true
human identity and purpose.

Individuals whom I have counseled over the years who
utilized work as the survival mechanism it was designed
to be somehow recognized work as a means of staying
emotionally alive despite the odds against them. If their
marriage was falling apart, they always had their work.
If their kids were giving them a hard time, meaning could
always be found in work. When serious illness struck, you
would hear, "I can't lie around, I've got to get back to
work." But it wasn't the *job* they were referring to, since
most of them hated their jobs. It was *work*. Work was the
high road to meaning for these individuals and, as such,
enabled them to survive. It was the *process* that concerned

them rather than the product. The product was a consideration, yes, but it was not the necessary or overriding one. They were thus primarily concerned not with the *social* function of work—the production of goods and services to assure physical survival—but with its self-validating function.

Without some emotional or "psychic" connection to our jobs, they remain only jobs, and our capacity to develop and strengthen the work survival mechanism is diminished. If we are to believe Freud's dictum that mental health is inexorably connected with our ability to love and to work, the importance of developing this mechanism to its highest level becomes even more apparent.

As with the love survival mechanism, the work mechanism has specific strategies that you can use in order to implement it effectively. The specific strategies I mention below may not be the right ones for you. Select the strategies that are appropriate for *you*. If those I mention here are comfortable, then use them. If not, discard them or modify them in some way. The strategies are a *vehicle* for implementing the survival mechanisms, not an end in themselves. The exact number of strategies you use to implement and develop the work survival mechanism, as with the love mechanism or any other, is unimportant. If one strategy is sufficient, then you need not develop additional ones. In general, I have found that the average person needs between three and five strategies to effectively implement each survival mechanism.

Work Survival Mechanism Strategies

Strategy #1: Personal Interest

Perhaps the single most important factor in effectively developing the survival mechanism of work is *personal interest* in the work itself. I believe this single factor does more to differentiate work from a job than all others combined. Unless we maintain a close emotional tie with our work, it will soon lose its meaning for us. When that happens, work becomes a job.

Personal interest in our work is, in my view, directly connected to childhood interest and fantasies. Generals Douglas MacArthur and George Patton were always "playing soldier" as young boys. The great heart surgeon, Michael deBakey, loved "playing doctor" and healing things as a child. Picasso dabbled in paints when he was barely old enough to hold a brush. The great aviation pioneer, Amelia Earhart, loved airplanes as a young girl. All these great achievers found meaning and purpose in their work and went on to develop their work survival mechanisms to high levels. They were able to do this because the strategy they used was *personal interest.* Think of the vast numbers of "also-rans" among artists, physicians, and business persons: do you see the same burning, all-absorbing interest in them as you do among those I mentioned?

Early childhood interests are usually, although not always, fairly accurate indicators of directions we should consider for our life's work. Early verbal skills may point the way to a career in law, the ministry, teaching, writing, or sales. Interest in math and the physical sciences frequently develops into engineering, computer, medical, or architectural careers. Remember, however, the actual career pursued is *not* what develops the work survival mechanism. The specific careers are merely vehicles toward that end. What develops the survival mechanism of work is the *emotional* or *psychic connection* to the specific career or job. It is the degree to which we are validated and confirmed as human beings that causes this survival mechanism to grow and flourish. The greater our intimate connection with career or job, the greater the strength of this mechanism. The weaker that connection, the weaker this mechanism will be and, consequently, the lower our capacity to thrive as human beings.

In his classic book *Think and Grow Rich*, Napoleon Hill speaks of the importance of "singleness of purpose" in achieving our goals and dreams.[3] Clearly, it is to our advantage to have such single-mindedness, or "burn," as some have called it. But what if we have no burn or desire? What if we have never had any overriding interests as children, or as adults? How then do we develop this strategy of *personal interest?* I believe there are several possibilities.

First of all, give yourself six months to a year to get into a job—no more! If at the end of that time you do not feel comfortable and *fulfilled*, get out. Second, do not allow yourself to be swayed from your decision by anyone who does not have a *personal* interest in your welfare. Third, during your six- to twelve-month trial period, become as actively involved in as many aspects of the job as is practicable. Fourth, do not seek out other kinds of employment during your trial period. This will "contaminate" your efforts to obtain an objective decision. Fifth, *act* as if the job you currently hold will be the *only* job available to you—ever. This will force your unconscious mind to immediately start seeking alternatives if it rejects your notion. The famed hypnotherapist, Milton Erickson, M.D., made an important observation when he stated that we should trust our unconscious because it knows more than we do![4]

If you follow this line of thought and action, you should be able to develop the personal interest of which I'm speaking. The reason is that you are allowing yourself to become involved in the *process* of the job, not merely its content. This should result in your connecting with the job on an intimate level. You will then either feel validated and uplifted, or you will gradually experience what most people do: a sense of alienation and loss of self-worth. No one will have to tell you this. You will know it!

Strategy #2: Talent

A young woman in her late twenties was sitting in my office recently. She was making plans to open her own beauty shop and was excited about the prospect of doing something on her own. I remarked casually that she was fortunate to have the talent to do something like that. She immediately responded with, "Talent? I don't have any talent. It doesn't take talent to do what I do. Just guts!" She was correct about needing "guts" but dead wrong about not having any talent.

Everyone has talent. Everyone! The key is to discover where our talent lies and then to *believe* in it. Once we have done that, this strategy becomes one of the most productive in developing the work survival mechanism. Like personal interest, the talent strategy usually manifests itself in early childhood. As noted, the work force is filled with those whose early childhood talents blossomed and developed into careers of considerable magnitude. Many people in the arts, sciences, humanities, law, and education showed their native interest initially as very young children.

It is important to distinguish between talent and personal interest. We may have personal interest in something but little talent for it. When personal interest and talent are both present, we have a winning combination. By the same token, when one has a talent for something but *denies* personal interest, he or she is laying the groundwork for failure by destroying the work survival mechanism.

Discovering talent early, developing and protecting it, are undoubtedly among the surest ways of enhancing the survival mechanism of work. If we leave out any of these three factors, the strategy of talent loses much if not all its effectiveness in the development of the work survival mechanism. Of course, if we do not actively *believe* in our talent, we clearly lay the foundation for failure. And lack of belief is frequently manifested by sheer foolishness— often in the face of opportunity. The end result, as the following story reveals, is often tragic.

I recall with great sadness a young singer-friend in his early twenties. He possessed a great and golden tenor voice. His talent had been discovered at an early age, and his teachers expected great things from him. He worked hard at developing his gift, but then, in a moment of thoughtless abandon, he threw it all away. He mixed a few uppers with a few downers and gulped them away with vodka. He went into convulsions, and when the doctors had brought them under control, the golden throat was silenced forever. The young man had become a paraplegic, with residual nerve damage throughout his body. When I visited him in the hospital, he could barely speak, let alone sing. He had discovered his talent, he developed it, but he did not *protect* it . . . or *believe* in it.

Discover your talent. Develop it. Protect it. Believe in it. Then *use* it as a strategy toward developing your work survival mechanism.

Strategy #3: Practice

Practice makes perfect! Three words say it all. The great pianist Artur Rubinstein once said, "If I don't practice one day, I know it. If I don't practice two days, my friends know it. If I don't practice three days, the public knows it." Practice, as a work survival strategy, is important from the standpoint that, despite our best intentions, unless we practice our craft, our work survival mechanism declines. And with it declines the meaning that work holds for us. As work or any of the other survival mechanisms lose their meaning, we correspondingly lose inner strength. We then, of course, become vulnerable to external forces and the possibility of emotional collapse.

As with talent, the capacity to practice can be enhanced. The key is to avoid procrastination. Procrastination is, indeed, the "thief of time." Don't put it off. Do it now! The practice strategy is a powerful one because we can learn to control it. You'll notice that the strategies I mention are those we can *consciously control*. Perhaps the most readily controlled of all the strategies is *practice*. We can decide when to do it, for how long, how often, and how intensively.

For a number of years I had the opportunity to study vocal music. My teacher gave me numerous exercises that seemed boring at the time. It was difficult for me to link them with the finished product—a well-placed vocal tone. But somehow I had faith that, if I kept practicing, I would eventually convert those exercises into what I wanted to do with a song.

During what seemed like an endless process, I learned not only the value of practice but also of *repetition*. The more I did the vocal exercises, the easier they became. Soon I realized that repetition and *persistence* evolved into a kind of *intensity*. Ultimately, it was the intensity that carried over to my singing and that I felt in performance and projected to the audience. I remember with humility and deep satisfaction the many memorable performances I have been able to give over the years as a result of deploying the practice strategy in strengthening my work survival mechanism.

Remember, "if you don't use it, you lose it." Although the practice strategy can be effectively used with *all* the survival mechanisms, I believe its most salient use is within the mechanism of work.

Strategy #4: Motivation

Motivation, as a concept in human functioning, has been discussed thoroughly in both the professional and the self-help literature. Abraham Maslow treats motivation as a central theme in his analysis of "self-actualization."[5] Others, including Sigmund Freud and Carl Jung, have dealt with motivation as a major concept in their psychological theories of human personality development. Denis Waitley defines motivation as "motive in action,"[6] saying that there are two kinds: *penalty motivation* and *reward motivation*. As we might expect, the former is rooted in fear of sanction while the latter derives from the hope of benefit or reward to the doer. Interestingly, Waitley goes on to state that "Both 'Penalty Motivation' and 'Reward Motivation' cause stress."[7] Stress, however, according to Waitley, is not the issue. It is how we *respond* to the so-called stressors and the degree to which they motivate us to move our lives forward that constitute the central issue. In this sense, stress can be either good or bad . . . the choice is ours!

Despite literary attention, however, the concept of motivation remains elusive. At the risk of adding to the confusion, I offer yet another slant on the concept. To me, motivation represents a *strategy*. And like strategies mentioned throughout the book, motivation is a concept that can be developed and used to enhance the survival mechanism of work.

Motivation is not a fixed state or condition. Like talent, personal interest, and practice, motivation can be nurtured into a finely-tuned instrument for personal growth and happiness. We do this by developing a *desire* to achieve that can be satisfied only by achieving!

Before entering the therapy profession, I sold life insurance. It was among the most interesting and enlightening pursuits I have ever undertaken. Once a fellow agent asked me if I would go out on a cruel, wintry night and travel to some remote region just to sell an insurance policy. I hesitated for a moment. Impatiently he retorted, "Paul, if you hesitate even for a second, then you're not really motivated. You don't really have the *desire!*"

I have often thought of his remark. It truly exemplified his own genuine desire and motivation. If you go, you have the desire (motivation). If you don't go, or you hesitate, you don't have it. Simple.

How then does one become motivated? Listed below are four suggestions to help you.

1. Set yourself performance standards that are realistic. People frequently set unrealistic goals ... goals that, at their particular point in life, are unattainable. When these goals aren't achieved, they become discouraged and feel that setting future goals is futile. In short, they give up.
2. Develop habits of self-reliance. "You make it happen!" No one will do it for you. As you cut your own path in life you will acquire the mental toughness to move successfully through the challenges life presents.

3. Stay away from controlling people. Don't fall into the trap of allowing them to run your life. It is virtually impossible to become a motivated, mature person when you lean too heavily upon others or, worse, allow *them* to lean too heavily upon you.
4. Do what D.H. Lawrence suggests when he says: "You might as well take the lightning for once, and feel it go through you. You might as well accept the thunderbolt and prepare for storms. You'll not get vitality any other way."[8]

Strategy #5: Commitment

The final strategy to develop and strengthen your work survival mechanism is *commitment*. As with motivation, commitment is often misunderstood and thus loses its strategic possibilities. When you understand it clearly, the commitment strategy can be used systematically to enhance your work survival mechanism.

Commitment, according to John Gardner, means the "striving toward meaningful goals, not necessarily the attaining of those goals."[9] Such commitment, however, requires not only self-discipline but *self-less* discipline as well.

Commitment to any worthy cause is in itself an ennobling virtue. When it is combined with the kind of self-less discipline required in truly productive work, commitment is elevated to an art form. By committing ourselves to the joyous pursuit of our work, we become artists who paint the pictures of our own destinies.

Basic Life Elements Affected by
the Work Survival Mechanism

First, life meaning;
second, self-image;
third, inner strength;
and fourth, personal control.

NOTES

1. Viktor E. Frankl, *Man's Search for Meaning* (Boston: Beacon Press, 1962), p. 70.

2. Roderic Gorney, *The Human Agenda* (New York: Bantam Books, Inc., 1972), p. 414.

3. Napoleon Hill, *Think and Grow Rich* (Greenwich: Fawcett Publications, 1960), pp. 33-47.

4. Sidney Rosen, ed., *My Voice Will Go With You: The Teaching Tales of Milton H. Erickson, M.D.* (New York: W.W. Norton, 1982), pp. 57-74.

5. Abraham H. Maslow, *The Farther Reaches of Human Nature* (New York: Penguin Books, 1971), p. 289.

6. Denis Waitley, *Seeds of Greatness: The Ten Best Kept Secrets of Total Success* (Old Tappan: Fleming H. Revell, 1983), p. 173.

7. *Ibid.*, p. 174.

8. Vivian de Sola Pinto and Warren Roberts, eds., *The Complete Poems of D.H. Lawrence* (New York: Penguin Books, 1971), p. 559.

9. John W. Gardner, *Self-Renewal: The Individual and the Innovative Society* (New York: Harper Colophon, 1964), p. 98.

SURVIVAL MECHANISM INVENTORY # 2
WORK

Inventory Statements	SA 5	A 4	U 3	D 2	SD 1	Score
1. I view my work as fun.						
2. When I'm working, I see myself as creating something.						
3. My parents enjoy/enjoyed their work.						
4. I usually experience a feeling of personal growth when I'm working.						
5. Rarely do I see my work as a job.						
6. I can recall my first work experience as positive.						
7. If I could live my life over, I would do the same kind of work as I'm doing now.						
8. My work is self-validating.						
9. Very infrequently do I envy what others do to earn a living.						
10. If I were independently wealthy, I would voluntarily do my work.						

Rating
Check Appropriate Box

SM Strength Quotient =

Key

SA - Strongly Approve
A - Approve
U - Undecided
D - Disapprove
SD - Strongly Disapprove

10 - 24 Weak
25 - 34 Average
35 - 50 Strong

6

Survival Mechanism #3:
Play

> When I'm playful I use the meridians of
> longitude and parallels of latitude for
> a seine, and drag the Atlantic Ocean for
> whales. I scratch my head with the
> lightning and purr myself to sleep with
> the thunder.
>
> —*Mark Twain*

PLAY, LIKE WORK, is a major survival mechanism. We spend more time in play, or thinking about play, than we realize. Play is not only an enjoyable pastime, it is also a vital source of energy and self-renewal.

Hans Selye, the eminent authority on stress, has stated that we have only a limited amount of energy, and once that specified allotment is used up, it cannot be replaced.[1] I contend, however, that if we obtain what we need from play, the actual drain on our energy pool will be reduced substantially. Thus, instead of losing energy to stress and anxiety, we will preserve it through play.

Play comes in many forms. It can mean different

things to different people, and it ranges from an organized activity like a tennis match to an informal game of checkers. It can be exhausting or very relaxing. Sometimes play is a solitary experience, at other times a highly social one. Regardless of how we define play, from a survival perspective play is fun used for serious purposes.

One thing is certain: play has become a part of our socio-cultural fabric, from organized sports and games to music and camping. We participate in play at home, in school, in parks, and at every organizational and institutional level imaginable. Play is rooted deeply in our social order because it fills a basic human *need* and, as such, represents a major survival mechanism.

Play has many ramifications as a survival mechanism. Instead of trying to cover all of them, I will focus on play as a survival mechanism whose major purpose is the *preservation of life energy.*

Chronic stress and anxiety, as Dr. Selye observed, can produce severe, irreplaceable energy loss. Play, in my opinion, can greatly reduce that loss by reducing a person's anxiety level. This reduction results in increased inner strength—one of the four basic life elements.

The story of Norman Cousins's life-threatening bout with crippling rheumatoid arthritis is now legendary. In the midst of a brilliant career as a writer and editor of the *Saturday Review,* Cousins was stricken with a degenerative and potentially fatal collagen disease.[2] Refusing to accept this grim prognosis, Cousins, with the kind help and understanding of his physician, undertook a course of "self-treatment" that healed him. A major part of that treatment was the use of humor and laughter.

By watching funny movies and old Candid Camera clips, Cousins gave himself daily doses of healthy laughter. In effect, he *played* every day! The end result was a full recovery and a faculty position at the University of California Medical School, where he continues to teach about the healing benefits of humor and play.

As the saying goes, "What is one person's work is another person's play," and vice versa. If, however, we can make play and work one and the same, we grow and prosper. We find the winning combination that enhances life rather than draining and depleting it. Play, like love and work, is one of the three basic social functions of human behavior. Play is, however, an *optional* type of activity, and although it may not sustain life in the same manner as work and love, it clearly helps to *enrich* it. And perhaps enriching life's quality is, in the final analysis, its purest definition.

Play has a spontaneous nature. It is free and joyful. Although we might associate it with competitive sports, play is itself not competitive. It does not seek to dominate. Instead, like love and work, play's overriding and central social function is *self-validation*. As Dr. Roderic Gorney has aptly stated, "Play will comprise that part of the self-validating function which explores and exercises the person's potentialities for the joy inherent in the activity . . . "[3] According to Dr. Gorney, play is performed "for its own sake."

It is play's element of joy that, in my opinion, *preserves energy* and increases our inner strength. By experiencing joy in our play, we reduce the inevitable anxiety and stress that is bound to come to each of us on a daily basis.

When play becomes work—a "job"—it loses its healing quality. This is why so many people fail in business ventures. They may have a good idea or product, but when they attempt to sell or promote it, they fail. Failure comes not because the product or idea is poor but rather because the *fun* or play element has gone out of it. We think, erroneously, "Now that I'm in business, (instead of having fun) it's time to 'get serious.' " A major cause of the forty-five to sixty percent of annual marital failures, can, I believe, be traced to couples taking themselves and their relationships too seriously. They forget to play. The fun is gone.

Keep play in your life and you will not only have more energy, you will be a much happier and more prosperous person. Below are listed several strategies to help you develop and strengthen your play survival mechanism. Remember, these are only suggestions. Try to think of others that may prove even more useful to you *personally* as you enhance this mechanism.

Play Survival Mechanism Strategies

Strategy #1: Associate with Positive, Up-beat People

To enhance your play survival mechanism, it is vital that you associate with friendly, enthusiastic people—supportive people, not "downers." No matter how positive and optimistic you think you are, when exposed on a consistent basis to negative individuals you tend to get pulled downward. This phenomenon rarely, if ever, works in reverse. No matter how sure you are that you can "lift" someone who is chronically down to your higher, more optimistic level, ultimately the downward forces seem to win out. If you doubt this, just ask the spouse of any alcoholic how successful he or she has been at changing the other person's drinking habits.

BEWARE! The "Poisonalities"

When I was in my early twenties and studying voice, my teacher used to emphasize the importance of attitude in proper vocal production. He also believed one's attitude was directly connected to relationships. He enjoyed reminding me that some of my relationships were not the best, and he frequently urged me to get rid of the "Poisonalities" in my life. His little play on words has remained with me and serves as a helpful reminder every time I catch myself slipping into a negative relationship.

When we are receptive, the positive and upbeat people we meet have a way of lifting our spirits. They encourage the *playfulness* inherent in each of us. We experience joy when we are around them. They enable us to preserve our energies instead of dissipating them. I encourage you to seek out positive individuals and watch your play survival mechanism gain strength. Stay away from the nay-say-ers—those who say "It won't work; you can't do it; it's too late." Instead, *go out of your way* to find the upbeat, positive-thinking folks who believe in you and your goals and dreams. Remember: some people are "Poisonalities." The antidote to them is to surround yourself with positive thinkers.

Strategy #2: Seek Out Positive Experiences

The second strategy is seeking out and developing positive life experiences. A positive life experience is one that is uplifting and self-validating. Any experience that diminishes self-esteem in *any way* is a negative life experience.

Any relationship—be it friendship, marriage, employee-employer, or parent-child—that brings a sense of joy and mutual fulfillment is, by definition, a positive, self-validating one. Positive relationships will spawn positive life experiences; negative relationships will inevitably foster negative experiences.

A few years ago I worked with a middle-aged couple in pre-marital counseling. Both had been previously married and had come to me to "check out" whether they were doing the right thing. Curiously, both were from broken homes, both had previously married people from broken homes, and both retained the same unrealistic expectations for the second marriage that they had for the first.

Essentially, both were courting disaster a second time! Instead of positioning themselves to experience a positive relationship the second time around, they were doggedly pursuing exactly the same negative life course. Despite my repeated warnings, they proceeded to marry each other. Within two months, they were experiencing problems, and within six months they were separated. One year from the date of their marriage, predictably, they were divorced again. As with so many "Hollywood marriages," it would not surprise me if this couple repeated this pattern yet a third, fourth, and fifth time.

Seek out positive people and positive life experiences. They will pay you dividends in the long run, the most important of which will be the strengthening of your play survival mechanism.

Strategy #3: Find Something to Smile About

Scientific studies have shown that it takes more emotional and physical energy to frown than to smile or engage in hearty laughter. In addition, when we smile or enjoy a good "belly laugh," our entire physiological system is involved in a positive way. When we hear a funny story our diaphragms are called upon to discharge gusts of laughter. Our musculo-skeletal systems go limp. We relax and "let go."

When we frown or become angry, we experience a negative physiological response. We acquire headaches and backaches. We feel tense and experience a loss of energy. Our breathing becomes shallow and tight, and we suffer a loss of oxygen to the brain. This series of events results in poor thinking and diminished emotional control. Under such conditions we are bound to make poor judgments and suffer lowered self-esteem. Each of these negative outcomes is preventable simply by learning to smile!

A colleague-friend of mine is a master story- and joke-teller. He has a million of them! Frequently, when burdened with difficult cases, he'll visit or phone me and ask if I've "heard the one about . . . ?" Invariably, I haven't. He then proceeds to tell me (even if I don't want to know!), taking obvious delight in doing so. Although unaware of it, he uses the "smile strategy" to strengthen his play survival mechanism. I am convinced this simple strategy makes him a survivor.

The next time you're feeling burned out, try this little experiment. Pick up the nearest *Reader's Digest*, turn to the section entitled, "Laughter, The Best Medicine," and read some of the stories and anecdotes. Notice how, within seconds, your mood is elevated. You may not be rolling on the floor with laughter, but your mood *will* improve, although perhaps only slightly.

Dr. Raymond Moody, in his book *Laugh After Laugh*, views humor from three basic perspectives: physiological, psychological, and social.[4] He points out that humor and laughter integrate these three aspects of human functioning and are related directly to our sense of *total* health.

Humor provides us with a "natural high." Sometimes a good laugh enables us to feel good even when we don't want to! We respond as we do when the physician hits us on the knee with his rubber hammer: every time he taps us in a particular spot, we have the predictable "knee-jerk" reaction. Sometimes we need to give our emotional "funny bone" a good tap!

A growing body of indisputable research underscores the definite, clear-cut connection between humor, smiling, laughter, and our physiological responses. And those responses, in turn, affect our moods. When our moods are positively affected, our physiological responses are in turn also positively affected. This healthy, growth-producing cycle strengthens our play survival mechanism. We become healthier, happier, and more productive individuals as a result.

Strategy #4: "Get Physical!"

Drs. William Glasser, Kenneth Cooper, and others have studied the effects of running and other aerobics on both physical and emotional health. In his book *Stations of the Mind*, Glasser states that *both* runners and meditators, during the course of their "addictive behavior," release endorphins in their brains.[5] These naturally-occurring chemicals produce a "high" in the runner or meditator that negative addicts obtain only artificially. In contrast to negative addicts, who continuously become weaker as a result of their addiction, Glasser reveals that positive addicts gain inner strength.

To advance Glasser's theory one step further: the degree to which *any* physical activity, running or otherwise, is *fun*, will determine the degree to which one's play survival mechanism will be strengthened.

In addition to just plain having fun, gaining inner strength and preserving energy should be our ultimate purpose in engaging in any physical activity. If running, for example, is a joyous experience, it will *automatically* strengthen our play survival mechanism. If it is not fun, if instead it is drudgery, stop doing it and find another activity.

A good friend of mine is a runner. He runs about six to eight miles a day. Every day! He loves it. Whenever I see him he's "up." Nothing ever seems to get to him. If he has a problem, he seems to handle it with ease. What's truly remarkable about him is his capacity to play. Running has become a vehicle for him to develop and strengthen his play survival mechanism—*and he doesn't even know it!* He has been doing this for years and has gotten emotionally stronger with time. In addition to increasing his energy level and inner strength, running seems to have sustained and strengthened his three other basic life elements: *control, self-image, and life meaning.*

Strategy #5: "Get Organized!"

Man is, by nature, a social creature. It is practically impossible to obtain a true understanding of homo sapiens when studied in isolation. Almost every activity imaginable occurs within a larger group context. Even the lone fisherman enjoys comparing his "catch" with that of his fellow anglers. It is thus understandable why involving ourselves in organized group activities might occasion joy and fulfillment.

Countless group activities are available in which participation strengthens our play survival mechanism. The activity should be *organized* only because, if we are left to choose at random the groups in which to involve ourselves, we are likely to make the activities more isolated and less group-oriented. This is not to say that isolated activities are less beneficial toward developing the play survival mechanism. They clearly are not, as I will show in the next section; however, as much as we are social, group-oriented creatures, we still tend toward isolated activity if we feel threatened or shy. Seeking out the organized group can help prevent this tendency and, concurrently, afford a unique and productive way of strengthening the play survival mechanism.

An organized, well-run group has a *positive contagion* factor associated with it. Many people who have experienced a sales rally or religious revival meeting will attest to this phenomenon. There is something very exciting and energizing about four or five thousand people all shouting, singing, laughing, or swaying in unison. It gets the juices flowing and the muscles moving!

As exciting as a large group can be, smaller groups also serve to develop the play survival mechanism. This is one reason the "coffee klatch" and bridge club are so popular. Who can deny the popularity of BINGO groups, large or small? Committees and various types of social clubs and fraternal organizations, such as Knights of Columbus, Masons, and Kiwanis, are extremely successful for the same reason.

For many years I have run parent support groups. At the outset, I always ask what members hope to gain by their attendance. Although a myriad of reasons are normally given, rarely do any parents remotely suggest joining the group to enhance their play survival mechanism. Despite the "serious nature" of these groups, I have yet to observe members *not* enjoying themselves in the process!

Alcoholics Anonymous has, for decades, fostered support groups that have sustained countless thousands of recovering alcoholics and their families. Although members' purposes in attending AA meetings are deadly serious, most depart such meetings feeling reassured and comforted. Subsequent meetings are then anticipated and can, for many, become enjoyable *social* experiences.

I know people who are members of informal groups that regularly meet in each other's homes to play bridge or poker. Several clients of mine would never dream of missing their weekly BINGO! I know of several others who, with friends or associates, attend either a movie, concert, or play practically every weekend. Many are involved in informal sports activities.

There is almost a magnetic quality that causes some groups to attract and hold its members. During the time I was actively involved in performing music, I had the good fortune of associating with various choral groups around the country. Some of them were church and temple choirs while others were community-based professional and semi-professional ensembles. We performed everything from *Bach's B Minor Mass* to *The Sound of Music*.

It always intrigued me that people not only joined these groups, they often remained members over long periods of time—some of them for life. It wasn't until years later that I realized people stayed around not so much for the music or performances as for the camaraderie, friendship, and sheer fun inherent in the group itself. Whenever there happened to be a "stellar performance," well, that was "frosting on the cake."

Participants simply enjoyed singing in these choirs, and as they did they *unconsciously* strengthened their play survival mechanisms. How exciting it would be if more of us *consciously* took the initiative and joined more of these groups. Life could truly be a song!

The list is endless when it comes to groups, large and small, physical or non-physical, organized or non-organized, that one can join to enhance the play survival mechanism. The significant factor in all these groups is the mutual contagion effect on members and the all-important element of fun. Consciously or unconsciously, people join these groups for personal development, friendship, the need to belong, and the pure joy of it. More important, they join to increase the strength of their play survival mechanisms.

Strategy #6: Learn to Play "Solitaire"

Psychologists tell us that some of our most vivid and lasting memories are formed in early childhood. One of mine is that of my great-aunt Martha. I can still see her sitting comfortably in her favorite chair in front of a mahogany coffee table, playing for hours on end her favorite game—Solitaire.

It didn't matter what the weather was, or the state of the world, or how many worries she had. When Martha played Solitaire, every care, every problem seemed to melt away for her. I know she didn't realize it and I, as a six-year-old, *definitely* didn't realize it, but when Martha played Solitaire, she was strengthening her play survival mechanism.

Countless solitary activities and hobbies like card-playing, knitting, coin and stamp collecting, bird-watching, swimming, canoeing, body-building, yoga, and karate can serve as excellent means of strengthening the play survival mechanism. People who engage in these pursuits invariably experience an increase in the four basic life elements in addition to the preservation of their energy levels.

The other day, while driving to an appointment, my eye caught the message on a bumper sticker on a car ahead of me. It read simply: "I'd rather be fishing." I found myself nodding in agreement and smiling at how aptly that brief message offered the sentiments of countless people who read it.

Why is sport fishing so popular? Because it's *fun!* I was only a boy of nine when my father took me to the rocky shores of Lake Erie in Cleveland, Ohio, and helped me cast my first line into those choppy waters. Even now, forty years later, I recall the sheer joy I felt when I hooked and landed my first yellow perch. I felt a surge of *inner strength.* I felt in *control* when I landed that perch. My *self-esteem* was showing when I announced to my mother that I caught that fish . . . *by myself!* For that nine-year-old, life took on new *meaning.* The pattern was to be repeated countless times in the intervening years.

Although this book is not a treatise on fishing, it is important to note that fishing, in my opinion, comes as close to meditation (without meditating) as any activity I know. One can literally forget the world when engrossed in this sport. If for no other reason than that, I heartily recommend it to all who can endure the long hours between bites! It's amazing how such a solitary and tranquil activity can produce such strength of character.

Basic Life Elements Affected by the Play Survival Mechanism

First, inner strength;
second, personal control;
third, self-image;
and fourth, life meaning.

NOTES

1. Hans Selye, *Stress Without Distress* (New York: New American Library, 1974), pp. 26-29.

2. Norman Cousins, *Anatomy of an Illness as Perceived by the Patient* (New York: W.W. Norton, 1979).

3. Roderic Gorney, *The Human Agenda* (New York: Bantam Books, 1972), p. 456.

4. Raymond A. Moody, *Laugh After Laugh* (Jacksonville: Headwaters Press, 1978), pp. 5-16.

5. William Glasser, *Stations of The Mind* (New York: Harper & Row, 1981), p. 253.

SURVIVAL MECHANISM INVENTORY # 3
PLAY

Inventory Statements	SA 5	A 4	U 3	D 2	SD 1	Score
1. I am friendly most of the time.						
2. I can laugh easily.						
3. Rarely do I take myself too seriously.						
4. I see the world as a playful environment.						
5. When things go wrong, I'm able to chuckle and say, "Forget it."						
6. I find joy in my daily activities.						
7. I can be happy even when the world seems sad.						
8. It is easier for me to laugh or smile than cry or frown.						
9. My parents were/are able to find joy in life.						
10. I remember being happy when I was nine years old.						

Rating
Check Appropriate Box

Key

SA - Strongly Approve
A - Approve
U - Undecided
D - Disapprove
SD - Strongly Disapprove

SM Strength Quotient =

10 - 24 Weak
25 - 34 Average
35 - 50 Strong

7

Survival Mechanism #4: Creativity

In creating, the only hard thing's to begin;
A grass-blade's no easier to make than an oak.
—*James Russell Lowell*

FROM ANCIENT TIMES, creativity and the creative impulse have had a positive effect on mankind. In some cases creativity even included healing power. Both pre-literate and early literate societies used music, dance, drama, and song to dispel evil spirits and cure the sick.

The Old Testament relates how King Saul called upon David and his famous harp to chase away his evil moods. The ancient Greeks saw a clear connection between art, beauty, and health. They would frequently, for example, hold dramatic enactments to cleanse the inner spirit.

People's creative urge can be traced easily from their ancient roots through the Middle Ages and the Renaissance up to modern times. One can readily argue that the creative urge is something we all possess to varying degrees.

Viktor Lowenfeld, an influential theorist in the field of the therapeutic use of art education, states: "Creativity is an instinct which all people possess, an instinct which we use primarily to solve and express life's problems."[1] Creativity and the creative process are among the most influential of all the survival mechanisms when it comes to enhancing one's self-esteem and gaining inner strength and personal control. In addition, I believe that, as we gain fuller awareness of our creative powers and use those powers more effectively, we also perceive greater meaning in our lives.

John Gardner, noted psychologist and writer, points out that creativity is more than one's "I.Q." or the ability to master a creative medium like music or painting. Mastery, he states, does not equate with originality. And it is originality that is the core of creativity. True creativity is a *process*, and that process is not responsive to mere conscious control; instead, the conscious and unconscious minds must work in harmony to achieve it. Gardner goes on to say that creativity is rooted in our earliest childhood and family experiences and that, without the proper environmental influences, our creative talents and impulses will not find release.[2]

I recall vividly how my own interest in and love for music and, in particular, singing, was generated in my home. My parents had come to America as children themselves, my father being fifteen and mother only twelve years of age. They left their native Romania and Hungary and, like so many others of their era, were destined to never again see their homeland or loved ones.

My father was always a hard-driving man whose chief ambition was to be a "good provider" for his family. He was a survivor, to be sure, and did it primarily by brute force. My mother was the quieter, gentler, more spiritual parent. After realizing she probably would never again return to her beloved Hungary or see her own dear parents, she devoted herself to raising her six children, studying the Bible, attending church and, most important, pursuing her *music*.

My mother also loved to recite, in Hungarian, poetry by the great Hungarian poets. Countless times she stood before hushed church congregations and, in her inimitable way, gave dramatic recitations that would bring tears to the eyes of her listeners.

Music, however, remained my mother's true vehicle for self-expression. When she sang, you could hear something indescribably beautiful in her voice, something iridescent. It was not only the vocal tone that touched you but the special *meaning* her voice carried. It was filled with passion and compassion.

I never realized until years after her death that that meaning was the real reason my mother sang. Through her music she found a sense of meaning and self-esteem unavailable to her by any other means except, perhaps, her deep religious faith.

Music became, for my mother, the vehicle for gaining not only meaning and a sense of self-worth, but also a means of achieving control and inner strength out of what otherwise might have been a chaotic existence. The creative outlet of music was her chief survival mechanism. Without it she could not have had the emotional and physical energy to successfully meet the demands of six growing children and a marriage that lasted forty-seven years.

Creativity may be more essential to life than we think. William Glasser, in his enlightening book *Take Effective Control of Your Life,* states: "from an ancient survival standpoint, the ability to create is by far the most important function of our behavioral systems. No species that shuts down its creative system could compete successfully against those who never stopped creating."[3]

Learning how to tap the creative resources within us requires persistent effort. We often discover that creative solutions evolve from those thoughts and dreams, already a part of us, that need only be brought into clearer focus through concentrated mental energy.

Dr. Glasser underscores this point by stating that the source of our creativity lies in our ability to "reorganize" the "familiar organized behaviors."[4] He is referring here to the basic, simple, everyday things we do, say, think, or feel. By reorganizing these everyday activities, we learn a new approach to old problems and obstacles.

Glasser goes on to say that this reorganizational ability is an "intangible process" that is difficult to describe, but upon close scrutiny it becomes visible as a "maelstrom of jumbled feelings, thoughts, and potential actions that are in a constant state of reorganization."[5]

This is simply Glasser's eloquent way of saying that we are all in a constant state of evolving as human beings. The incredible part of this evolution is that we may or may not be aware of the process as it is occurring. Creativity, then, represents humankind's physical, emotional, and spiritual evolution. Or, in William Glasser's words, "Creativity is the creation of something new that has never before existed in the life of its creator." To me, this represents an incredibly exciting idea and one that should hold great promise for each of us. The cliche of the 1920s, "Every day in every way I am getting better and better," may have a new validity for us, not only as individuals but for our species as well.

The major reason I believe creativity is so important and exciting is that, as we achieve it, we go right to the heart of strengthening our self-esteem, a basic element of our emotional lives. Without self-esteem, it becomes difficult, if not impossible, to develop the other three basic elements. And, as I pointed out earlier, *all four* elements, like the survival mechanisms themselves, are interconnected and mutually interdependent. Each element *must* be strengthened to assure success of the others, and self-esteem, or self-image, is the plumbline for the other three elements.

Perhaps the above statement can be further reinforced by the advice of the famed child psychologist Dr. Bruno Bettelheim, who said, "The absence of self-respect is a central issue in all functional disturbances. The most important task of therapy is not to have the patient gain insight into his unconscious, but to restore him to a high degree of self-esteem."[6] We could argue effectively that achieving this end is the central purpose of developing the survival mechanisms.

Be Willing to Pay the Price

Achieving creativity is an excellent means of developing self-esteem and strengthening as well the other basic life elements. As much as creativity can aid us in our quest for personal happiness, however, we must be prepared to pay a price for creativity itself.

Several years ago I was involved in a business venture with a highly creative and successful individual. He also possessed more than his share of good common sense. He was fond of reminding me to "stay in the creative stage" and not to sit around and count paper clips when I could be out in the trenches. "Get out there and *make* it happen, Paul. Nothing happens until you *make* it happen!" he would say. What a leader he was! What an inspiration! Perhaps the greatest lesson I learned from him was that a definite, unmistakable price must be paid for any kind of worthwhile success. And no matter how we may try, there is no negotiating the price! To be creative is to be successful, and every successful person is, by definition, a creative one. He or she *willingly* pays whatever price is necessary for success.

There are, of course, degrees of creativity in us all. Not everyone can be a Michelangelo or DaVinci. We can't necessarily sing like Luciano Pavarotti or run a marathon in record time. And neither do we need to. Each of us, however, in our own way, can remain in the creative stage and in so doing make our unique contribution.

Creativity Survival Mechanism Strategies

Strategy #1: Openness

To become creative individuals, we must develop the personal qualities that creative people possess. John Gardner has defined four distinct qualities of creative people.[7] These qualities can be developed and used as survival strategies to strengthen the creativity survival mechanism. The first quality is *openness*.

People who are open with themselves and others are "the luckiest people in the world." They are truly free, for they have nothing to hide. The saddest people, by contrast, are those who go around pretending to be happy but all the while hide behind a mask of false bravado and self-righteousness. They have long ago closed their hearts and minds to the beauty of the world and the goodness inherent in others. Their self-doubt and suspicion of others serve only to increase their emotional distance from the kindness that would surely come their way if given a chance.

Open people, on the other hand, are a joy to be with. They exude a warmth and honest humility that puts others at ease. They do not have to be phony because they are self-assured without having to prove it. The truly open and creative person, in Gardner's words, possesses a "freshness of perception" and an "unspoiled awareness"[8] of him- or herself and of reality.

Strategy #2: Independence

The second quality that Gardner finds in creative people is *independence*. Creativity requires, in fact *demands,* independence. Some of the greatest thinkers, writers, musicians, artists, and scientific minds in history were also among the most fiercely independent people.

Constraints can inhibit and, in some cases, even destroy the creative impulse. As a therapist, I witness this inhibiting tendency among parents who fear their children's growing up. Because of their low self-esteem, many parents try to make their children feel inadequate and keep them in a dependent position in order to feel adequate and independent themselves. This charade doesn't do much for either the parent or the child. Eventually, the child catches on and resents the parent's intrusion. The parent, in turn, feels unappreciated and rejects the child. Both are losers in the struggle for self-esteem, inner strength, personal control, and perception of life's meaning.

Independence *in any relationship* is best achieved when each party is able to "let go" of the other person, to enable personal growth and maturation to occur. Each must be willing to risk personal loss, disappointment, and failure in anticipation of a greater gain in strength for the creativity survival mechanism. Unless this happens, until we stop "playing it safe" or worrying about what others might think or say, the struggle for survival and prosperity will be lost. Instead we must, as Gardner states, become visionaries. We must see the "gap" between what *is* and what *could* be.[9]

Strategy #3: Flexibility

Gardner's third quality is *flexibility*. Creative individuals have developed the art of "playfulness" as they go about the business of living. They can remain "detached" from conventional, rigid categories of the way life should be lived. They can readily endure ambiguities and paradoxes, both internal and external, both conscious and unconscious.

During the course of therapy sessions, I frequently try to incorporate humor or personal interest stories and anecdotes as a means of alleviating tension. I can tell quickly if a person is open or flexible by the manner in which he or she responds to such interventions. Many times a person reacts with suspicion or confusion to an obviously humorous incident or story; this person is usually far too serious about himself and the world.

Flexible and creative people are able to "go with the flow." They don't spend a lot of time or energy being "up-tight" about situations or other people simply because they are different or have differing views. Flexible people are not obsessed with the "rightness" of their way as opposed to the "wrongness" of yours.

Unfortunately, many neurotic families operate in an "up-tight" manner. Each member, in his or her rigid way, believes he or she is "right" and everyone else is "wrong." This attitude produces serious problems for other family members and for the family as a system. I'm convinced, in fact, that closed, rigid, up-tight families—those in which dependence is not only encouraged but *demanded*—have produced more neurotics than all the rest of society combined. Many parents who are so-called "heads" of such households are very quick to point the finger of blame at "society," the schools, the evils of the drug culture, negative peer groups, and other distractions, but shirk their own responsibilities to care for and nurture their children into responsible adulthood. Some simply don't want to take the time and effort required for the job. Many of them simply don't have what it takes because they have never learned, from their own parents, what it means to survive and prosper.

Rigidity, whether within individuals, families, corporations, or entire nations, produces what social scientists refer to as *closed systems*. Closed systems are generally characterized by randomness, stagnation, and eventual death. To strengthen the creativity survival mechanism, we must develop the quality of *flexibility*.

Strategy #4: Finding Order in Chaos

The fourth quality Gardner has identified is the creative individual's capacity to find order in his experience. This kind of person can synthesize all that life may dish out, *good or bad*. As you may recall, two important qualities of a healthy ego are *assimilation* and *integration*. The creative person is comfortable in abandoning old habits and patterns and forging new ones. As the creative individual goes about performing daily activities, he or she does so with zeal and drive. Creative people are absorbed in their work. There is a passion in what they do. Creative people have a "sense of destiny."

Because of inability to deal with stress or anxiety, many people are all too often ready to "throw the baby out with the bath water." As soon as a problem emerges, or plans don't work out just right, non-creative people are ready to quit. Creative people, on the other hand, are always solution- rather than problem-focused. As if by magic, they zero in on finding a way *to* their destination rather than finding a way *out* of their problem. The creative person says, "I've caught my second breath; let's try again . . . a different way." The non-creative person says, "I can't stand the heat; I'm tired; It won't work; Let's quit."

The "quitting attitude" is what causes these individuals to continue losing in their struggle for personal happiness. Since they are all too willing to "jump ship" the minute the waters get a little choppy, their lives seem never to have any order. Every time they quit, every time they start a new project without completing what they've already started, they get a little further behind. Their lives become a little more chaotic. They lose the struggle for survival a little more.

To strengthen the creativity survival mechanism you must develop the quality of *finding order in chaos*.

Strategy #5: Association with Positive, Creative People

The fifth strategy to achieve the creative impulse and strengthen the creativity survival mechanism is association with creative, positive people. This is perhaps the single most important way to strengthen creativity.

Having worked with emotionally disturbed persons over many years, I can honestly say that the worst thing such a person can do is to associate with other emotionally troubled people. Despite my exhortations and even protests to the contrary, however, these individuals invariably seem to find each other. Neurotics seem to gravitate to other neurotics . . . schizophrenics to schizophrenics, drug abusers to other drug abusers, and so forth. Indeed, there is truth to the time-worn saying, "Birds of a feather flock together!"

What these unfortunate souls have in common is their inability to learn from their mistakes. They seem destined to repeat the same old patterns over and over again. The hallmark of their existence is their capacity for losing. This observation has led me to the unshakable conclusion that losers attract losers and winners seek out other winners.

The population with whom I work comes from a wide

cross-section of humanity. Some of its members are well-to-do, even wealthy, while others are poverty-stricken. Some are very disturbed, others fairly healthy. After years of clinical assessment, one thing I have discovered for certain: *The poor can't help the poor, and the sick can't help the sick!* Without the four basic life elements remaining essentially intact, most people, regardless of ethnic, cultural, religious, or socio-economic standing, are powerless to assist their fellow humans in any significant way.

Some people might argue that such a statement on the powerlessness of emotionally disturbed people is a cliche or gross generalization based on anecdotal evidence. Even if this were true, we must then ask the question, "How do cliches become cliches?" The answer, I believe, is that they are essentially valid. Truth always has, and always will, withstand the test of time.

Strategy #6: Believe in Yourself

Creativity can be developed by learning to believe in yourself. Belief, or having the capacity for what Dr. Robert Schuller calls "Possibility Thinking,"[10] represents a vitally important strategy for development of the creativity survival mechanism. Although I will cover the subject of belief in more detail in a future chapter, I must make a statement on it here.

Not only do most of us not believe in ourselves, we refuse even to see the possibilities that are presented to us on almost a daily basis. Why is it such a difficult task to believe in ourselves? Why, when possibilities are presented, do we deny them or feel we are unworthy of them? The answer to these questions, of course, is rooted deeply in both our personal philosophies of life and the sociocultural and familial systems in which we were brought up— all of which constitute our self-image.

If we perceive ourselves as losers, we deny ourselves the rewards intended for winners. Countless cases bear out this statement. Think of such celebrities as Marilyn Monroe, Janis Joplin, Len Bias, Mario Lanza, John Belushi,

Elvis Presley, and Mercury Morris who, despite every advantage, lost out on their great potential. Just when their flame started to burn at its brightest, it was extinguished by tragic failure.

I believe these individuals lost out, in most cases, because of an unconscious wish and *need* to fail. This unconscious wish, of course, is rooted in the basic life element of self-image. If the self-image says "I *am* a failure; I have *always* been a failure; I will always *be* a failure," then that self-image will be borne out in fact . . . *every time!* It is a self-fulfilling prophesy.

If you doubt the power of mental programming, positive or negative, consider this statement made by Angela Lansbury, famed star of stage and screen: "If you tell yourself over and over again that there's no limit to the creative power within you, that's about all there is to it."[11] That remark was made more than thirty years ago. Considering the success of Ms. Lansbury in the ensuing years and her status as a major star today, it seems to have had staying power indeed!

There are countless creative activities that individuals can undertake. These may range from simple tasks like gardening or painting the house to those of greater complexity like learning to play the piano or writing a best-selling novel. Many have found great joy and strength in painting portraits or landscapes, while others have utilized their creative talents in photography, journalism, or dance. The creative outlet itself is not the important thing. Exercising it is!

If a person suffers from a poor self-image, he or she will not exercise any creative energies simply because that person believes he or she is not worth it. How many times have you suggested to people that they take up drawing, or playing a musical instrument, or writing, and heard the self-denigrating statement, "Oh, *I* wouldn't be able to do *that!*"—as if to say practically *anyone* could do it, but certainly not they. Such statements, rather than implying a sense of shyness or modesty, invariably reflect low self-esteem and lack of belief in the self.

Over the years, I have encountered scores of people who were failing in life. Many of them, when given the choice between opportunity and certain failure, consistently and predictably chose failure. Are people who choose failure over success from some strange planet? Quite the contrary. Many of them are upstanding citizens, intelligent in every way . . . except one: *inside, they feel like failures!*

Choosing failure, when examined superficially, seems a strange choice indeed, but when we view our mental apparatus on a deeper level, choosing to fail may in fact be quite understandable and predictable. When we perceive ourselves as failures, when we can't or won't believe, when we refuse to see possibilities—even when they're staring us in the face—then choosing failure becomes a logical choice. The choice to fail is *syntonic* with our self-image. It fits. Success does not.

There is, however, another factor underlying our lack of belief in ourselves. This factor is far more insidious and damaging to a person's self-image and belief than all others combined. It is the *combined effect of sociocultural and familial deprivation.* Any activity, any event or force, that robs a child or young person of the opportunity to exercise his or her native worth, whether in society or the family, should be viewed as a lethal charge against that young person. Clearly, economic deprivation could easily be included in my discussion here. Although its importance cannot be denied, this factor, in my opinion, is more readily overcome than sociocultural and familial ones. Outlining a way to overcome them is, unfortunately, beyond the scope of this book.

Building our self-esteem demands that we choose success. I looked on in utter disbelief recently when one internationally known television evangelist stated that any quest for self-esteem was satanic! Countless millions of people, young and old, heard that remark. What kind of mental programming does such a statement foster? When we live in a society or culture that frowns on individual achievement (even viewing it as "satanic"), or when we grow up in a family that denies our native abilities, we lose our creative impulse. We lack belief in our own uniqueness or talent simply because there is no need for it. When and if this occurs, our creativity survival mechanism atrophies and dies.

In Socialist or Communist bloc countries, individual initiative and innovation is abrogated in favor of the group. The same is true for some families. When one member emerges as "different" or "special," the family, as a group, may tend to deny or ignore that member and ostracize him or her unless the member relinquishes any personal quest for achievement and independence. This pattern can occur within organizations and on the corporate level, too, when an employee strives for personal advancement.

The creative impulse exists within each of us. It is our birthright. Never let anyone tell you that to sing, or play a musical instrument, or write, or dance, or paint, or act is something you have to be "born with." *We were all born with it!* Exercising that birthright is what counts. As we learn to do this more effectively, we automatically strengthen our creativity survival mechanism. Along with it, we also strengthen the four basic life elements, thus securing our personal happiness and prosperity. Again, the formula is simple. *Doing it is the key!* Stay in the creative mode, and express that creativity in a style and manner that is uniquely your own.

Basic Life Elements Affected by the Creativity Survival Mechanism

First, self-image;
second, life meaning;
third, inner strength;
and fourth, personal control.

NOTES

1. Quoted in Larry K. Brendtro and Arlin E. Ness, *Re-Educating Troubled Youth: Environments for Teaching and Treatment* (New York: Aldine Publishing Co., 1983), p. 255.

2. John Gardner, *Self-Renewal: The Individual and the Innovative Society* (New York: Harper Colophon Books, 1964), pp. 33-34.

3. William Glasser, *Take Effective Control of Your Life* (New York: Harper & Row, 1984), pp. 92-93.

4. *Ibid.*, p. 88.

5. *Ibid.*

6. Bruno Bettelheim, *A Home for the Heart* (New York: Bantam Books, 1975), pp. 21-22.

7. Gardner, pp. 35-40.

8. *Ibid.*, p. 35.

9. *Ibid.*, p. 36.

10. Robert H. Schuller, *Move Ahead with Possibility Thinking* (Old Tappan, New Jersey: Spire Books, 1967).

11. Claude M. Bristol, *The Magic of Believing* (New York: Pocket Books, 1948), p. 160.

SURVIVAL MECHANISM INVENTORY # 4
CREATIVITY

Inventory Statements	Rating *Check Appropriate Box*					
	SA 5	A 4	U 3	D 2	SD 1	Score
1. I see myself as a creative person.						
2. I believe that *everyone*, not just artists, musicians, and sculptors, can be creative.						
3. I would not define creativity as something mainly "in-born."						
4. I remember a time while still in grammar school when I created something in which I took pride.						
5. My parents and teachers recognized my creativity as a child.						
6. I would be willing to withstand public criticism rather than give up a creative enterprise.						
7. In my opinion, creative people are happier that non-creative ones.						
8. If I had my life to live over, I would strive to be more creative.						
9. My parents were/are creative people.						
10. Creativity is something that is in the eye of the beholder.						

Key   SM Strength Quotient =

SA - Strongly Approve   **10 - 24** Weak
A - Approve   **25 - 34** Average
U - Undecided   **35 - 50** Strong
D - Disapprove
SD - Strongly Disapprove

8

Survival Mechanism #5: Recognition

The love of praise, howe'er conceal'd by art,
Reigns more or less, and glows in ev'ry heart.
—*Edward Young*

WHILE SEEKING INFORMATION on the subject of recognition in human relationships, particularly as it relates to self-esteem, I was fortunate enough to come across a little book by Les Giblin entitled *How to Have Confidence and Power in Dealing with People.*[1]

In a chapter called "How to Cash in on your Hidden Assets"[2] I found the results of an interesting study. Here Giblin cites J.C. Staehle's surveys conducted on the "principal causes of unrest among workers." Below are the causes Staehle found, in order of their importance:

1. Failure to give credit for suggestions.
2. Failure to correct grievances.
3. Failure to encourage.
4. Criticizing employees in front of other people.
5. Failure to ask employees their opinions.

6. Failure to inform employees of their progress.
7. Favoritism.

In citing Staehle's research, Giblin notes that each of the "seven causes" is related to "failure to recognize the importance of the employee."[3] Giblin accurately observes that this "failure to recognize" syndrome sends an all-important message to the individual employee: "Your work isn't very important." A bottom-line translation of this would be, *"You* aren't very important. *You* don't count!"

Although Staehle conducted his surveys more than thirty years ago, time has not diminished their validity. Current research dealing with job recognition and praise continues to support the notion that above all else, workers value being appreciated.

Jane Ciabattari, in an article in *Working Woman,*[4] reveals the findings of a 1986 survey of female employees in which 7,800 responses were tallied. More than fifty-three percent stated that their companies fail to make them feel important or recognized. In noting the factors that account for a satisfying job, the respondents listed "Management that makes employees feel they are important as individuals"[5] as among the most critical.

In further support of the need for recognition on the job, John Stoltenberg writes, "Feeling unrecognized by your supervisor can take some of the glow off an otherwise very rewarding job."[6]

The importance of recognition and praise, of course, extends far beyond the workplace and digs into the heart of the way we feel about ourselves as human beings. After analyzing nearly a thousand "compliments," researchers made a rather startling discovery. They found that, whereas people generally value receiving a compliment on their appearance/attire, performance, possessions, and such matters, their deepest satisfaction comes from what they receive the *least*. The authors state: "Although people reported few compliments on their personality or *worth as a person,* they rated these as the *most meaningful"*[7] (emphasis mine).

Other studies support the notion that to be recognized—on and off the job—means being valued for who and what we are as individuals. And without a doubt, that same recognition is the quiet strength that supports and sustains the four basic life elements.

The same principles that operate in relation to Staehle's "seven causes" in the work system also operate in social and family systems. A parent who fails to credit his or her child for a good suggestion or a job well done, for example, is saying to the child: "Your ideas don't count. Your work is irrelevant. After all, you're merely a child." Accolades that same child receives when an adult fall on deaf ears, since the adult's self-image is incapable of accepting such recognition. A person who openly criticizes a friend in front of other people is saying, "You aren't important enough for me to worry about your feelings of possible humiliation."

Truly, one of the most unfortunate aspects of human nature is that we fail to recognize one another for our endeavors and for our individuality. Paradoxically, each of us craves recognition in practically all that we say and do.

Dr. David J. Schwartz, renowned author of *The Magic of Thinking Big*, points out: "Everyone, yes everyone—your neighbor, you, your wife, your boss—has a natural desire to feel he is 'somebody.' The desire to be important is man's strongest, most compelling non-biological hunger."[8]

When you think of it, Schwartz's words are truly astounding: "man's strongest, most compelling non-biological hunger" *is the desire to be recognized.* Notice, Schwartz refers to the need for recognition as a "hunger." This corresponds with what Dr. Eric Berne calls "recognition hunger" in his landmark book, *What Do You Say After You Say Hello?*[9] Dr. Berne states that this hunger is "the quest for special kinds of sensations which can only be supplied by another human being." Researchers, he reveals, have noticed how both baby monkeys and human infants need more than their mother's milk: "They also need the sound and smell and warmth and touch of mothering or else they wither away, just as grownups do if there is no one to say Hello to them."[10]

As with the other survival mechanisms, the recognition mechanism is directly connected to and interrelated with the four basic life elements. I believe it is within the recognition mechanism, however, that the four elements are *most acutely affected.* When a supervisor fails to recognize a worker's efforts, for example, the worker will suffer a loss in all four of his or her life elements: inner strength, control, self-image, and life meaning. When a parent fails to provide proper recognition to a child, the child will suffer loss in all four elements and *probably to an equal degree in each.*

When any one of the four basic life elements is diminished, the result is a loss of self (ego). This loss threatens the individual's emotional survival. With this in mind, one can readily understand why recognition plays such an important role among the survival mechanisms. And yet, despite its importance to us, recognition remains a rare commodity. Why this paradox?

Most of us fail to receive and give adequate amounts of recognition for one reason: *faulty perception.* We fail to perceive the other person as being important to us. As David Schwartz points out, our attitude is: "He can't do anything for me. Therefore, he's not important."[11]

We will explore the matter of perception more fully when we consider the survival mechanism of perception. For now, however, I'll elaborate on the subject as it relates to the survival mechanism of recognition.

David and Goliath

To this day, I can still remember the Bible stories my mother used to recite. She was a great student of the Bible and frequently called upon stories from both the Old and New Testaments to make a point or influence my thinking in some way. I always welcomed these stories and, as a small child, was influenced greatly by them. One of my favorites was the story of David and Goliath.

David was a member of the tribe of Israelites, whose enemies were the Philistines. In the camp of the Philistines was a great giant named Goliath. He strutted around mightily, intimidating everyone and screaming challenges at anyone who might dare to fight him. One day David, a young shepherd, grew weary of Goliath's bullying tactics and took up his challenge. Certain that he would be killed, everyone tried to persuade David not to fight the giant. David would not, however, be dissuaded, and the battle date was set.

Goliath was to the Philistines what the MX missile is to any modern-day army. He represented awesome power. He was invincible. He was the embodiment of all that the Philistine army meant to the Israelites . . . death and destruction. For David to face him in a showdown was more than anyone could ask. But despite Goliath's imposing presence, David was not intimidated.

You can just imagine how Goliath must have looked to little David. His shoulders must have seemed like small mountains jutting out of his back, his legs like pylons balancing a huge torso aloft like some enormous inverted pyramid. He stared down at the little shepherd with burning, hate-filled eyes. He was Goliath, and David was the morsel whom he would crush . . . or so he thought!

This famous Bible story is, of course, familiar to practically everyone. If you recall, David selected five smooth stones and, with one of them placed neatly in his sling, flung it at Goliath. The stone crashed directly into the giant's forehead, and the Philistine hero fell to the ground dead.

This story, with all its melodrama, illustrates the importance of the recognition survival mechanism. First, Goliath never *perceived* David as important and, as a result, refused to *recognize* him. He did not recognize the cunning and courage of the young shepherd and paid for it with his life.

Second, the great throngs of the Philistine army also

failed to recognize David as any kind of threat to the mighty Goliath. They, along with their "hero," judged him by his diminutive size. After all, what could a mere boy do against a giant who had already killed far worthier combatants? Third, and perhaps most important, the faulty perception and lack of recognition of David by Goliath and the Philistines ultimately cost them their freedom and survival, for in their bravado they had foolishly agreed to be the Israelites' slaves if David prevailed over Goliath!

Failure to recognize another person's worth merely because we erroneously believe that person to be unimportant to us can and *will* undermine our own survival by weakening the four basic life elements. First, like Goliath, we lose inner strength. Second, we lose control, just as the Philistines lost control over their freedom. Third, when we lose our freedom, we also lose self-esteem. And finally, with the loss of self-esteem comes the loss of life meaning. A pretty steep price to pay merely for not recognizing the worth of another individual, wouldn't you say? Adolf Hitler was a child abused and unrecognized by his parents. Will the world ever be able to forget it?

Recognizing others is simply another way of validating them . . . of making them feel important. If Goliath had recognized David, who knows what direction the course of human history might have taken? But this is only half the story. It is equally important that "others do unto us as they would have us do unto them!"

Allow me to explain the above re-phrasing of a well-worn Biblical passage. When we are told to "Do unto others as we would have others do unto us," we must, in order to carry out this injunction, *know* what we wish to have done to us. Otherwise we may be quite upset with the outcome!

In order for Goliath to have accorded David proper recognition, he should have done three basic things: first, *perceived* David as important; second, *noticed* David for who he was—that is, a distinct personality; and third, *not lorded it over David* or tried to impress him with his own self-importance. Goliath's downfall lay in his lack of *respect* for David.

Had Goliath done these three simple things, he would have done unto David what he wanted David to do unto him. As it turned out, of course, Goliath did none of these things. Instead, he did the opposite. Goliath was, in fact, so enraged that David came to him with a "stick" that he baited David, inviting the shepherd to come out so that he could kill the boy.

Aren't these three items the ones we would have others do unto us? Don't we all wish others would perceive us as important? Aren't we pleased when we're noticed? Don't we appreciate others' not lording it over us? Indeed, these are the three things *I* would have you do unto *me* if I had any say in the matter!

In order for any of us to have these three things "done unto us," we must first place ourselves in a position to increase the likelihood of their occurrence. When we do this, we are utilizing three of the most important recognition strategies, ones that will enhance the mechanism of recognition and consequently the four basic life elements.

Recognition Survival Mechanism Strategies

Strategy #1: Associate with Perceptive People

It is important to the development and growth of the recognition survival mechanism that we associate with people who perceive us as important. They must see us as having intrinsic worth. Their attitude toward us should be: "WOW! She's unique. She's special. She is somebody!"

In order for this to occur, we *must* associate with people who have the *capacity* to notice us. Unfortunately, however, most people lack accurate perceptive powers. They have deluded themselves into believing that they see and hear accurately, but their perception is usually blunted by what they *want* to see and hear—or, in some cases, by what they *don't* want to see and hear. Their defenses go up, and they block out the truth in favor of a less-threatening image. Sad, but true.

Have you ever noticed a friend's or neighbor's attitude toward your desire to move ahead socially or economically? All too often, it goes something like this: "I want you to get ahead, as long as you don't pass me by." What the person is really saying is: "I have an image of you as being 'average.' As long as you don't do anything to threaten or change that image, I'll be your friend. If you do change it (and threaten me in the process) . . . *watch out!*"

Why is it so vital that we are perceived as important by others? Simply because to be honestly and openly recognized elevates the self-image. To have one's self shot down, to be thought of as "average" or unimportant, means a loss of self—a shrinking of self-esteem. Weakness in the recognition survival mechanism weakens the self and diminishes inner strength.

To be perceived as important by others means we must surround ourselves with individuals who have the *capacity* to notice us. They must be able to see our intrinsic worth . . . to be able to think we're "somebody." Despite what you may have heard to the contrary, *no one* really likes to be thought of as "average." After all, what is "average" other than the "best of the worst and worst of the best"? Undoubtedly, you have seen a picture of a large group, such as a high school graduating class, or of a crowd at a sporting event, in which you knew you were included. Whose face did you look for immediately in the picture? *Yours*, of course! I would do exactly the same. Most people would. It is only natural for us to seek ourselves out from among the throng. Why is this?

Perhaps the most important reason we seek ourselves out from among thousands of faces is that we view ourselves as unique personalities . . . and we are. It is thus a natural tendency for us to want others to perceive us in the same way. In short, we all want to be *noticed*.

When someone says to us, "What an elegant tie you

have on today," what we think is: "He noticed me!" When someone asks us to deliver a speech or write a paper for an important function, we think: "She noticed me!" This notice is significant for developing and strengthening our recognition survival mechanism.

Les Giblin cites a research study, conducted at the University of Michigan's Survey Research Center in Ann Arbor, in which foremen who showed interest in their workers got more work than bossy-type supervisors who didn't notice their staff and merely tried to force them to work harder.[12] In other words, individual attention directed toward workers made them feel recognized and valued as *individuals* rather than as mere cogs in the corporate machine.

The less we feel like "things" and the more we feel like unique individuals, the stronger our recognition survival mechanism becomes. And as it strengthens, so do the four basic life elements.

Strategy #2: Stay Away from "Prima Donnas"

The comic Rodney Dangerfield has built his entire career around the expression "I don't get no respect!" Perhaps the reason for his success rests on the premise that most of us can identify with this sentiment. Most of us feel undervalued by others.

It is unfortunate but true that most people don't receive the respect and recognition they deserve. The reason for this is simple. In order to *give* respect and recognition to others, we must first have *received* it ourselves. Unless we learn early in life that we are valued as individuals, it becomes difficult, if not impossible, to value others later as adults. Virtually every major psychological theory dealing with human growth and development supports this fact. Adults who were not valued by their parents as children feel threatened by others whom under normal circumstances they would value and admire.

It is therefore vital to seek out the company of those individuals with whom you can feel comfortable and who will value and respect you for who and what you are. Stay clear of people with over-inflated egos . . . individuals who will rarely notice you or respect you no matter who you are or what you accomplish in life. In fact, the *more* you are or the *more* you have achieved, the less you are likely to be valued by such individuals.

THE PRINCESS WHO GOT HER FEET WET Several years ago I worked with a teenage girl who came from a broken home. Her mother was a highly trained professional who rarely spent quality time with her daughter. The father, although living in the same city, displayed only passing interest in the girl and continued to engage in a "cold war" with his former spouse.

I tried desperately to reach this youngster, but her mother, with whom she lived, showed only disdain for my most valiant efforts. Her attitude toward me reflected a lack of even common courtesy. With every breath she seemed to be saying: "I don't respect you or your training or your experience or your ability to help me or my daughter." What discouraged me even more was the fact that my relationship with her daughter was positive and potentially productive.

In time, it became increasingly clear that my efforts to help this family were doomed. What became even more evident and dangerous was the mother's highly narcissistic nature. To her I was not the only "scum of the earth"; others were scum as well before her perfect, pristine princess eyes. Unfortunately, her own daughter was included in that group. Each time I tried to point out some positive achievement by her daughter, the mother found a way to minimize it. Any virtue she might possess had to have a vice somehow connected with it, any positive, an automatic negative.

One day our princess came into the office dressed to kill. Her daughter had been truant from school and was threatened with suspension. I hoped to elicit the mother's assistance in working with school officials, but all she could talk about was how the rain had ruined a pair of expensive shoes she had recently purchased. I got the feeling that those shoes were far more important than her daughter or any ideas I had about helping her.

After a while, I began to realize that this woman's entire life was self-centered. And, as is befitting most prima donnas, she immediately dismissed *anything* that caused a deviation from that central, all-consuming focus. It was virtually impossible for her to respect me, her daughter, or anyone else—*especially herself*. She never received recognition and respect as a child; how could she give it to others?

As with the other survival mechanisms, lack of feeding and nurturing produces atrophy and eventual death in the recognition survival mechanism. As the mechanism dies, so do the four basic life elements. To sustain these elements, we must find ways to develop and strengthen them.

Strategy #3: "Let Your Little Light Shine"

When I was a youngster, church attendance two or three times a week was a must. Regardless of how I might have felt about it at the time, those experiences left an overall positive effect on me. One of the experiences I recall vividly was learning to sing hymns and children's religious songs. One of my favorites was "This Little Light Of Mine." The words went something like this: "This Little Light of Mine, I'm gonna let it shine; This little light of mine, I'm gonna let it shine, let it shine, let it shine." There were umpteen verses, all of which were about as complicated and profound as the one noted above. But that song, in all its simplicity, has stayed with me for a lifetime, because the song embodies an important truth.

In the world of showbiz, it is crucial that entertainers obtain exposure to their public. Unless they get their names, faces, and talents in front of an audience or camera—unless they "let their little lights shine"—no one will ever notice them, no matter how great the talent. Exposure is also an important strategy if we are to strengthen our recognition survival mechanism.

Unlike show business, however, where an entertainer

might justifiably worry about *over*exposure, non-show-business people seeking to enhance and strengthen their recognition survival mechanism need not have this fear. I first became aware of this principle a number of years ago while working with a group of parents around problems they were having with their teenagers.

During one of the sessions I noticed that one parent, Cynthia (an especially quiet, non-assertive member of the group), was trying to make herself heard by tentatively beginning a series of half-formed questions and comments. Despite her repeated attempts, however, no one seemed to notice her. Cynthia was quite shy (one of her main reasons for joining the group), and the fact that she made an effort to express herself was in itself a significant achievement. I finally asked the group members to take note of Cynthia's efforts to be heard, which they did. But when everyone was listening, Cynthia could not bring herself to speak. It was obvious to me that she would need to do something more to release the wonderful human being that struggled silently within her.

The following week Cynthia arrived early. She carried a paper bag and was wearing a broad smile. "What's in the bag, Cynthia?" I asked as I greeted her.

"Oh, you'll see," came the friendly reply. Other group members began arriving shortly. As I greeted them I noticed that Cynthia was busying herself arranging the contents of her bag on an attractive plate that she had brought. I soon heard other group members "oohing" and "ahing" over the plate's contents—scrumptious-looking chocolate-chip cookies! "And they look homemade!" exclaimed one member.

"They are," said Cynthia, smiling with obvious delight at the immediate recognition directed toward her. "I baked them this morning." That day, all of us enjoyed yummy, home-baked chocolate-chip cookies.

The following week, Cynthia again honored the group with more of her culinary skills by bringing in melt-in-your mouth home-baked zucchini bread. Everyone went wild over it! Amid the pleasantries shared by all, I noticed an interesting phenomenon occurring: Cynthia was freely interacting with the other group members! Her previous inhibitions were gone! She was talking, laughing, joking, and generally involved. She was later able to share a painful experience from her early childhood with the group, and she accepted feedback without retreating into her customary emotional shell.

As the weeks and months passed, Cynthia's reputation as a baker par excellence grew, and so, too, did her sense of being recognized. She discovered that, by allowing her "little light"—her talent as a baker—to shine and be nurtured by the group, she could achieve the recognition that enhanced her four basic life elements. Most notably, her self-image improved dramatically, and with it emerged a more assertive, self-confident woman. Cynthia must have put something extra special in those chocolate-chip cookies!

Strategy #4: Psychotherapy

Perhaps one of the surest means of gaining recognition is through the process of psychotherapy. Ever since Freud discovered that by merely listening to people he could assist them with their problems, psychotherapy has been in the vanguard of healing modalities.

The reason "talking therapy" is so helpful is that, in the process of sharing one's hurts and disappointments, people gain for themselves *recognition* of who they are. In other words, sharing anger, fear, guilt, or sadness with a skilled therapist—while having intrinsic cathartic value—may serve the more basic function of offering the client a vehicle for self-validation.

During family therapy sessions I am routinely confronted with having to arbitrate among family members who compete for my attention. Not infrequently parents, grandparents, children, aunts, uncles, and others act as siblings striving for any meager crumbs of recognition from the therapist. Berne's concept of "recognition hunger" again comes to mind.

As children, most of us were so starved for recognition that now, as adults, when we get a small taste of it, we act like half-starved wild animals—willing to kill for even a morsel of what we never received.

Sadly, many otherwise well-trained therapists do not fully understand how important recognition is to their clients. Many of them are so in need of recognition themselves that their own emptiness pre-empts their ability to be truly helpful. This phenomenon can perhaps best be observed in therapists who dissipate vast energies on getting their clients to like them. If they fail at this, they feel they have failed also as therapists. Indeed they have, but not for the reasons they think!

When someone is fortunate enough to work with a mature, skilled clinician (one whose emotional needs can be better met outside the therapy session), his or her opportunities to enhance the recognition survival mechanism improve considerably.

Whether in individual, group, or family therapy, a competent therapist knows *how* and *when* to give a client the recognition he or she needs and desires. Such recognition has the ultimate healing goal of strengthening the client's four basic life elements. It is *never* directed at giving false hope or, even worse, placing the client in a position whereby his or her energies go into meeting the unfulfilled needs of the therapist.

Although it may ultimately prove helpful for therapist and client to share a liking for one another, therapists who *need* to be liked by their clients (before they are helpful) place the cart before the horse. If therapists' energies are directed toward providing competent therapy, their clients will probably like them anyway!

Unfortunately, many therapists have significant unfulfilled recognition hunger, reflecting their unmet needs, which simply cannot be met (and should not be) while attempting to help others. Therapists who are serious about their craft need to be willing to "pay the price" and enter their own therapy. In my opinion, this should be a bottom-line requirement of anyone seeking an advanced degree with the goal of becoming a professional therapist. It is remarkable how few clinicians, while eagerly selling their product to unwary clients, are willing to buy that product *themselves!* They then wonder why clients never change.

Basic Life Elements Affected by the Recognition Survival Mechanism

First, self-image;
second, inner strength;
third, personal control;
and fourth, life meaning.

NOTES

1. Les Giblin, *How To Have Confidence And Power in Dealing with People* (New York: The Benjamin Co., 1956).

2. *Ibid.*, p. 24.

3. *Ibid.*

4. Jane Ciabattari, "The 12 Key Ingredients of A Satisfying Job," *Working Woman*, vol. 2 (October 1986), pp. 49-50.

5. *Ibid.*

6. John Stoltenberg, "Ten Ways to Fall Back in Love with Your Job," *Working Woman*, vol. 10 (November 1985), pp. 136-137.

7. Mark L. Knapp, Robert Hooper and Robert A. Bell, "I Really Loved Your Article, but You Missed Your Deadline," *Psychology Today*, vol. 19 (August 1985), p. 26.

8. David J. Schwartz, *The Magic of Thinking Big* (New York: Cornerstone Library, 1965), p. 113.

9. Eric Berne, *What Do You Say After You Say Hello?* (New York: Grove Press, 1972).

10. *Ibid.*, p. 21.

11. Schwartz, p. 114.

12. Giblin, p. 26.

SURVIVAL MECHANISM INVENTORY # 5
RECOGNITION

Inventory Statements	Rating — Check Appropriate Box					
	SA 5	A 4	U 3	D 2	SD 1	Score
1. To be recognized for my own worth is important to me.						
2. My parents and other important adults recognized me as a child.						
3. I feel that I have been appreciated for who and what I am.						
4. I believe recognition is vital to a healthy self-image.						
5. People who can acknowledge their need for recognition are emotionally strong.						
6. I have no problem recognizing others for their achievements.						
7. It is *easy* for me to accept a sincere compliment from someone.						
8. I believe being able to accept a compliment is *always* a good indicator of a positive self-image.						
9. My parents valued each other unconditionally.						
10. If we look for it, we'll discover intrinsic worth in most people.						

SM Strength Quotient =

Key

SA - Strongly Approve
A - Approve
U - Undecided
D - Disapprove
SD - Strongly Disapprove

10 - 24 Weak
25 - 34 Average
35 - 50 Strong

9

Survival Mechanism #6: Perception

> If the doors of perception were
> cleansed, everything would appear to man
> as it is—infinite.
>
> —*William Blake*

WE OFTEN THINK OF SUCCESS as swift and unanticipated. Countless stories about people in the entertainment business, politics, professional sports, and other so-called "high visibility" professions create in the public mind the idea that these people somehow achieved instant, meteoric success. That view of success is, however, usually an illusion, a myth readily believed by the masses as a result of media hype and public gullibility.

What is an illusion? The professor of adult psychopathology at my graduate school continually reminded me and my fellow students of the distinction between an illusion and a delusion. He pounded away at it so often I have never forgotten the distinction. "Remember," he thundered, "an illusion is a *misperception* of reality. . . . A delusion is a *false belief* held true despite evidence to the contrary." Only years later did I fully appreciate his emphasis on this distinction.

Most of us believe (or want to believe) in the validity of what William Glasser calls "the pictures in our heads."[1] These are the firmly ingrained mental photographs or images we all possess of who we are and what we need for satisfying our deepest longings. Each of us believes that the degree to which we meet and sustain these needs and images ultimately determines the amount of personal happiness or discontent we will experience during our lifetimes.

Unfortunately, many of us maintain illusions or misperceptions of reality. We cling tenaciously to these misperceptions because we want to believe them. We think that they will somehow give us strength or control or self-esteem or even meaning. If we maintain these illusions for extended periods they become *beliefs*—beliefs that are in truth delusions.

Once we become delusional, we find ingenious ways of defending our delusions and, as a result, lock them in for life. A number of years ago when I was a staff member of a large psychiatric hospital, I conducted a tour for psychology students from a nearby university. As our group approached the schizophrenic ward, one of the students began staring with pity at one of the more disturbed residents. As the student passed by, the patient suddenly blurted out, "What the hell are you looking at, man. . . . At least I *know* I'm crazy!" The young student was shocked and quickly retreated.

I recall this incident whenever attempting to illustrate the perception survival mechanism. That patient actually perceived himself as in a superior position because he "knew" (believed) he was crazy. In his disturbed thinking, the rest of us were also crazy, but we didn't *know* it, and that made us more vulnerable and somehow inferior.

The patient rationalized and justified, via his misperception, his otherwise powerless position. He turned his illusion into a delusion in order to accommodate an inner picture he held of himself as an adequate, strong, even superior person. In reality, he could not get out of the hospital. But his misperception somehow justified his being there. Having so justified his position, he no longer had a *need* to get out. In fact, for this patient it was the student who needed to get *in*—if he could only know it!

Perhaps nowhere do misperceptions occur more frequently than in marriages. Why do people marry? They do so, of course, for many reasons, both conscious and unconscious. But the fundamental reason most of us marry, I believe, is to have our most basic and deepest emotional needs met.

Glasser states that we are driven by five basic needs or forces. These are the need to survive and reproduce, the need to belong—to love, share, and cooperate—the need for power, the need for freedom, and the need for fun.[2]

Stop for a moment and think how these five needs correspond to what you look for in your marriage, or in your non-marital relationships if you are single. Undoubtedly you are hopeful, consciously or unconsciously, that somehow these needs will to some degree be met in that relationship. Whenever a marriage "goes on the rocks," more often than not it is a direct result of these five needs going unmet.

When we analyze Glasser's "five needs" we see that they correspond closely with the ten survival mechanisms covered in this book and with the four basic life elements that these mechanisms sustain. Applying this correlation to the more than one million marriages that fail annually, we are forced to deduce that the reason they fail is related directly to weakness in our survival mechanisms and the corresponding failure in the four basic life elements. Clearly, since the survival mechanism of perception is so closely interconnected with marital success and failure, if we enhanced that mechanism we could help reduce the divorce rate. Thus, as long as we hold onto misperceptions of what we need as against what the other person is capable of giving, we will continue to fail, not only in marriage but in all life's endeavors involving relationships with people.

The Case of Mark

During the close of my graduate internship, I was coming to the end of therapy with several clients at an adolescent psychiatric clinic. Mark, a handsome fifteen-year-old, although superficially pleasant and outgoing, had an underlying brooding anger that threatened to erupt when his needs were frustrated. And despite Mark's seemingly confident smile, he suffered from low self-esteem.

One day I informed Mark I was leaving the clinic, graduating and thus ending my year-long relationship with him. Although Mark appeared to understand and accept what was happening, I sensed a reservation and disappointment in him.

The following week Mark failed to show up for his scheduled weekly appointment. This was unusual, since he had missed only two appointments all year, one due to illness and the other when he was on vacation with his family. When I called his home, his mother said she did not know his whereabouts and thought he was with me.

The next week Mark showed up but offered no explanation for his absence the previous week. Throughout the session he barely put two sentences together. For a talkative boy, this was also atypical behavior. Again the following week Mark was a "no-show." Calling his mother produced an identical response: whereabouts unknown. I was becoming increasingly troubled by what seemed to be a pattern of Mark's angry withdrawal from me as a result of my terminating his sessions. I had no idea, however, of the degree of his anger or the way he was *perceiving* my departure!

Two days later I was sitting in Dr. Milton Roswell's quiet, relaxing office. Dr. Roswell, a leading child psychiatrist and analyst, served as a part-time consultant to our clinic. I always enjoyed speaking with him because he gave not only astute observations about, and insights into, difficult cases but also practical help that could come only from long years of experience. In explaining my dilemma to Dr. Roswell, I stressed the fact that several weeks before my planned departure, I had taken great pains to "prepare" Mark for my leaving the clinic, stating that my tenure as a student was ending and I would, in fact, be leaving not only the clinic but the area, assuming a new job in a different city.

Dr. Roswell was wise beyond anything that the framed degree certificates that hung on his office wall indicated. He studied me kindly for a moment and then asked, "Paul, may I ask you a personal question?"

"Sure, anything, Dr. Roswell," I replied eagerly.

"But you've got to answer me *honestly* . . . no hedging." I was now a little more than curious as to what might be forthcoming. Looking directly at me he asked, "Paul, do you *really love* Mark?"

At first I thought I had misunderstood his question. "Do I what?"

"Do you *love* him? Do you *really love* him?"

"Do I *love* him?" I responded incredulously, still not believing I was hearing him correctly.

"Yes . . . *LOVE! LOVE! LOVE!*" came his impatient response.

"Well . . . I . . . eh . . . ," I stammered as I tried to squirm out of the question. "I don't know if love . . . eh . . . I guess it depends on what you mean by love," I finally mumbled.

But Roswell was relentless. "Paul, for heaven's sake, just answer the question! Do you *really* love Mark? Yes or no?"

With my back now squarely against the wall I finally was able to say, "Well, I guess if it's between love and not love, well, then I would have to say I love him. Yes!"

Dr. Roswell was now wearing his familiar, sly smile and looking steadily at me. "No you don't, Paul."

"But, Dr. Roswell, I . . . ."

He held up his hand to stop the empty protest. "You see, Paul, you don't *really* love Mark, because if you *really loved* him, you wouldn't leave him!"

Do you know how it feels when you hear, for the very first time, the absolute, undeniable truth? When every ounce of phoniness has been stripped away and you find yourself naked as a jaybird standing in the middle of Times Square? Well, that mildly describes how I felt when Dr. Roswell hit me with that statement. But even then I did not want to *hear* what he was saying.

"Dr. Roswell, you don't understand. I'm not just abandoning Mark. I'm graduating. I have a family to support. Surely Mark understands that. He's an intelligent kid. I can't stay with him when . . . ."

Holding his hand up once again he continued, "Paul, it doesn't matter two hoots how *you* see this, how great or logical your reasons may be. The *only* thing that matters is how *Mark* sees it!"

I learned more about perception in that twenty-minute consultation than I learned through all the books and lectures on psychology during my entire graduate school experience. Even now, years later, the lesson remains intact.

The way we perceive our reality truly is in the eye of the beholder. As I was to discover later, Mark's reality, indeed, was that I was leaving *him* . . . not graduate school, the clinic, or anything else. No amount of rational explanation by me would ever change that reality or his perception of it. The only person who could change it was Mark. Fortunately, he was able to do this as, together, we struggled through the painful separation. Only then, and on *his terms*, was Mark able to differentiate my leaving from the way I felt about him as a person. Only then was he able to know that, despite the leaving, the love remained.

As Mark became able and willing to "give up" his erroneous belief—his misperception—of my not loving him enough, we could see his self-image, inner strength, personal control, and life meaning return. When he gave up that misperception he was able to strengthen his perception survival mechanism. But to achieve this, Mark had to do something most of us find impossible to do: he *had to change.*

To change constructively, we must learn to negotiate

and compromise our differences, our feelings, and our perceptions. We must learn the fine art of moderation, of balance. Strengthening the survival mechanism of perception can be achieved when we alter or abandon our faulty perceptions for more realistic ones. As we learn to do this effectively, we enhance our four basic life elements.

Perception Survival Mechanism Strategies

Strategy #1: Self-Acceptance

It is unfortunate that most of us judge ourselves (sometimes harshly) according to what others think—or what we think they think. We rarely see ourselves for our inherent worth. Our self-image is thus frequently compromised through the eyes of others. We believe that the way "they" perceive us is more important than what and whom we see . . . through our *own* senses. If we are to enhance our perception survival mechanism we must alter this erroneous belief. We do this by *accepting ourselves*—"warts and all"—no matter what.

Of course, this is easy to say but extremely difficult to do. Unfortunately, we live in a world where we are judged by our peers. This judgment sometimes takes on a harsh, even cruel tone that can crush our spirit and will. I work in a profession that purports to have "unconditional regard" for every human being. With amazing frequency, however, those very clinicians who are so accepting of their clients can also be among the most rigid, judgmental, and rejecting toward their own colleagues. They can also be equally harsh, punitive, and unforgiving toward themselves.

To strengthen the perception survival mechanism, we must allow it room to be itself. For this to occur *we* must also be ourselves. The phoniness must be stripped away and our true, honest selves permitted to emerge. In addition, we must forcefully resist being judgmental toward ourselves and others. We must also scrupulously avoid associating with judgmental people who, because of their low self-esteem, seek out ingenious ways to hurt and hinder our growth. When we remain in the presence of such people for any extended time, our perception survival mechanism is weakened and with it the four basic life elements.

Recently I spoke with a young mother regarding her career goals. She had spent her entire life trying to please other people, and she felt that in the process she had sold herself out. This left her feeling hurt and extremely angry. Only recently has she been able to take stock of her life and initiate the changes that enabled her to begin a career in accounting, a career that, because of her chronic fear and self-doubt, she had abandoned. While I was discussing these issues with her, she abruptly stopped her train of thought and said, "You know, I always used to believe that I had to be responsible for *everything*. Now I realize, for the very first time, that I don't have to be responsible for everything, that others have their responsibilities, too. I've allowed others to make me feel overly responsible, and that has robbed me."

Several days later, while reflecting on what she said, the thought occurred to me that what happened to this woman is precisely what happens when we continually subject ourselves to people with low self-esteem. The only way they can feel good about themselves is by demeaning, humiliating, judging, condemning, criticizing, complaining, and maintaining grudges against others. In short, they rob us of our self-worth so that theirs might prosper. Such individuals are the emotional leeches of this world, the human parasites who, because of their own chronic pain and disappointment, spew their anger, hatred, and rage upon the innocent. To subject ourselves to them keeps us from being self-accepting and self-forgiving—ingredients necessary to strengthen our perception survival mechanism.

Strategy #2: Learn To Negotiate!

Learning to negotiate our differences is one of the most effective ways of strengthening the survival mechanism of perception. Successful negotiation is, however, frequently a difficult task. Success in negotiation requires a number of factors. The most important is maintaining a *non-reactive posture* during negotiation. Achieving this posture requires controlling our emotions. It means putting into action the prayer, "Lord, help me to keep my head when others all around me are losing theirs."

The degree to which we can "keep our cool" in emotionally tense situations will determine the extent to which we negotiate successfully. And our ability to negotiate directly affects the strength of our perception survival mechanism. The better we negotiate, the stronger this mechanism becomes.

The ability to negotiate well is linked closely with perception. Thus, if our perceptions are accurate—that is, if we see ourselves and others in relation to our true needs and the capacity of others to meet them—we will enhance our ability to negotiate successfully. As this ability increases, so will our capacity for more accurate perception. The end result is strengthening of our perception survival mechanism and a happier, more productive life.

It is crucial that we *see ourselves* as successful negotiators. Since all of life is one big negotiation, we must maintain an image or vision in our mind's eye of achieving what our hearts desire. To strengthen the perception survival mechanism, therefore, we must believe it is already strong and that our perceptive powers are *already* present within us. Indeed, as we have learned, the power of belief can reach into all aspects of life. And its relevance extends not only to the survival mechanism of perception but to *all* survival mechanisms.

The two basic life elements most significantly affected by successful negotiation are inner strength and personal control. Every time we negotiate successfully, we strengthen these two basic elements, because they are the elements closest to the hypothalamus, the segment of our brain regulating behavior and such important emotions as anger and fear. When we negotiate successfully, we learn indirectly to use the hypothalamus to gain increased power and control over our emotions and even, to a degree, our autonomic nervous system—respiration, digestion, blood pressure, body temperature, heart rate, and so forth.[3]

Strategy #3: Learn To Communicate Effectively!

Communicating effectively is one of the most necessary of all the survival strategies. The art of communication is with us from the moment we are born. As infants, we learn to communicate our needs for food and comfort through the mechanisms of crying, whining, whimpering, burping, gurgling, and a host of other rudimentary sounds. Crying and other distress signals bring us attention from caregivers and reinforce within us forever that age-old truth, "The squeaky wheel gets the grease."

We use countless methods to communicate our needs, some verbal, others non-verbal. Some are direct, others more subtle. Sometimes we are calmed by others' communications and sometimes we are upset by them. Communication can be clear and concise or confusing and contradictory. Communication can heal us and it can hurt us. One thing is certain: it is virtually impossible *not* to communicate.

Some people would argue with this last statement and say, "I can do it. I can avoid communicating. You just watch me. I'll sit here with my arms folded and remain silent." Such a person is, of course, communicating *non-verbally*. What is a person who sits in silence with his arms folded saying to us? "I'm angry. I'm hurt. I'm stubborn." His posture sends out messages, or *metacommunications*, that, though unspoken, are heard clearly. Some of the loudest messages are silent!

Leopold Stokowski, famed conductor of the Philadelphia Orchestra, was renowned not only for his musical genius but equally for his fiery temperament. On one occasion, during rehearsal, an oboist missed his cue. Stokowski suddenly stopped the orchestra, stared at the poor oboist and, with the long index finger of his right hand, pointed at the petrified man for what must have seemed like an eternity. Stokowski never uttered a word. He merely pointed and stared angrily. That oboist never missed his cue again! No one seeing that long, bony finger pointing unwaveringly at him could misperceive Stokowski's demand for perfection when it came to music.

Whether verbal or non-verbal, overt or covert, learning to communicate clearly is vital to the growth of the perception survival mechanism. When communication is clear and unambiguous, our perception of the message being sent increases. When communication is fuzzy or contradictory, the perception survival mechanism becomes confused and unreliable. The statement below illustrates this point. After you've read it, decide whether you have any question in your mind about what is being said.

You say you understand what you think I said.
What you don't realize is that what you heard is not what I meant.

No wonder we don't communicate clearly! This classic illustration of ambiguous communication underscores how readily misperceptions occur. The statement can mean anything or absolutely nothing ... *simultaneously!*

Effective communication, however, involves more than learning to express yourself clearly. I was struck recently by the following story, told by Leo Buscaglia during one of his inimitable television talks on human relationships.[4] After one of Dr. Buscaglia's lectures, a woman from the audience approached him and asked excitedly to speak with him. He agreed graciously and began to listen to this woman's tale of woe.

For nearly a half-hour she related problem after problem, while Dr. Buscaglia uttered not a word. Finally, after pouring out her heart, the woman exclaimed, "Oh, Dr. Buscaglia, thank you so much . . . .You've been such a big help!" Then she left. Although Dr. Buscaglia had said nothing to the woman, he helped her in a most significant way—he *listened!*

Real communication is always a two-way street ...

talking *and* listening. How many times have you met someone who "talks your ear off" but couldn't care less about listening to what *you* have to say? Many people pretend to listen but in reality are daydreaming, wishing we would finish what we're saying so they can once again start their own avalanche of words.

We also encounter people who appear to listen but don't "hear" what we're saying. They listen superficially to our words but miss our meaning . . . our message. This occurs often when teenagers try to share something important with their parents, who then respond with an unwelcome lecture instead of an empathetic ear.

I cannot overemphasize the importance of listening as an essential component of the communication survival strategy. Learning to listen improves our ability to communicate effectively. As we become more proficient listeners, we acquire clearer perceptions of others, and they in turn gain clearer perceptions of us. When we listen, we provide the buffer that tempers the noise of our own excessive verbiage, and we are then able to truly "hear" what others are saying. This process gives others a sense of self-worth and, for us, it affords yet another way to strengthen our perception survival mechanism and with it the four basic life elements.

Strategy #4: Refuse to Stereotype People

Stereotyping others is one of the most destructive forces to act upon the survival mechanism of perception to impede its growth. Stereotyping is holding a mental picture about the way events should or should not unfold. It is maintaining prejudicial views on the way others should act, be, think, and feel, and then using those views to limit, label, categorize, and force another individual into a fraction of his or her true self.

Stereotypical and/or prejudicial behavior can be either positive or negative. The *New English Dictionary* defines prejudice as "a feeling, favorable or unfavorable, toward a person or thing, prior to, or not based on, actual experience."[5] Unfortunately, however, the normal breed of stereotyping is almost always negative. The capacity for human thinking and creativity is virtually limitless. But when we label people, categorize them, or *overgeneralize* about them, we force them to become miniatures of themselves. As psychologist Gordon Allport stated succinctly many years ago, "Overcategorization is perhaps the commonest trick of the human mind. Given a thimbleful of facts we rush to make generalizations as large as a tub."[6] Stereotyping diminishes a person—and us—by blunting the interchange that might otherwise have been possible between us. Limiting others, labeling them, maintaining iron-clad stereotypes of them victimizes them and adds to the maelstrom of human misery and alienation.

Perhaps you are aware of someone who has been victimized by our society's tendency to categorize and limit because of age—one of the ways stereotyping and prejudice have a field day. In fact, even *you* may have been victimized by this form of stereotyping. The process of "age stereotyping" generally follows a definite, clear-cut sequence that goes something like this: When we are young children and teenagers our parents say, "You can't do that, you're not old enough." Then, when we become "middle-aged," society joins in and says, "You're too old to do that. Act your age!" Finally, when we are old and soon to die, we hear a stentorian chorus shouting, "You should have done that when you were young; why didn't you?"

The perception survival mechanism depends on growth at all levels of development in the human life cycle, regardless of age. Young children and adolescents, if they are to successfully negotiate the path into adulthood, need the encouragement of parents and teachers. Those of us in our so-called "middle years" also need encouragement and approval from those close to us at home and at work. We need to know that others think we are still vital and have much to contribute. The aged should, as in oriental cultures, be valued for what they have achieved and contributed. They should be looked up to as teachers and counselors to the rest of us more actively engaged in life's day–to–day struggles.

How sad it is when we misperceive others and believe that "what we see is what we get." Such a view is destructive and alien to the life force. We would all do well to begin anew and accept others as they are and for who they are.

During my graduate training, one of my professors, a geriatric psychiatrist who had for many years worked with the elderly, said that he was frequently asked why he worked with old people. His answer was simple and direct: "Because some day I too will be old, and when I am, I want somebody to be kind to me."[7]

His candor struck me as I realized that the commodity most valued and least available in our society is *human kindness.* We all need to realize that without it our perceptions of each other will at best be blurred. At worst, they will drive us insane. Instead of openness and honesty, we will find ourselves overwrought with suspicion and self-doubt. Instead of acceptance and understanding, we will find ourselves plagued with the useless emotions of envy and anger. Rather than sharing in the common goals of our fellow humans, we will be lost in isolation and despair. Our acts of human kindness toward each other can help us eradicate these evils from our individual and collective lives.

When we stereotype others and refuse to see them for their intrinsic human worth, we undermine the growth of our own perception survival mechanism and ultimately our self-esteem. Each time we make statements like "He's too old to cut it any more," or "She can't do the job, she's only a woman," we not only announce to the world that we suffer from a low self-image, we inadvertently perpetuate and *increase* that low self-image.

Doggedly maintaining our stereotypical thinking is both ironic and self-destructive, since stereotyping decreases the strength of the perception survival mechanism. And it is, of course, our survival mechanisms that enhance and sustain the four basic life elements, one of which is self-esteem. A lessening of strength in *any* of the ten survival mechanisms automatically brings with it a corresponding decrease in the four basic life elements.

If we would stop wasting our vital energies criticizing and stereotyping others because of their age, sex, race, or group affiliations (most of which are unchangeable anyway!), our survival mechanism of perception would strengthen dramatically. This strength would in turn result in the enhancement of the four basic life elements, especially that most vital one of all: self-esteem.

The origins of most of our misperceptions and hence our stereotypical thinking lie in our early lives. Our ability to perceive clearly is related intimately to our families of origin and the role they played in our formative years.

Most people who suffer from low self-esteem, powerlessness, loss of control, and meaninglessness come from families where nurturing and emotional support were severely lacking. Their subsequent deficiencies in the four life elements in turn breed the misperceptions and stereotypical thinking that then haunt them throughout life, infiltrating practically every aspect of their feeling, thinking, and behaving. They wander aimlessly through life, threatened in relationships at all levels and misperceiving the world and its inhabitants—both human and otherwise—as somehow dangerous.

It is sad to say, but the only measure of protection you have from the negative influences of those suffering from low self-esteem is to stay as far away from them as possible. The main reason for this is that, because of their poor self-image, such individuals will readily *take* from you but rarely *give* to you. Because we are preoccupied with defending ourselves against them, takers invariably have the tendency to blunt our perceptions, soon causing us to project our fears (real or imagined) onto all relationships and life circumstances, including those that are perfectly innocent. As this pattern becomes entrenched, we soon lose our ability to perceive clearly. The cycle is then ready to repeat itself and become even more deeply rooted.

People with low self-esteem tend, for example, to engage in stereotypical thinking. So a young person with low self-esteem may stereotype an older person as "over the hill" and soon cease to communicate with him or her. As their relationship becomes increasingly distant, the older person, in self-defense, begins stereotyping the younger one as "naive and arrogant" and also ceases to communicate. Soon an emotional "cold war" is raging. Stereotypical and paranoid thinking becomes standard fare. The firmer and more deeply entrenched this kind of thinking becomes, the wider the emotional chasm between the two people. And with the emotional distance comes even more paranoia and further stereotyping.

It is truly pathetic that this kind of scenario is enacted at practically all levels of our society because, in large measure, of the irrational stereotypes people hold of one another.

Basic Life Elements Affected by the Perception Survival Mechanism

First, self-image;
second, inner strength;
third, personal control;
and fourth, life meaning.

NOTES

1. William Glasser, *Take Effective Control of Your Life* (New York: Harper & Row, 1984), pp. 19-30.

2. *Ibid.*, pp. 5-18.

3. Kenneth R. Pelletier, *Mind As Healer, Mind As Slayer: A Holistic Approach To Preventing Stress Disorders* (San Francisco: Delacorte Press, 1977), pp. 46-48, 54-58; Judith Hooper and Dick Teresi, *The Three-Pound Universe* (New York: Macmillan, 1986), p. 35.

4. "Give Love: Leo Buscaglia In Niagara Falls," WNED/PBS, Buffalo, March 12, 1990.

5. Quoted in Gordon W. Allport, *The Nature of Prejudice* (Garden City: Doubleday Anchor, 1958), p. 7.

6. *Ibid.*, p. 9.

7. Dr. James S. Jacobsohn, in a lecture April 1970 at Case Western Reserve University School of Applied Social Sciences, Cleveland.

SURVIVAL MECHANISM INVENTORY # 6
PERCEPTION

Inventory Statements	Rating Check Appropriate Box					
	SA 5	A 4	U 3	D 2	SD 1	Score
1. I value people because of their individual qualities rather than prejudging them by superficial stereotypes.						
2. I think it's okay not to have black or white answers to important life questions.						
3. Parents must send clear-cut messages to their children.						
4. In order to really understand what life is all about, we should strive to be open with our fellow humans.						
5. People who are open may risk being hurt but will also experience personal growth as a result.						
6. In the long run, it is important for me to keep a dialogue open with someone even though I may disagree with him or her.						
7. I believe the opinions of small children are important and should be listened to by parents.						
8. I have definite, clear-cut opinions about important life issues, but I am open to new ideas.						
9. Even though life may sometimes be frustrating, I always manage to keep my eye on the goal.						
10. I would rather see myself for who I am than go through life pretending.						

SM Strength Quotient =

Key

SA - Strongly Approve
A - Approve
U - Undecided
D - Disapprove
SD - Strongly Disapprove

10 - 24 Weak
25 - 34 Average
35 - 50 Strong

10

Survival Mechanism #7: Friendship

I praise the Frenchman, his remark was shrewd—
How sweet, how passing sweet, is solitude!
But grant me still a friend in my retreat
Whom I may whisper—solitude is sweet.
—*William Cowper*

YEARS AGO, when I was just beginning to work with troubled families, I found myself frustrated trying to motivate people to become involved in therapy. I couldn't understand why they would resist coming in and talking about their problems or why they cancelled appointments or simply didn't show up. Initially, I thought they were resisting me. Gradually, I came to the realization that it was only their *perception* of me that was the problem.

Most people would like to see themselves as being in control of their own lives. Going to a therapist diminishes that sense of control. I finally decided that if somehow I could change the way they perceived me, I would have better luck getting people to come in and trust me with their problems. To do that, however, would first require a change in the way I perceived *myself*.

Through trial and error, I gradually came to the conclusion that people weren't looking for therapists. Instead, although not consciously aware of it, what they sought were *friendships*. Indeed, what most clients seek in a therapist is a friend—someone in whom they can confide *comfortably* and who can gently lead them out of their pain. As long as the therapist can keep his or her role in perspective, this perception by clients should present few, if any, real problems. It's when the therapist loses sight of his or her primary function that problems arise.

Once I understood the simple but basic premise that people wanted to see me as a friend, *not as a therapist*, I was able to rid myself of any illusions of what *I* thought my clients wanted or needed. Furthermore, the issue of motivation resolved itself because, even though I resisted becoming a "friend" to clients, I managed to remain "friendly" with them. This, I discovered, was all they needed or wanted to keep up their interest in therapy. (A good therapeutic relationship is based, in part, on the therapist's objectivity. Clinicians who attempt to form conventional friendships with clients inevitably lose this essential treatment tool.)

The fact that people seek out counselors and therapists as "friends" is in itself a sad commentary on the human condition. Although there are more than 250 million people in the United States, loneliness and human isolation remain chronic problems. More suicides are caused by unrelenting loneliness than perhaps by any other single factor. And yet, ironically, although we crave friendship and human closeness, we are either too burdened or fearful to achieve either.

Life without true friendship is like being lost in the desert without water. It can be meaningless and even fatal. Although our material survival needs may be met, when we are immersed in our own isolation and loneliness life tends to have a hollow ring for most of us.

Perhaps you have never thought of friendship as a survival mechanism. If not, try for a moment to imagine life without any meaningful social relationships whatsoever. Imagine being forbidden to speak to anyone in a friendly manner—and their being forbidden to speak to you—under threat of death, while at the same time, everyone else can intercommunicate freely. Imagine yourself in this situation for the rest of your life. Wouldn't that be a living hell? Could you survive such a burden? Could anyone?

Emile Durkheim, the noted French sociologist, coined the term *anomie* to refer to the sense of futility and isolation we experience when we are cut off emotionally or physically, or in both ways, from the mainstream of humanity.[1] Emotional cutoffs are among the worst kind. When such cutoffs occur, we literally wither and die. Prisoners of war are frequently isolated from their fellow prisoners because their captors know that, sooner or later, those kept in isolation will break. The same principle causes us to join groups and make friends—*emotional survival!*

Silence Is Golden!

William Wordsworth and Samuel Coleridge, two of the great Romantic poets of the late eighteenth century, were friends and colleagues. I have never forgotten a story I heard in college about these two literary giants. As I remember it, one cold and blustery winter's eve Wordsworth made the long trek to visit with his old friend Coleridge. The two men sat companionably before a roaring fire, saying not a word. After several hours of silence, Wordsworth arose and, as the story goes, put on his hat and coat, turned to Coleridge, and exclaimed, "Thank you, old friend, for a delightful evening of good conversation!"

True friendship doesn't require a continuous flow of words just to fill empty space. In fact, good friends need little to keep their relationship solid. It is the shared values, beliefs, and principles they live by that sustain people in a relationship and give it that enduring quality we call friendship. The relationship of George Burns and Gracie

Allen is one of the best examples of this. Despite all the hoopla of Hollywood, radio, and television fame, nothing could shake their relationship. George never had second thoughts about playing the "straight man" to Gracie's comic genius. She in turn always credited George. The kind of positive complementarity they enjoyed is what made their marriage work on and off the stage.[2]

A lack of positive complementarity is probably the major reason that more than half of all marriages currently being formed will, at some point, sustain a separation. Of these separations, the vast majority will occur some time within the first three to five years of the marriage and will remain permanent. People simply do not understand the importance of giving, as Carl Rogers put it, "unconditional positive regard" to one another.[3] *Nowhere is this more important than in a marriage.*

Some Strange Ideas about Marriage

Unfortunately, many of us enter marriage with all kinds of erroneous ideas as to what the other spouse is supposed to do . . . or be . . . to meet our needs. Ninety-nine percent of the time our expectations are unrealistic.

We expect our spouse to be both exquisite lover and flawless homemaker or provider. We expect him or her to be both marvelous conversationalist and sensitive listener. The wife should be both nurturing mother to the children and, in some neurotic cases, to the husband as well. The husband should be out there "bringing home the bacon" and, simultaneously, spending quality time at home with the wife and kids.

As I have noted when discussing the work survival mechanism, many jobs are "unnatural" experiences. Marriage also represents an "unnatural condition" for essentially the same reasons. Two people united in the bonds of marriage may have little in common other than their claim of mutual "love." And even if they have more than that in common, they will, a few years into the marriage, undoubtedly discover many *uncommon* factors present in their relationship.

A *common* expression among most couples experiencing marital discord is, "He (or she) wasn't like *that* before we got married!" Whenever I hear this, I instinctively want to respond, "Oh, yes, he (or she) was!" The spouse just couldn't see it. That's because we never discuss many of our expectations prior to marriage (a common error during courtship), or we hold these expectations unconsciously and become conscious of them only later. In addition, many of our romanticized notions about love and marriage blind us to truths about the object of our affections that would be obvious under less emotional circumstances. As we become increasingly aware of the discrepancy between our expectations, both conscious and unconscious, and the reality of their chances of fulfillment, our disenchantment with our marital partner and the marriage grows.

Perhaps one way of mitigating this discrepancy is for marital partners to accept the necessity of making long-term commitments. In so doing, they give each other the opportunity to bring their expectations more in line with reality. Adults who are immature or suffer from low self-esteem, however, generally fear making such commitments. To make and keep a lifelong commitment to another person requires a high level of maturity and *inner strength*. When these qualities are absent from the beginning, emotional cracks in the marital foundation develop shortly into the marriage.

As teenagers we form intensely bonding relationships. We believe these relationships are invincible and able to endure virtually any intrusion by our parents, teachers, and the "straight" adult authority world. If we fail to mature into adulthood and properly exchange these adolescent beliefs for those of the real world, they become permanently entrenched in our value systems. We then go through the remainder of our lives literally "living in the past."

When we neurotically insist on hanging onto the past and bringing it, along with our erroneous expectations, into the current reality of marriage, we court almost certain disaster. A couple with whom I worked recently kept repeating two phrases over and over—"I want, I want" ... and "My family was never like this!" They sounded like a duet without the harmony. Neither of them could really "hear" what the other person was saying. Neither was willing to *negotiate* his or her previously-held beliefs, values, and ideals. Negotiation would have incorporated what each person brought to the relationship into a true partnership. What they ended up with, however, was a forced union of two people each seeking what the other couldn't provide. Indeed, the degree to which a married couple can negotiate their differences determines the extent to which the marriage survives and prospers.

Have You Ever Seen an Ego?

To better understand the friendship survival mechanism, think of it in the broader context of *ego development*. The concept of ego development has been covered extensively by Sigmund and Anna Freud, Erik Erikson, Heinz Hartman, Melanie Klein, John Bowlby, and a host of others. These investigators have established that the ego represents "the self," or who we are and how we got to be that way. The self is a composite representation of all that has gone into us (or *not* gone into us!) from the moment of conception until the present time.

The great ego psychologists, including Erikson, Anna Freud, Klein, Hartman, and Bowlby have taken special note of the ego's flexibility—that it is much like a rubber band. As a result, the ego can withstand the considerable assault and deprivation that might be inflicted upon it by both the inner and outside world. It has the capacity to "bounce back" and start anew. When the ego becomes incapable of bouncing back, that means the assaults on it have been either too numerous or too severe or both.

We are all familiar with the person who, despite having suffered unbelievable misfortune as a child, such as gross maltreatment, abandonment, and chronic physical or sexual abuse, rebounds and goes on to live a productive and happy life. Such a person illustrates the ego's flexibility—its capacity to assimilate, integrate, and consolidate information and life events that, when looked upon at face value, would be catastrophic. Stories of multiple personalities, as found in the books *Sybil*[4] and *The Three Faces of Eve*,[5] illustrate this point.

Unfortunately, most people have little, if any, accurate understanding of the ego. After all, have you ever seen an ego? Most of us, when hearing the term, hear it in an erroneous context. We might, for example, overhear someone say, "He's got a lot of ego!"—implying the person is self-centered or arrogant. Or the term might be used in a more positive way: "It really takes a lot of ego to do that"—implying the person is very self-confident.

Although lay expressions of the term *ego* may indicate some of its real meaning, they are generally inaccurate and misleading. A wife complained to me recently about her husband's philandering. When I stated that perhaps this was related to his poor ego development (that is, his poor self-image), she immediately retorted, "Oh, no! That's the problem . . . he's got *too much* ego!" She clearly harbored an erroneous understanding of the term *ego*. A person who is self-centered, as the wife implied, rarely, if ever, has "too much ego" in the true sense.

The ego is one third of our mental apparatus, as defined and developed by Sigmund Freud and later elaborated upon by the so-called neo-Freudians and ego psychologists noted earlier. The other two thirds are the *id* and the *superego*. Understanding the id and the superego will help you understand the ego and therefore the important concept we call *trust*.

The Id—Your "Inner Desire"

Freud defined the id as representing our more primitive or instinctual self. I like to compare it with the old reptilian core as found in the limbic system of the brain. From it flows our deepest needs, appetites, and desires. Freud believed that the id was composed of *drives*—one being the *aggressive drive*, the other being the *sexual drive* or *libido*. Whatever we choose to call it, the id is the part of us that clamors for *immediate gratification*—"I want what I want and I want it now!" Present at birth, it remains with us to the grave.

The Superego—"Your Mommy and Daddy"

Think of these three mental processes as comprising an invisible pyramid. At the base we have the id. In the middle resides the ego. And at the top sits the superego. It's not called the superego for nothing, because to *everything* the id clamors for, the superego responds, "Yes," "No," or "Maybe." The superego, of course, is our conscience. It tells us what's right and what's wrong, what's good, what's bad. It is, in the final analysis, our mommy and daddy saying what we should or shouldn't do, say, think, feel, or be. Like the id, the superego can be a tyrant. What happens when an immovable object meets an irresistible force? A Muhammad Ali and a Rocky Marciano? The United States and the Soviet Union in a nuclear showdown? Enter the ego.

The Ego—"Meet Mr. Referee"

The ego is the mediating force or "referee" between the id and the superego. It says to the two warring ends of the pyramid, "Hey, wait a minute, fellas. Let's see if we can work this out peaceably. Let's not fly off the handle. Let's negotiate!" Can you imagine two great fighters like Ali and Marciano or two superpowers like the United States and the Soviet Union going head to head without a mediator to lay the ground rules or to call foul when necessary?

Likewise, can you imagine what happens when the id

and superego confront each other without an ego, or, almost as bad, with a weak ego? The result of such a confrontation is almost always disastrous. The reason is that the ego, in addition to being a mediator between the id and the superego, serves also as an *integrative* and *assimilative* force. It is like a strainer that weeds out, thins out, and refines information in a way that will make it acceptable to both the id and the superego. Perhaps one of its most important functions is that of *reality testing*.

A healthy ego says, "Yes, go ahead and do that. It will be good for you. You will not be hurt, nor will you hurt others." The end result is success and enhanced self-esteem. The unhealthy or poorly developed ego may say exactly the same thing, but the end result is failure and lowered self-esteem.

Trust, a product of healthy ego functioning, is a very fragile strategy that is subject to the demands of both the id and the superego. Without a healthy ego capable of withstanding these constant demands, trust in any relationship can easily be crushed. This is why so many marriages fail—*lack of basic trust.*

When trust is lacking, that means there is no healthy ego or only a very weak ego to support it. Since the id, ego, and superego are only theoretical in nature, assessing who has a strong or intact ego or superego and who hasn't is difficult. After all, when was the last time you saw an ego? And when was the last time you said "hello" to an id or a superego?

Essentially the best, and perhaps only, way to determine the degree to which another person has an intact, healthy ego, and hence a good level of basic trust, is by observing his or her *degree of judgment and behavior over time.* When people are consistently "messing up" or making bizarre statements or engaging in immature and contradictory behavior or acting out of control, then you can begin to suspect impaired ego development.

Although many ingredients comprise true friendship, let me offer here the six that I feel should be on any basic list. They are adapted from Alan Loy McGinnis's beautifully written book, *The Friendship Factor:* trust, honesty, transparency, appreciation, comfort, and capacity to listen.[6]

I have incorporated these into survival strategies to help strengthen your friendship survival mechanism. Remember, they are only *suggested* strategies and may or may not have relevance to your own life.

Friendship Survival Mechanism Strategies

Strategy #1: Learn to Trust People

Erik H. Erikson, the Pulitzer Prize-winning psychoanalyst, notes that children develop basic trust somewhere within the first year of their lives.[7] They do this when they look around and see their mother nearby, gaining comfort and security in the tentative knowledge that she is there if needed. Then, upon looking again, they are comforted further with the now more secure knowledge that their mother is *still* there. As this little sequence is repeated over and over, children gradually develop a basic trust that their mother will *always* be there as protector and provider.

Basic trust, Erikson contends, then solidifies as children move on to their school age and adolescent years. If their mothering and nurturance has been consistent and genuine, young people are then theoretically equipped to move on to satisfying and trusting adult relationships because of the stable foundation established in the first year of life.

If we accept Erikson's premise, we are confronted with a stark realization: most parents must fail to nurture their children sufficiently. This deficit shows up in the number of people we meet daily who, as adults, seem either to distrust us or to appear unworthy of our trust. These are the people who respond to us with suspicion and fear, those who seem determined to go out of their way to see to it that we *don't* "have a nice day!"

The inability to trust others is, in my opinion, indisputably rooted in faulty relationships developed early in life—probably, as many experts on child development have noted, within the first two or three years. Once the *learned pattern* of distrust is firmly entrenched in young children, it will probably remain there forever. All their subsequent relationships will be tentative, hazy, marred by conflict, or flawed in some way. They consequently view trusting relationships as "dangerous traps" to be avoided at all costs.

Learning to trust others, as a survival strategy, is of primary importance if we are to regain, sustain, and strengthen our friendship survival mechanism. As with all the survival strategies, this one must be consciously and consistently practiced. We can do this by associating with positive, helpful, genuine, and, most important, *trusting* people, those who are willing to give us the "benefit of the doubt" even when their patience with us may be exhausted. Doing less is to sell ourselves out.

People who are trusting will, if given sufficient opportunity, encourage a trusting relationship within us. Negative, distrustful, and fearful people will, in turn, promote these same emotions within us. Associating with positive individuals fosters a positively reinforcing cycle. As we observe others' trust in us, so will our own level of trust grow. As this growth occurs, we subsequently strengthen our friendship survival mechanism and with it our own self-esteem and personal happiness.

Strategy #2: Be Honest with Yourself and Others

A deepening silence fell over the room. A teenager sat there staring at me with hate-filled eyes, eyes filled with defiance and inner rage, with disappointment and fear. He refused to speak. I received no responses to the many well-thought-out questions I asked. Instead, he granted me only silent shrugs or an occasional grunt.

His father was in prison for rape and arson. His mother, a ragged prostitute and hopeless schizophrenic, lived in a flophouse. His only brother was in prison for killing a service station operator during a botched robbery attempt. What little family he had left refused to claim him as one of their own. He was, in the vernacular, "a throwaway child."

As I sat there staring back helplessly at this sixteen-year-old castoff from humanity, I couldn't help feeling somewhat hypocritical. Here I was, delegated by the so-called "powers of the state" to *cure* this incurable kid and somehow to "make OK" what society had already condemned. What a hoax! What a tragic paradox, I thought as I groped for words—*any words*—to somehow help convey my absolute frustration and sense of futility.

Finally, in the desperate silence, I blurted out, "Sammy, I've got to tell you, I really feel hopeless and helpless as to what to say or do. I don't really feel equipped to help you, because if I were you, I would probably react just as you are now. In fact, when I was your age, Sammy, I was going through some difficulties that didn't even compare with what you're going through right now, and I can remember how angry and misunderstood I felt. But at least I had a mother and father and family who cared for me and loved me. If I hadn't had that, Sammy, I honestly don't know what I would have done. Maybe I would be in prison today, who knows?"

For the first time, I could see his eyes come alive just a little. He gave me a long, questioning look that said, "Are you for real? Are you actually telling me something about *yourself*? Are you truly being *honest* with me?" In that moment, the moment of truth, I finally got that kid's attention. When I opened up to him and dared to be honest and *vulnerable*, then and only then did we connect in a spirit of mutual trust.

Honesty in any relationship is the glue that holds it together. Without it no friendship, no marriage, no employer-employee relationship can survive, let alone thrive. But honesty is not always easy. We must be willing to *risk* ourselves. Once achieved, however, the rewards of honesty far outweigh any risks involved.

Why Is Honesty So Difficult to Achieve?

The major reason most of us find it difficult to be honest in our relationships is our *fear of rejection*. This fear causes us to keep our emotional guard up. We buttress our relationships with others by pretending to be someone or something we're not or by *not* being who we really are. We fantasize somehow that this charade serves as our magical protective shield against possible rejection. When we allow this to occur, our fears rob us of the potential joy friendships can bring, and we destroy opportunities for personal growth.

Being honest means being vulnerable. When we feel weak inside (demonstrating poor self-image and poor ego development), we are less likely to risk ourselves with people or circumstances we perceive as threatening. Unfortunately, the less we risk, the weaker and more vulnerable we feel. This cycle keeps repeating until honesty is no longer viewed as a virtue but becomes instead a dreaded enemy.

We especially fear honesty when we have been hurt in past relationships. The pain associated with honesty becomes more than we can bear. I have heard countless couples in marital therapy express their pain and fear of remarriage in the statement, "Once is enough . . . . Never again!"

But honesty, paradoxically, is a crucial survival strategy. Without it, true friendship falters, and hence there can be no growth in our relationships. Phoniness in relationships is epidemic. It is a scourge, a plague that makes relationships wither long before the friendship stage is reached. The more we practice phoniness, the more natural and spontaneous it becomes. Soon, phoniness becomes real, and what is real becomes phony.

Developing the honesty survival strategy serves not only to make our friendships more genuine, it also increases our sense of inner strength and self-esteem. Gaining strength and elevating self-esteem are what promote happiness. When we add to this a sense of life meaning and personal control, we not only survive, we prosper as well.

Strategy #3: Be a Transparent Person

Several years ago I lunched with a group of colleagues who talked about young people growing up and going off to college, jobs, and marriage. At that time I had a son in college and a daughter about to enter it. One person at the table was asking all kinds of questions regarding college tuition, dorm life, and what it must be like to experience one's children "leaving the nest." When I tried to respond, I noticed that he made no effort to listen. Instead, he just kept talking, barreling away as if I weren't there!

In fact, the more he talked, the more animated he became, philosophizing and theorizing, never once acknowledging the fact that someone sitting at the table didn't have to theorize because he was living it! None of that seemed to matter. What mattered was for him to keep talking about *his* ideas, *his* philosophy, *his* life. Distrustful, negative, suspicious, fearful people usually have only one way of doing things, seeing things, saying things, and hearing things: *theirs!* To them, as we learned earlier, basic trust has long ago been lost.

Finally, after I had failed in several attempts to answer some of his questions, someone else at the table took note of the fact that I currently had a son in college and asked what it was like. I looked directly at my non-hearing colleague and again responded with my thoughts on the subject. Again he barely acknowledged one word I said. I felt as if he were looking *through* me to some invisible entity standing behind me. And despite my attempts to ward it off, a strange feeling of having been used and demeaned swept over me as I departed that day.

Each of us, I'm certain, has had experiences similar to the one just described—perhaps more of them than we care to recall! It is a sad commentary on relationships and communication practices when people truly don't acknowledge and appreciate one another. It is also a curious paradox that we expect, even demand, openness and sincerity in relationships and then, when we get them, we look through or beyond the responding person to someone or something else. When that person then closes the doors and windows to his soul, we become angry and resentful. But in truth, when this happens, we have only ourselves to blame.

Transparency in friendships is one of the most powerful ingredients toward making them wonderful experiences. Yet to be a transparent self leaves one open and vulnerable to exploitation. How can we best cope with this paradox? The key to preventing this from occurring is to recognize our own weaknesses as well as strengths. Thus, when confronted by self-centered individuals who voyeuristically look through us, refusing to affirm us, we must either physically or emotionally avoid them. Sometimes we need to do both. The least we can do is to limit the degree of our emotional openness and exposure to them if we find physical avoidance impossible. I have a little mental technique that I use routinely when I am exposed to the *emotional voyeur,* the person who would deny my very existence if I would let him. In the case of my luncheon colleague, as he rambled on I listened quietly and thought joyously to myself, "I have a whole world . . . a universe . . . that you don't know about—nor will you ever know!"

It is important to seek out friends who, rather than seeing us as ordinary windows to be looked through, appreciate us for the multi-faceted diamonds that we truly are. Our friends should be people who reciprocate our openness and who joyfully affirm those unique gifts we bring to the relationship.

When we are chronically exposed to the emotional voyeur, we are diminished both in personal strength and self-esteem. Our friendship survival mechanism languishes and our individual happiness declines. When we are with happy people—people who value our openness and transparency and who are in turn open and transparent with us—we grow in both inner strength and self-esteem.

Strategy #4: Learn to Appreciate People

With great wisdom and candor, the famed philosopher and educator John Dewey observed that the deepest yearning in human nature is "the desire to be important"[8]—to feel appreciated by our fellow humans. Unfortunately, most of us are either too self-absorbed, fearful, or lacking in basic trust to fully appreciate other people. As a result, we miss opportunities to strengthen our friendship survival mechanism, since this mechanism is heavily dependent on our ability to value and appreciate one another.

The only way to make, hold, and enhance friendships is by learning to appreciate people for who and what they are. The minute we start judging them for what we think they should or should not be, then we fail to appreciate others for their specialness. Others will in turn then fail to appreciate us.

Closely aligned with the ability to appreciate others is the factor of *friendliness*. Strengthening the friendship survival mechanism is based not only on our ability to appreciate one another but also on the degree of friendliness present when we interact with others. A smile not returned or a friendly "Good Morning!" that elicits only a grunt will weaken the friendship survival mechanism. But when we smile back (sometimes when it's not easy to do!) and return the "Good Morning!" we not only strengthen the other person, we also strengthen ourselves. Someone once said, "A forced smile is better than a sincere frown."

Keeping our friendship survival mechanism strong should be a top priority. If we allow it to weaken, we run the risk of becoming hostile and hurtful in our most important relationships. We become defensive and begin to feel unfriendly toward those whom we may love and cherish most. We may even begin to feel paranoid toward others whom we erroneously perceive as the source of our pain and suffering. We may irrationally believe that since pain has been inflicted on us, we need to inflict it on others.

Once we start such an unfortunate sequence, we victimize not only ourselves but often the innocent as well. As noted in the chapter on love, the opposite of the love survival mechanism is fear. The opposite of the friendship survival mechanism is *animosity*. Appreciating the other person for his or her intrinsic worth is an effective way to strengthen the friendship survival mechanism and eliminate from our lives the wasteful emotion of animosity.

How do we acquire the quality of friendliness? How do we eliminate the destructive and wasteful emotion of animosity? We need to understand that becoming a friendlier, more caring person takes time, patience, and effort. We really need to work at reaching out to another person . . . to touch him or her in the spirit of friendship.

As I write these words, I am thinking about someone who truly exemplifies the spirit of friendliness. He is a toll booth operator along the New York State Thruway. If awards for friendliness were being handed out, I would nominate him. He is always friendly and always kind, and he always seems to have a cheery greeting for everyone, rain or shine! He makes no extra money for his kindness or for taking extra time and effort with others. He simply does it. He honestly seems to appreciate everybody!

In fact, this man is so popular with motorists that he was recently featured in the local newspaper. When the curious reporter asked why the toll booth operator was always so cheery, he responded simply that he is just naturally a happy person. *And his happiness is contagious!* I always look forward to going through his toll booth just to see him smile and to receive his warm greeting. Can you imagine how many people he affects on a daily basis? And how many affect him in return? Wow! Now *that's* how to build your friendship survival mechanism!

It's sad but true that mutual appreciation among people is rare. The deficiency stems largely from our lack of trust. Indeed, without basic trust, truly appreciating another person is difficult, if not impossible. With trust, we not only appreciate others but discover that our friendships endure and prosper over the years.

Appreciating another person means affirming that person as a unique, special individual. One of the greatest "affirmers" of all time was Jesus of Nazareth. His great belief in and love for humanity is eloquently and majestically expressed in the moving, lyrical strains of the Beatitudes as found in "The Sermon on the Mount." If you have never read this famous section of the Bible, I encourage you, regardless of your religious orientation, to do so. You will learn more, more quickly, about what it means to appreciate and affirm people than from a thousand books on the subject!

Basic Life Elements Affected by the Friendship Survival Mechanism

First, inner strength;
second, self-image;
third, life meaning;
and fourth, personal control.

NOTES

1. Emile Durkheim, "Anomie and Suicide," in Lewis A. Coser and Bernard Rosenberg, eds., *Sociological Theory: A Book of Readings* (New York: The Macmillan Co., 1957), pp. 480-490.

2. George Burns, *Gracie: A Love Story* (New York: G.P. Putnam's Sons, 1988).

3. Carl R. Rogers, *On Becoming a Person* (Boston: Houghton Mifflin Co., 1961), pp. 47, 62-63, 283-284.

4. Flora Rheta Schreiber, *Sybil* (Chicago: Regnery, 1973).

5. Corbett H. Thigpen, *The Three Faces of Eve* (New York: McGraw-Hill, 1957).

6. Alan Loy McGinnis, *The Friendship Factor* (Minneapolis: Augsburg Publishing House, 1979).

7. Erik H. Erikson, *Identity: Youth and Crisis* (New York: W.W. Norton, 1968), p. 96.

8. Quoted in Dale Carnegie, *How To Win Friends and Influence People* (New York: Simon and Schuster, 1937), p. 44.

SURVIVAL MECHANISM INVENTORY # 7
FRIENDSHIP

Inventory Statements	SA 5	A 4	U 3	D 2	SD 1	Score
1. As a teenager I had as many as four or five good friends.						
2. I have a few good friends today.						
3. Friendship is important to me.						
4. My parents have (or had) two or three good friends.						
5. I believe good friends should be able to share their disappointment in us as well as their satisfactions.						
6. Whenever I lose a close friend, I am deeply affected.						
7. My parents are (or were) friendly toward each other.						
8. I feel a strong sense of commitment to my friends.						
9. I see myself as a friendly person.						
10. I feel uncomfortable around people with whom I cannot be myself.						

Rating — *Check Appropriate Box*

Key

SA - Strongly Approve
A - Approve
U - Undecided
D - Disapprove
SD - Strongly Disapprove

SM Strength Quotient =

10 - 24 Weak
25 - 34 Average
35 - 50 Strong

11

Survival Mechanism #8: New Experience

> Let the great world spin forever down
> the ringing grooves of change.
> —*Alfred Lord Tennyson*

ONE DAY SEVERAL YEARS AGO I received a call at my office from a former client. She was the young mother of a two-year-old child, calling long-distance from another state. She said that she had been in a terrible car accident in which her child was ejected and killed instantly on a busy interstate highway. The voice spoke to me as if coming from outer space. Although this stunning tragedy had occurred just two days earlier, she described it with chilling detachment.

I had worked with this woman for several months, and I remembered her case well. She wanted to move to Texas to begin a new life. Her former husband, a paranoid schizophrenic, had threatened to kill her and the baby. She wanted a change—some new experiences—far from the sadness and chaos of her former life. The change came about, however, all too tragically . . . and ironically.

New experiences in life need not be negative; they can be wonderful. But for us to enjoy and benefit from them *we must be willing to change.* Over the years, I have been both fascinated and dumfounded by people's unwillingness to change their habitually destructive feelings, thoughts, and actions. Despite the fact that their lives are not working, they doggedly hang onto old, worn-out patterns of living. Any efforts to help them change are instantly resisted. They even construct incredibly intricate rationalizations to defend the old patterns. When the pain in their lives continues unabated, they complain loudly and mournfully about what a miserable place this world is.

Why New Experiences?

The new experience survival mechanism is important for two reasons: it *regenerates* our spirits and prevents stagnation, and it *motivates and mobilizes* us to take action. Over time, the importance of these two factors has been powerfully driven home to me. I have been fortunate enough to observe these phenomena with hundreds of clients. Some were able to utilize new experiences and strengthen this survival mechanism, while others, having equal opportunity, wasted their chances and fell by the wayside.

Essentially, when it comes to new experience there are two types of people: those who suffer and seek change and those who suffer and *pretend* to seek change. The woman who so tragically lost her child is an example of the latter. She had spent the better portion of her adult life failing. It is important to note that she *chose* failure. It was not something forced upon her at gunpoint. She had the intelligence to change her negative patterns of life, but, as I shall shortly prove, she simply did not *want* that change, so her new experience survival mechanism never regenerated. Although she realized she was failing, her basic impulse was to keep failing rather than using the opportunity to achieve new growth.

As noted in the chapter on creativity, the impulse to

fail is frequently unconscious. This is why the survival mechanism theory holds such hope: through it we realize that we can *consciously* control our own destinies. When we sincerely desire change in our lives, we deliberately seek new experiences that in turn regenerate and motivate us to even further growth. Unfortunately, many people who suffer terribly only *pretend* to seek change. Their charade results in atrophy and even death of their survival mechanism of new experience.

One may wonder why the woman who lost her child only pretended to change, or why I might conclude that she chose failure. Certainly, we must assume she had no death wish for her child or that, while seeking a change, she somehow knowingly courted disaster. I contend, however, that because of her fear of change, she was unconsciously *forced* to maintain her old patterns of thinking, feeling, and doing. Those patterns in turn led her back to the failure image with which she had been accustomed to live. Because she feared change so greatly, choosing failure was easier for her. We are constantly caught in the struggle between the unconscious downward forces and the conscious upward ones. The former seek to keep us forever locked into the old patterns while the latter urge us to break them and forge new, more productive ones.

It is important to seek out *proper* new experiences. Many people strive for this but fall short simply because their intentions are wrong. As I learned later, for example, my client was really going to Texas to seek out an old flame who had caused her great pain in the past. Instead of true *new* experience, she was searching, compulsively, to *repeat an old, harmful experience.* Her need to repeat a hurtful event in order to gratify her negative self-image was more powerful by far than the courage she needed to summon real change.

Real Change Is Painful

Thousands of people pay therapists millions of dollars annually in hope of finding personal happiness. Most, unfortunately, will fail in their quest. They fail simply because they choose *not* to pay the price of *real* change. Perhaps the saddest lesson I have learned from clients is that the *vast majority of them are simply unwilling to change.* They come to therapy expecting the therapist to wave his or her magic wand and "make the world go away."

Although, as noted earlier, psychotherapy is a legitimate survival strategy, most clients use it erroneously. In their search for a "quick fix," they never learn how to properly strengthen their survival mechanisms. As their life failures continue, they grow disenchanted, quit therapy prematurely, and continue on their merry way to nowhere.

Therapists, no matter how skilled, cannot, unfortunately, fulfill the basic needs that should be met within the first five or six years of life. Only a nurturing, loving parent can do that. If, for whatever reasons, that kind of nurture doesn't occur, the client must obtain on his or her own those elements essential for survival. Therapy and therapist can help, but only as road map and guide . . . *not giver.*

The fantasy of the "quick fix," however, remains and appears evident within the general population. Because of the pain associated with change, the average person opts to remain unchanged. A person would rather complain than alter his or her life course, choosing, as Albert Ellis has observed, long-term pain for short-term gain instead of short-term pain for long-term gain.[1] Robert Schuller hit the mark when he said, "It takes guts to leave the ruts!"[2] Real change *is* painful. It *does* take guts to get out of the ruts.

When I finally understood this simple yet basic principle, it made sense that few people change. Change requires *strength*. It requires *guts!* And when we allow our survival mechanisms to atrophy and die (as most of us do), we lack the personal strength . . . the guts . . . that change requires.

Someone once said that good therapy is good education. And to be well-educated means we must change. Because of our weakness, however, change is often what we want least! I frequently recall a man who sat in my office complaining bitterly about life's misfortunes. After finally agreeing that he would have to work hard to improve his life, he looked me straight in the eye and said, "I'll work and work hard, but don't expect me to change . . . that's for *other* people to do." I could scarcely believe my ears! Needless to say, his life never improved.

Change, indeed, "is the name of the game." It is mind-boggling how few people want to understand and accept this one simple fact. We want our lives to improve but paradoxically think we can remain the same.

Any new experience, by definition, involves adaptation and change. And because change requires a certain amount of risk, most new experiences are viewed with a measure of apprehension. We fear the unknown. I was speaking recently with a friend who was contemplating a job change. Although he greatly desired a move, he said he probably would not follow through because it meant he would have to change his way of life. He agreed that he would be happier with a different job but said the chances of improvement were poor because of his fear of change and the unknown.

The new experience survival mechanism doesn't ask us to change; it *demands* that we change! That's because human beings are so prone to maintaining the status quo that they often need to be shocked in order to get off "dead center."

Frequently, it takes what Dr. Morris Massey calls a "Significant Emotional Event" to move us out of our homeostatic doldrums.[3] Such an event might include a major loss, such as serious illness, death of a loved one, separation, or divorce. On the positive side, it could include marriage, a job change, a geographical move, graduation, promotion, or winning the lottery.

Any kind of change can be stressful. It is the way we respond to change that counts. If we respond with fear, our new experience survival mechanism will atrophy and eventually die. If we welcome change as an integral part of life, this mechanism will be strengthened and with it the four basic life elements.

Each day provides us with new experiences, both good and bad, that become part of us . . . locked forever in the depths of our unconscious. New experiences are self-renewing and exhilarating. Even the seemingly simple, mundane task of getting out of bed each day represents a new challenge. How will we greet the new day? Will we welcome it with optimism and hope? Or will we meet it with dread and pessimism? Each day at work is a new experience. We can view it with an attitude of "I'm going to *make* this a good day!" or, "Oh no! How am I going to get through this day?" The choice is ours. *Attitude is everything!*

New Experience Survival Mechanism Strategies

Strategy #1: Fight Fear with Force

We are all familiar with the statement, "Experience is the best teacher." Although most of us are willing to accept the wisdom behind that time-tested truth, probably few of us are willing to act on it. The single most prevalent reason for our inaction is *fear.*

To enter into new experiences or adventures means to risk ourselves. And with the thought of risk comes anxiety and fear. Even the most daring and brave among us sometimes suffer the pounding heart, sweaty palms, and disorientation caused by fear or anxiety.

James Lincoln Collier states that "the new, the different, is almost by definition scary. But each time you try something, you learn, and as the learning piles up, the world opens to you."[4] If we try, we can "desensitize" ourselves to the fear, much the same way we acquire immunity to snake bite if we take regular doses of antivenin.

The best way to fight fear is by *going into the fear.* Do the thing you fear and watch fear flee. Several years ago a man in his early thirties came to see me. He was an alcoholic and, as with most alcoholics, he struggled with pervasive fears and worries. Although having enormous talent, he was so immobilized by fear that his ability to act was greatly diminished.

I asked him what he feared most. He stated that his greatest fear was losing his very tentative sobriety and with it his shaky marriage. He told me his wife was a tyrant who gave him little credit, and were it not for his fears of being alone he would have left her years ago. I told him what he already unconsciously knew: he would have to do the thing he feared. He would have to *force* himself to leave his wife and face the fear of "falling off the wagon." After long and agonizing months of deliberation, he decided that leaving was, indeed, what he *had* to do.

Several months later, he was like a different person. He had acquired a new job, returned to college, and improved his relationship with his children. And he didn't "fall off the wagon!" His new experiences of living and making it on his own had strengthened his survival mechanism, and he did it by *going into the fear*.

Strategy #2: Fly with Your Own Flock

When embarking on a new experience it is always better to do so with like-minded people. The reason for this is simple: *Your interests will be supported and sustained by those who see things your way.* Doing something new or daring can be a difficult task at best. If you lack sufficient support and encouragement, your efforts may be doomed to failure even before they get off the ground. This particular strategy plays a crucial role in developing the new experience survival mechanism.

To illustrate how this strategy works, consider the multi-level marketing system used by various direct selling organizations like Amway, Shaklee, and Mary Kay. I have made a study of multi-level marketing techniques, and I can tell you *they work*.

Individuals who join such organizations as distributors are supported by an entire "army" of co-distributors. They congregate, sometimes numbering into the thousands, for rallies, seminars, retreats, and other functions.

Their organization forms a mutual support network in which distributors swap stories, share triumphs and defeats, and basically stick together in sort of a "network of hope." The many shared slogans serve to remind members of their common linkage. During the course of building his or her business, the distributor is constantly gaining new experience, not just related to the business but *personally* as well. I have spoken with many individuals who have told me that their primary objective for becoming distributors was for "personal development." In effect, although they may not be conscious of it, these individuals utilize the distributor experience to build their new experience survival mechanism. The strategy of "sticking together" seems to be their primary strategy . . . and it works!

Strategy #3: Marriage

Although marriage is an obvious vehicle for gaining new experience, most of us would never characterize marriage as a "strategy" to strengthen the new experience survival mechanism. We consider marriage as an institution through which we share our lives with a person with whom we have fallen in love. Period! On a deeper level, however, I believe we marry in order to enhance and strengthen the new experience survival mechanism. That may sound somewhat presumptuous. Let me explain.

Marriage, perhaps more than any other institution, is fraught with uncertainty. If ever a great unknown existed, certainly it is marriage! When we marry, we traverse from the known to the unknown, from the secure to the uncertain. Marriage involves *risk*, and risk is what strengthening the new experience survival mechanism is all about. *All* new experiences require a certain amount of risk.

Sensing that risk-taking is essential to achieve the new experience that will strengthen this survival mechanism, many of us, despite our apprehension, are more than willing to enter marriage as a vehicle to achieve this end. Using marriage in this way can, however, be a deadly trap . . . as so many have discovered. Several years ago, one of my clients was so intent on utilizing marriage as the vehicle to enhance his new experience survival mechanism that he dashed from one relationship to another. At one point he was divorcing his current wife, reuniting with his first wife, and starting a new relationship with a third woman he had recently met at work—all at the same time. He had plans to either remarry his first wife, marry the woman he had met just the week before or, if all else failed, maybe not go through with the divorce from his current wife! On top of this, he wanted me to agree to any decision he might come up with. When I didn't, he flew into a rage, called me a charlatan, and quit therapy.

Although we hunger for new experiences, we need care and sound judgment when selecting the vehicle to obtain them. Marriage for the sake of new experience alone is like getting sick just so we can visit the doctor. Both are self-defeating. When we enter marriage out of a genuine love and positive regard for the other person, we then can anticipate enhancing the new experience survival mechanism without negative consequences either to our partner or to ourselves.

A successful marriage is like a wonderful journey that two people undertake together and from which both can grow. When a couple engages in such an adventure, the result is that both partners will experience growth in this survival mechanism and, correspondingly, individual self-esteem. In addition, the partners will gain personal strength and control over their lives and, perhaps most important, *meaning* from the marital bond.

Strategy #4: Maintain a Future Orientation

Perhaps one of the deadliest plagues ever to face the human race is now sweeping the land. It is far worse than anything in recorded history. Its relentless march covers the continent like some giant, suffocating fog. It cannot be seen; it is only experienced. No one seems able to escape its menacing grip. There is no known cure, no means of prevention. Its overwhelming power respects no socioeconomic, racial, or cultural barriers. It transcends every value system. Its force is unstoppable. Its impact on humanity is unmistakable. Its final objective: destruction of personal happiness and prosperity.

What is this horror that, as I write these words, threatens our very survival? Is it AIDS, or cancer, or heart disease? No, it is not. Since it is my belief that such a menace has no known counterpart in modern history, I had to coin a new word to describe this pestilence. I call it *Immutanitis*. *Immutanitis* is a neologism I invented when I came to the horrifying realization that our emotionally overburdened society, in the process of creating "burnouts," was also creating a new breed of homo sapiens. This new breed, because of its degree of burnout, has been transformed into a mutant-type creature who no longer lives life as would a normal human being. Instead, this creature merely *imitates* life. So I combined the word *imitation* with the word *mutant* to form the term *Immutanitis*.

Immutanitis describes a condition or illness in a human who, because of the chronic and sustained nature of his or her burnout, is no longer recognizable as human.

If there is a tragic commonness among our species, I would have to say that, to a greater or lesser degree, we all are afflicted with this plague. Many of us infected with this highly contagious and, if untreated, emotionally fatal disease may be unaware of its symptoms. And knowing what the symptoms are is critical if we are to continue living our lives productively. I therefore feel compelled to alert the reader to the symptoms of this dreaded killer.

THE SYMPTOMS OF IMMUTANITIS Here are some of the more common and pervasive symptoms of immutanitis: Laziness. Apathy. Boredom. Emptiness. Victimization. Passivity. Dependency. Procrastination. Non-organic muteness. Treating white as black. Treating black as white. Treating good as bad. Treating bad as good. Forgetting when remembering is needed. Remembering when forgetting is needed. Thinking when feeling is required. Feeling when thinking is required. Inaction when action is needed. Action when inaction is needed. Poor impulse control. Poor frustration tolerance. Poor reality testing. Inconsistency. Paradoxical and contradictory thinking. Happiness when there should be sadness. Sadness when there should be happiness. Being troubled by truth. Being joyful over lies. Anxiety when there should be security. Security when there should be anxiety.

Although these are common symptoms of the illness, the most common characteristic among severely afflicted victims is the degree to which they are *past-oriented*. It is a cliche, for example, that the "Good Ole Boys" sit around the bar and talk about their past glories and victories. Bruce Springsteen, the famous rock star, sings about this in his hit song "Glory Days."

To effectively strengthen the new experience survival mechanism and thus eradicate the disease of immutanitis, we must be *present- and future-oriented.* The past is dead. Let it rest in peace. New experience requires that we live in the present and make judicious, worry-free plans for the future. The reason most of us don't develop this all-important survival mechanism to its fullest is that we're stuck with what was and fail to see what is and what could be.

Looking back over the thousands of clients I have attempted to help through the years, I would have to say that probably eighty-five to ninety percent were plagued with the disease of immutanitis. Although the degree of their suffering varied, each of them was unable to develop his or her new experience survival mechanism to its fullest because of chronic obsession with past events, failures, problems, and faded dreams. Had these clients been able to "let go" of the past and move on, their personal growth would have been enhanced tremendously.

Strategy #5: Think like a Winner

The case of the woman who lost her child was one involving the *negative* use of new experience. She was an individual who *thought* she was changing. Instead, because of her poor self-image and a lifetime of negative programming, she was pulled back into a previous pattern of defeat and self-destruction. She *thought* she was making positive choices, but instead she made fatal ones.

The following story, by contrast, relates a far different outcome. It depicts the use of new experience in a positive light. It is a story of courage and tenacity, of winning rather than losing, of life and hope rather than death and despair.

I first met Reginald when he was an outstanding high school athlete. He was tall and powerfully built. And he ran like the wind. He was a perfect wide receiver. Any college football coach would consider him a godsend and give just about anything to get him. One coach was lucky enough to do just that.

"Reggi," as he was known to his friends, did not always have things going his way. He came from a troubled past. Because of depression, failure in school, and inability to control his temper, he wound up in a residential treatment center for troubled youth.

But deep inside, Reggi was a winner. Deep inside, courage burned. Even as a youngster, he would not be held down. By the time he was a sophomore in high school, he was a starter on the varsity football and basketball teams and an honor roll student. He had conquered both his depression and his temper and went on to stardom in college football and graduation with a 3.8 average. Today Reggi, no longer the tense, forlorn eleven-year-old who entered the scary world of residential treatment, is a starting player for one of the National Football League teams. You have undoubtedly seen him many times, still running like the wind, as you cheered your favorite team on Sunday afternoon or on Monday Night Football.

WHAT IT TAKES TO BE A WINNER What makes a winner? In a word, *attitude*. A winner's credo is: "I can if I think I can!" But winning is really a combination of factors working in close harmony. Without a winning attitude no one can win . . . on or off the football field. One must also have the *motivation*, the sincere desire to win. It must be a *burn* residing deep within that keeps us going . . . *no matter what*.

Winners also *believe* in themselves. Indeed, without

belief, even our grandest dreams crumble. Then there is *courage*, that elusive quality that so troubled the lion in the Wizard of Oz. Hemingway once beautifully defined courage as "grace under pressure." But even grand courage will not make winners of us if we lack *tenacity* and commitment to our goals.

A chicken and pig were walking along the highway. Along the side of the road was a large billboard that read: "Stop at Joe's Diner for a breakfast of bacon and eggs." The chicken stopped and exclaimed, "Hey, Pig, let's stop and eat. I can provide the eggs and you the bacon." The pig stared at the chicken for a moment and then responded, "Yeah, Chicken, easy for you to say. For you it's all in a day's work . . . for me it's *total commitment!*" When we commit to our goals, we should be prepared to go all the way.

Once a winner has made a commitment, that person is prepared to take *action* toward achieving his or her goals. The Bible tells us that "many are called, but few are chosen." Indeed, many *think* they have all the qualities of a winner, but when it comes time for action they are nowhere to be found. Such individuals are fully prepared to "talk the talk" but woefully inadequate when it comes time to "walk the walk."

Finally, winning always demands *change*. If we are unwilling to change, we are unwilling to win. A winner will always and unhesitatingly "do whatever it takes." Winners don't allow fear of the unknown to hold them back. Indeed, they welcome the fear! And if changing themselves is required, they will do it. No questions asked! But to change means embracing new experiences. It means "going into the fear." It means risking. In the final analysis, achieving lasting change in our lives means *less talk and more action!*

Basic Life Elements Affected by
the New Experience Survival Mechanism

First, life meaning;
second, self-image;
third, inner strength;
and fourth, personal control.

NOTES

1. Albert Ellis and William J. Knaus, *Overcoming Procrastination: Or, How to Think and Act Rationally in Spite of Life's Inevitable Hassles* (New York: New American Library, 1977), pp. 35-36, 54-55.

2. Robert Schuller, *The Be-Happy Attitudes* (Waco: Word Books, 1985), p. 40.

3. *What You Are Is Where You Were When*, Morris Massey, CBS/Fox Video, Farmington Hills, Michigan, 1982.

4. James Lincoln Collier, "Anxiety: Challenge by Another Name," *Reader's Digest*, December, 1986, p. 114.

SURVIVAL MECHANISM INVENTORY # 8
NEW EXPERIENCE

Inventory Statements	SA 5	A 4	U 3	D 2	SD 1	Score
1. I look forward to new experiences that may enhance my life in some way.						
2. I have a certain amount of anxiety whenever I embark on a new experience.						
3. I am able to overcome normal fears that new experiences may create.						
4. My parents encouraged me to have positive new experiences during my childhood and adolescence.						
5. If I were invited to take an all-expenses-paid trip to Europe, I would do it.						
6. I was able to overcome a very *negative* new experience I had as a child.						
7. I enjoy meeting new people.						
8. I believe that new experiences enable us to grow as individuals.						
9. I would encourage my own children to have new, growth-enhancing experiences.						
10. By the age of twelve, *most* of my experiences, I would say, were positive.						

Rating
Check Appropriate Box

SM Strength Quotient =

Key

SA - Strongly Approve
A - Approve
U - Undecided
D - Disapprove
SD - Strongly Disapprove

10 - 24 Weak
25 - 34 Average
35 - 50 Strong

12

Survival Mechanism #9: Spiritual Belief

> If ye have faith as a grain of mustard seed, ye shall say unto this mountain, Remove hence to yonder place; and it shall remove . . . .
> —*Matthew 17:20 (King James Version)*

FROM EARLIEST RECORDED HISTORY and even from prehistoric times, we have evidence of the spiritual beliefs people used to sustain themselves in their struggle for survival. Such evidence extends from the ancient cave dwellers to the Greeks, Romans, Teutons, and Celts. Ancient humans feared being killed by a volcano, earthquake, flood, or some other natural catastrophe. If the forces of nature weren't endangering their existence, some evil spirit or demon might be threatening to destroy them. In order to cope with these fears of death and annihilation, humans developed belief systems in forces more powerful than the forces of nature and the unknown. *They developed belief in gods.* Ancient people worshiped the spirits of mountains, sky, trees, water, and fire, assuming that divinity resided in those natural entities. Anthropologists call such early forms of worship *animism* and *animatism*.

If we compare these early spiritual precepts with modern-day forms of spirituality we see that their essential purpose has remained unchanged: to provide humanity with that same sense of security, peace, hope, and wonder that sustained our forebears. The essence of spirituality that existed within our early ancestors resides within us, too, and it can serve to enhance our lives when we discover it and learn how to release its power.

Unfortunately, most of us maintain a view of our inner spiritual beliefs that is limited and circumscribed by the *form* these beliefs take rather than seeing spirituality as a *process*. Once we acquire a view of the process, we broaden our horizons for personal growth. Understanding spirituality as a process leads to our embracing it as a more expansive panorama, allowing our prejudices to fall away and making room for acceptance of our fellow humans.

Achieving spiritual growth involves more than adherence to religious dogma or ritual, more than embracing one specified belief system or combination of systems. Spirituality is, in the words of mythologist Joseph Campbell, the "divine presence within us."[1] To grasp this presence we must first become aware of it, and to become aware of it we must gain the courage to enter the unknown world of our soul, or innermost self. For most of us, to enter that world is to look squarely into the face of fear.

We all possess our own unique methodology when embarking upon this inward journey. The goal, however, is always the same. A Hindu worshiping the universal spirit of Brahman breathes into his or her soul the same spiritual power that the Jewish people feel when the cantor sings. When the lone runner "hits the wall" and is released from pain, the same inner healing is experienced as comes to the Trappist monk who spends every morning in silent meditation.

There is no set formula for developing our spiritual belief survival mechanism. We strengthen it when we walk quietly and reverently among the ancient redwoods, even as did our forebears when they worshiped the spirits of the majestic forests and verdant groves. We strengthen it, too, when we go quietly into the silence of our own thoughts and feelings or when we reach out and offer healing to the land and its inhabitants. Our spiritual belief survival mechanism gains strength when we witness the miracle of a young child accepting the truth that there *is* love in the world, and when we actively participate in that truth.

The Inner War and Emptiness

Some of the bloodiest wars the world has ever known were fought because some people had the mistaken notion that they had found the perfect answers to humankind's spiritual needs and wanted to foist those answers upon others. These wars tend to obscure the lesser known conflicts that go on daily in the lives of average people, conflicts that comprise the *inner war* or struggle that keeps us from experiencing the joy that was meant for us. Because of this inner war, the war of our own thoughts, feelings, and perceptions, we rarely obtain the spiritual "high" that comes so readily to the mystic. We can, however, taste this magic if we are willing to pay the price for it. "And what," you ask, "is the price?"

Emptiness. The price of fulfillment . . . of fullness of spirit . . . is emptiness. When you empty yourself of the preconceptions of what life should be and allow life to be what it *is*, you will have gained emptiness. As I use the term here, emptiness does not imply creating for yourself a sense of neurotic defeat or despair, nor does it mean a self-imposed exile from who you are. Emptiness means, instead, the state of mind that you achieve by purging yourself from your fears, anxieties, perfectionism, and sense of self-alienation by entering the darkened chambers of your real self. To enter this labyrinth, you need courage, and to acquire courage you must connect yourself to a higher power.

Once you have achieved this emptiness, you will have room to grow . . . to experience life in a totally new dimension. For the first time, you can be truly filled—not with the old food from your childhood that may have poisoned your dreams for happiness, but with new nourishment from a world you long ago abandoned, but a world that never forgot you or gave up on you.

To tap into the richness of life that is out there, to make it your own, you must go into the fear—that savage, horrifying fear that wells up in you each time you reach for personal fulfillment, for happiness. You must understand that fear. You must study it . . . up *close.*

How close is close? So close that the distinction between past and present becomes academic, so close that your earliest childhood memories become as current as the thought you have at this moment. When you go into your fears, when you *own* them, you must go back to the original demons, those monsters created within the family crucible. Life as you know it today, for better or worse, had its origins in your family. That's where the inner war began and where your spiritual legacy came from, generations old and deeply embedded in your unconscious mind.

In order to progress through this inner struggle it is sometimes necessary to "unlearn" the destructive or limiting lessons of childhood—to sweep the "cobwebs from the attic"—before true spiritual growth can begin. Psychiatrist M. Scott Peck relates, in his book *The Road Less Traveled*, two fascinating cases that illustrate this point.[2] First, in the case of Kathy, Dr. Peck tells of the way he helped a young woman overcome the debilitating guilt and fears instilled in her by her mother in the guise of religion. In order for Kathy to grow spiritually, she had to go into these deeply rooted fears and learn to let go of them. This was a long and arduous process, requiring great strength and persistence. Once Kathy was free (empty) of these old destructive forces, she was gradually able to learn to enjoy a normal, independent, happy life.

In the second case, that of Theodore, Dr. Peck describes a man who had given up, in adolescence, any formalized observance of spiritual belief. His life was dull and joyless. Through intensive psychotherapy and profound soul-searching, Theodore slowly allowed himself to tap into the inner essence of spirituality that lay dormant within him but that he had previously denied. He eventually regained his lost spiritual belief on a more mature and fulfilling level and went on to study for the ministry.

What is it, then, that enables a human being to yearn after and strive for spiritual self-fulfillment, as Kathy and Theodore did? What life force comes into play that, despite overwhelming opposition, refuses to give up? I believe it is the spiritual self, that part of our humanness that connects us with a power greater than ourselves.

Everyone Has the Need to Believe!

Many human beings invoke daily the name of some deity, greater power, or higher consciousness in an attempt to lead more fulfilling, less stressful lives. These supplications represent a universal *need* to believe in someone or something, to hang onto a force or power greater than ourselves in times of great stress or catastrophe. We activate our spiritual selves when ordinary means of coping with disaster appear futile.

Some people may go along for years without ever thinking about spiritual beliefs, but in the moment of crisis they seem to reach out for something or someone bigger than themselves. The expression, "Oh, God!" appears to be almost instinctive among modern-day cultures in situations fraught with sudden tragedy or trauma, whether said to one's self or to a loved one.

Indeed, such an expression manifests itself so readily precisely because its source is a part of the deepest core of our innermost being . . . our spiritual selves. Viktor Frankl, for example, believes in the existence of an "unconscious spirituality," as he explains in his book, *The Unconscious God*.[3] He states that we can, by *conscious* choice, call upon this sense of the spiritual to transcend ourselves, our fears, and our self-doubt. Even though repressed for many years, this spiritual or "transcendent unconscious," as Dr. Frankl calls it, is ever with us and will manifest itself if we choose to acknowledge its presence.[4]

As a result of my personal and clinical experiences, I agree with Frankl's view. I have noticed in my own and others' families that, as we grow older, our spiritual beliefs and commitments tend to grow stronger. Although I grew up in a religious home, my siblings and I, with the exception of my oldest sister, who is an ordained minister, spent little time on religious issues once we entered our twenties. Although our basic faith in God remained secure, our energies seemed to go elsewhere. As we entered our forties, however, spiritual themes once again began to run through practically everything we said and did. And even now they continue to grow stronger each day.

I believe this conscious shifting back to our spiritual roots as we grow older underscores Frankl's unconscious God theory and our need to realize that, despite our wanderings, there is a force deep within us still *in charge*, still *in control*, and still directing us back to our beginnings. The biblical parable of the prodigal son, in which Jesus stated "For this my son was dead, and is alive again; he was lost, and is found"[5] carries tremendous emotional weight from a survival standpoint. We all need to believe that, *despite* our wanderings and despite the distance we may have strayed from the fold, we can still be welcomed "home" with love. If we can know and believe this, then all is well since, in the final analysis, such knowledge places us *in control* of our lives.

It seems that the older we get and the closer we come to that ultimate loss of control, death and the unknown, the more powerful is our need for spiritual belief to maintain control over our lives. Because of our human frailties, we are always in a struggle between being in control and losing control over what happens to us. When we feel secure and in charge, we tend to rely on our own powers.

But when our sense of personal control is threatened in some way or the loss of control is imminent, *then* we return to our spiritual belief survival mechanism.

Indeed, our spiritual beliefs do offer us a means of gaining control over our lives. As long as we have some spiritual foundation, we feel we are in charge even when our world may be crumbling. This foundation has a way of seeing us through even the most difficult of times. With spiritual strength within us we can hope, and with hope, there is always a new, brighter tomorrow.

Control over our destinies and hope for tomorrow— who could ask for more? This is why spiritual belief is such a powerful survival mechanism. But it does even more than provide us with hope and control. It also gives us inner strength, a sense of meaning and, in some cases, a self-esteem that enables us to carry on in a frequently burdensome, pain-filled world.

Countless individuals, through their spiritual belief survival mechanism, have strengthened *all four basic life elements*. And they have done so sometimes in the midst of hardship and tragedy beyond that which most of us could endure. They are the true survivors . . . those brave warriors who could accept that all things are possible even in the face of deepest doubt. They are the ones who teach us that if, through our spirituality, we find meaning and purpose in life, we will, *no matter what*, "make it through the rain."

How One Mother Used her Spiritual Belief to Survive

It is a source of continuous wonder to me how some people in the most dreadful of circumstances lift themselves up and come through with flying colors. Sometimes it seems that this effort is nothing short of heroic. A client of mine, the mother of four children, did this recently. When I first met her she had just come through a bitterly contested divorce. Her oldest daughter, an attractive fifteen-year-old, was heavily into drugs, and the second oldest, a twelve-year-old son, was mentally retarded. A nine-year-old son was emotionally disturbed and required placement outside the home.

One day last summer this woman came to see me and said that were it not for her faith in God and the strength she derived from it, she would probably have had a nervous breakdown long ago. The following week, as if by some malevolent plan, her five-year-old daughter, a beautiful child in whom she had placed great hope, was struck down by a drunk driver and killed instantly.

The tragedy left this woman numb with despair. The child in whom she had placed her last hope had been taken from her. Her marriage was gone. Her other children were at great risk. She was without a job and, because of her financial situation, would soon be evicted. The average person would have collapsed under far less devastating circumstances.

When I saw her after the funeral, however, she smiled at me and with courage I will never forget said, "Paul, as long as God stays by my side, I'll make it." It was as simple as that. Once again I was reminded of Hemingway's beautiful definition of courage: *grace under pressure.*

Faith can indeed move mountains! But how is such faith acquired? What are the specific ingredients, the strategies, we need for developing our spiritual belief survival mechanism? How can we use this belief to weather life's sometimes inhuman struggles? How do we navigate the treacherous waters and sail through the storms that threaten to capsize our hopes and dreams? Perhaps the next section will help answer some of these questions for you.

The Fear Factor

Faith and Fear Cannot Coexist

Webster's Third New International Dictionary defines faith as "the act or state of wholeheartedly and steadfastly believing in the existence, power, and benevolence of a supreme being."[6] This definition represents the meaning of "faith" as I use it in this section. If you accept this definition, however, you must further delineate for yourself the nature of this "supreme being," finally grappling with the faith question within your innermost thoughts.

Someone once said that faith and fear cannot coexist. If we are filled with fear, then we cannot claim to have faith in a supreme being. If we claim to have faith and remain fearful, we deceive ourselves. There is a growing body of research to support the theory that individuals who are optimistic, hopeful, cheerful, and full of faith in a supreme being or higher power are usually less fearful and have fewer worries. In addition, these same people generally maintain a higher level of physical health and energy. In contrast, the research increasingly links hypertension, heart disease, gastrointestinal problems, and even cancer to individuals who are highly stressed, anxious, and fearful.

Some of the research findings in recent years have been so conclusive in correlating anxiety, stress, and worry with physiological illnesses that to deny it is tantamount to waving a red flag of ignorance high above one's head. Almost equally significant has been the correlation between having faith in a higher power and remaining free of debilitating fears or worries. In fact, as a result of some of these findings, one could almost say we could "will" ourselves a worry-free and fear-free life merely by developing a sufficient amount of faith!

From research as well as from my own clinical observations, I have concluded that the single greatest enemy of the spiritual belief survival mechanism is *fear*. And its greatest antidote is *faith* in a power greater than ourselves. To banish fear from our lives means to develop as much faith as possible. The spiritual belief survival strategies I will discuss below can help you achieve this end. As this occurs, the four basic life elements will *automatically* be strengthened. Remember, personal happiness is a by-product, not a goal, of our ability to sustain and strengthen the four basic life elements.

What Are You Afraid of?

Some of you will remember the great stunt man of the 1970s, Evel Kneival. In his day, he was a daredevil's daredevil! At one point, after breaking several bones for the umpteenth time, he visited his psychiatrist for advice and consolation. As the story goes, he told the psychiatrist that he didn't know why he continued to do his life-threatening stunts and thought he should stop before he was killed.

The psychiatrist looked at him for a moment and then asked Evel if he was ever afraid when he performed some of his death-defying stunts. The stuntman responded that, indeed, he was—"scared to death!" Considering his answer, the psychiatrist then told Evel that his fear was the healthiest part of him. The implication, of course, was that what Evel did might be crazy, but his fear reaction was sane.

Some fears are normal and healthy. Others are not. We should be afraid of a charging lion, especially if it's hungry! We should avoid, however, maintaining morbid, neurotic forebodings of some vague thing that might happen to us someday . . . maybe. Such fears or anxieties are unhealthy.

There are many kinds of fear. Here is a partial list: fear of rejection, fear of failure, fear of disability, fear of death, fear of poverty, fear of people, fear of fear, and fear of success. This does not, of course, even take into account the many debilitating phobias that afflict thousands of people daily.

Many people frequently confuse the concepts of fear and anxiety. Fear is more of a biologically determined emotion, causing us to flee or want to run away when our immediate physical safety or survival is threatened. It is what we feel when that lion is charging us. Fear represents a perceived *external* danger or prospect of harm. Anxiety, on the other hand, is an emotional response generated from *within* us. It is what we feel when our self-esteem is threatened or when we are faced with the prospect of losing love or the approval of someone important to us. In this sense, anxiety is the prospect of not being liked. It is what we feel when we sense we are about to be rejected or humiliated in some way.

It's true, however, that the distinction between fear and anxiety is essentially academic in that the two are closely interrelated. When we feel anxious, we normally experience irrational fears, and when we fear something or someone, our anxieties tend to increase as well.

The Role Learning Plays in Our Fears

Most people retain a misconception about the way the fear reaction is acquired. Technically, we are born with only two fears: the fear of falling and the fear of loud noises. It can safely be said that all other fears and anxieties are *learned*. We can therefore define fear and anxiety as a discomforting, learned, habitual pattern of reaction to situations or persons we perceive to be dangerous.

When we are confronted with an immediate danger, most of us react with what is known as the "fight-or-flight response pattern." Depending on the degree of danger we perceive, we choose either to flee from the danger or stay and fight it. Dr. Herbert Benson in his best-selling book, *the Relaxation Response,* points out that if we do neither— that is, if we neither flee nor fight—all the adrenalin discharged to meet the threat becomes bottled up and produces a stress reaction that can cause serious physical problems, including hypertension and heart disease.[7]

Usually it is not our fear but our *response* to it that makes all the difference. In reacting to fear, it is important to remember that we are not passive recipients of fear— it is not something done to us. Whether we realize it or not, we play an active part in the fear syndrome by the way we *choose* to respond to it. When we run from our fears they gain a stranglehold on us. Choosing to face them squarely, however (even when our knees are banging together), tames most of our fears and gives us power over them.

The causes of fear and anxiety are many. Examining a few major ones will help you gain a better understanding of your own fears and the way your faith can combat them.

Internal Causes of Fear

Many of our worst fears stem from both conscious and unconscious factors—including situations in childhood, family, and current life. Probably the vast majority of these situations are not fearful at all to the average person. To many of us, however, they evoke great, lurking demons seeking to devour us. Why do some people have such terrible fears and anxieties while others do not? The answer rests in our earliest childhood training and life experiences.

Chronic negativity, stress, and anxiety occurring within an insecure home atmosphere can produce not only excessive fear but unrelenting guilt as well. This fact has been consistently documented in study after study. Among the most striking research evidence comes from studies of the adult children of alcoholics, most of whom carry with them, like some kind of emotional albatross, the fears, worries, guilt, and rage engendered from growing up in an alcoholic family. Only in recent years has this tragic phenomenon been exposed and victims offered help through ACoA (Adult Children of Alcoholics) and similar organizations.

Many leading family therapists and researchers, including Murray Bowen, Salvador Minuchin, Carl Whitaker, and others[8] have cited the emotionally disturbed family as the breeding ground for fears, worries, guilt, and shame. Those unfortunate enough to have been raised in a troubled home tend to acquire many irrational fears simply through continuous exposure to such an environment. Once they become a part of us, fears, worries, guilt, pervasive anger, and other negative emotions acquired and internalized in childhood usually persist tenaciously throughout our lives.

In some cases, our fears are precipitated by an over-worked conscience (superego). When, as young children, we have been made to feel excessively guilty or overly responsible for parents who, out of their own neurosis or ignorance, simply didn't know any better, we are likely to develop fears, anxieties, and phobias that can cripple us as adults.

Many of our worst fears are unknown to us. That's because most of what occurs in our lives between birth and six years of age is repressed. If, for example, we have a frightening experience at the age of three, we are likely not to recall it consciously as an adult. The reason for this is repression, one of the major defense mechanisms identified by Freud. We repress, Freud said, unpleasant, anxiety-provoking life events, and they become part of our unconscious.

The unconscious, however, forgets nothing! The unpleasant or frightening event may, indeed, be out of sight, but it is never completely out of mind. Sometimes it is not a singular event that is repressed but a series of traumatic events—as might occur among physically or sexually abused children over an extended period. These children usually grow up to be fearful, anxious, and insecure adults. Although the terrifying memories of their ordeal may be mercifully repressed, the actual pain lives on in the recesses of their unconscious mind, periodically bursting through into conscious awareness.

External Causes of Fear

We need only pick up the daily newspaper or turn on the eleven o'clock television news to have fear strike our hearts. The uncertainty of nuclear war is ever-present. Famine and violence pervade Third World countries—to say nothing of our own country! Hostage-taking, war-provoking incidents in the Middle East, the powder keg in South Africa, the horrors of the AIDS epidemic that is expected to kill hundreds of thousands of people in the years ahead . . . the frightening litany is endless.

If we're not menaced by the prospect of global catastrophe, plenty of external factors right here at home breed fear. Inflation, taxes, deficit spending, insider trading, corporate and political corruption—all serve to gnaw away at hope for a secure financial future for the large majority of Americans. Average citizens feel they are working harder and harder for less and less. This condition produces not only fear but chronic frustration as well. Is it any wonder "burnout" has reached epidemic proportions?

Both global and national pressures have placed most Americans under enormous personal and interpersonal stress from which there appears to be no escape. These pressures have taken their toll on marriages and family life. The divorce rate now stands at around half of all married couples, and researchers who have studied the situation estimate that, of the remaining half, between fifty and eighty percent are "emotionally divorced"! This statistic is even more staggering when we consider the tragic ramifications to the children involved in those marriages, to say nothing of the "hidden" socio-economic losses produced by such conflict.

Another external cause of fear is the speed of modern day life. It appears that, as our technology has progressed and intensified, our ability to keep up and lead happy and resourceful lives has declined steadily. Perhaps hardest hit by this phenomenon is the family. The stresses and anxieties placed on married couples by increasing technology are so intense that marital problems now rank among the three most common reasons prompting individuals to seek therapy. Moreover, divorce has now replaced death of a spouse as the prevalent reason for dissolution of a first marriage.

This situation has created new societal conditions and attitudes. Remarried families now constitute a fifth of the total population, equating to approximately 48 million individuals whose lives are directly affected by remarriage. This means that millions of people must begin life anew, often in a traumatic context. Countless thousands are unable to survive the wrenching changes involved. With their energies depleted, these people have succumbed to a "give up and give in" attitude that manifests itself in the broad spectrum of symptoms currently plaguing our society.

Among the victims of social and family upheaval are children and young people. Here are a few samples.

I'll start with sexual abuse. A recent report indicates that as many as ten percent of all boys and twenty percent of all girls are victims of sexual abuse. Most studies suggest that in the United States every year, between 200,000 and 400,000 children are victimized sexually.

Suicide is on the rise. The current rate of suicide among young people is five thousand per year. The National Center for Health Statistics predicts that by the year 2000, suicide rates for teenagers and those in their early twenties will increase at such a rate that more than 10,000 young people between the ages of 15 and 24 will be killing themselves each year! Suicide is now the third leading cause of death in this age group and is one of the ten leading causes of death in *every* age group. In the age group five to fourteen years, it is the *seventh* leading cause!

Next, consider teenage pregnancies. More than a million teens become pregnant out of wedlock each year. Of these about 30,000 are girls under the age of fifteen. Most of these young women never finish high school; the majority are unemployed and on welfare. In fact, teen mothers now constitute the fastest growing group in the welfare population.

Alcoholism is prevalent. Current studies indicate that there are between nine and thirteen million alcoholics in the United States. For every person with an alcohol-related problem, four family members are affected. This means that between thirty-six and fifty-two million Americans are in some way directly affected by alcoholism. The problem, of course, spills over to the work system. Drug and alcohol abuse affects between fifteen and thirty-five percent of the American work force and costs the economy at least 200 billion dollars a year in direct and hidden expenses.

Job-related stress is a major problem among workers and employers alike. Worker's compensation claims for anxiety, depression, and more serious psychiatric illnesses are, in many states, among the fastest growing component of work-related insurance claims. These stress-related claims were *four times* as high in 1985 as they were in 1980. Some insurance officials estimate that about fifteen percent of all occupational disease claims nationwide are stress-related.

Clearly, these statistics cause us fear and uncertainty. They also, however, *reflect* anxieties that we ourselves have placed upon society as a result of our own internal stresses. And perhaps, as boring as statistics can be, they speak a compelling message: *it's time to slow down and smell the roses . . . before it's too late!*

How One Woman Learned to Control her Fears

Although fears can result from both internal and external factors, most fears are generated from within. Fear of rejection and fear of failure are among the most important and dreaded of all our fears. Interestingly, both these fears are interconnected with a third fear: the fear of domination. That's because when we are rejected we tend to see ourselves as being dominated by the rejecting *person*. We feel that our existence is denied. Similarly, when we fail, we see the *situation* as dominating us.

Several years ago I worked with a young woman, Mary, who was consumed by her fears. Most of these fears were rooted in early childhood experiences that left her with very little self-esteem, inner strength, personal control, or life meaning. She exhibited all three fears: fear of failure, fear of rejection, and fear of being dominated.

Although already in her mid-thirties, Mary continued to live with her parents. Her pervasive fears had debilitated her to the point that she felt she would surely fail if she chose to live on her own (something she very much desired). Since fear of failure was paramount in her mind, Mary avoided moving to her own apartment, even though to do so would have been a major achievement for her. Each time she avoided moving, her sense of failure increased, and with it her parents' admonitions that she was a "big girl now" and should not allow her childish fears to control her life.

Each admonition served only to deepen Mary's sense of rejection by her parents. "They don't love me any more," she thought. "If they did, they would want me to stay. I must really be a failure if my own parents want to kick me out!" Then Mary would make up her mind that she must move out . . . no matter what. Each time she "decided," however, her fear of failure loomed, and she would retreat. With each retreat came even greater feelings of failure.

As this vicious cycle became entrenched, Mary grew increasingly aware that she was being dominated by her obsessive fears of failure and rejection. Soon the fear of being dominated took on a life of its own, leaving her all but immobilized.

After working with Mary for several months I learned that these three fears: fear of failure, fear of rejection, and fear of domination, had controlled her every waking hour since her childhood. The way she had endured the long years of pain and struggle was truly beyond comprehension! Each time she tried to establish a life of her own, apart from her parents, these same three fears prevented her from doing so. Time and again she tried to improve herself vocationally or educationally, but the three fears remained, mocking her and waiting spitefully to "prove" how inadequate she was.

As my therapeutic relationship with Mary developed, I learned that, despite the pain and poor self-image with which she struggled, Mary had somehow maintained a deep sense of spirituality that manifested itself in subtle ways. Whenever she became depressed over her inability to move out on her own, for example, she would read inspiring books or watch an uplifting movie or television program. At other times she would spend an evening with positive, upbeat friends. These little strategies enabled Mary to get through the rough times . . . to survive.

When I observed the spiritual reserves Mary had developed (most of which she was unaware of), I encouraged her to do *more* reading of inspirational works and *more* watching of enjoyable and positive movies and *more* associating with upbeat friends. Soon, as Mary gained awareness that these activities contributed to her personal happiness, she began to do more of these things on her own. This increased Mary's spiritual power and gave her the necessary courage to face what turned out to be her greatest fear, *the fear of her own success.*

Once Mary understood that the fear of success was indeed her most ominous fear, she did what she knew she had to do . . . she went *into* the fear. She decided that, once and for all, *she* would control her fears and no longer permit the fears to control her. Mary forced herself, despite extreme discomfort, to move into her own apartment. Although her parents disapproved of the apartment's location, Mary was able to keep her fears of parental rejection at bay. She also controlled her feelings of inadequacy long enough to make her move a reality.

Despite a difficult first two weeks, once on her own Mary was able to establish herself, finally, as an independent woman capable of making her own way in the world. As the reality of her independence dawned on her, she understood, for the first time, what it meant to be free. Her fears of failure, rejection, domination, and success were things of the past. The decision to "take action" was all she had needed to activate her real self and release a life that had been imprisoned for so long.

Today Mary has a new, vibrant life. She feels like, and *is*, a success! She was able to strengthen her spiritual belief survival mechanism by acquiring the necessary courage and determination. Once that was acquired, her fears and anxieties, which until then had controlled her life, began to melt away. The end result was the sustaining and enhancement of the four basic life elements. To her complete amazement she was, for once in her life, able to experience true happiness!

Spiritual Belief Survival Mechanism Strategies

Strategy #1: Take Time To Pray

Prayer. The word evokes images of a quiet, serene chapel on a distant hillside. It may be a cathedral towering majestically on the banks of the Rhine or Tiber. It may be the distant echo of the first prayer learned as a small child:

> Now I lay me down to sleep,
> I pray the Lord my soul to keep;
> If I should die before I wake,
> I pray the Lord my soul to take.

Prayer can mean tranquility and peace. It can manifest itself through words or the strains of a mighty pipe organ. It can be the choir singing on Sunday morning, or the cantor's song at temple, or the soft summer breeze gently caressing the lilac trees. It may be a poem or a beautiful story.

For some people, early memories of prayer can mean fear and sorrow—a harsh voice commanding you to "Say your prayers because you're in hot water!" or a priest giving the last rites to a dying person.

Indeed, prayer means different things to different people. But one fact remains almost universal: people tend to pray when they feel that all conventional means of help have been exhausted. When they are especially stressed, lonely, afraid, sad, troubled, or in crisis, prayer seems their only way out.

Even when a physician announces that a cancer has spread and there is no hope, we still have hope: we can still pray. And in prayer there is power. The ability to lean on our prayers and on the prayers of others gives us an inner strength and resolve. By giving us hope, our prayers serve to strengthen our spiritual belief survival mechanism and with it the four basic life elements.

The key behind successful prayer is belief that it can be effective. If we believe this, chances that our prayers will help us are good.

Prayer can be a formal ritual, such as kneeling at an altar in a sanctuary, or informal, as when walking in the forest and "communing with nature," as did Thoreau. From a survival standpoint, it doesn't matter how people pray; it matters only that they engage in prayer and believe that their prayers can have effect. When this occurs, our spiritual belief survival mechanism is strengthened.

"I pray for him all the time. I pray he is safe. I pray he'll come home before something happens to him." These were the words of a distraught mother telling me about her seventeen-year-old son who had run away from home. "How have your prayers helped you?" I asked her. "They've helped me a great deal," she said. "They've helped me *survive*. I really believe that!"

Prayers can be highly elaborate, lengthy supplications or one-word invocations to a higher power. It doesn't matter. What matters is that we believe that the power we are communing with can help us.

You recall the short prayers I learned from Dr. Price, which I shared with you in an earlier chapter. These brief affirmations of faith had enormous power in my life because I *believed* they would. I never doubted. Not once! The meaning and belief with which we imbue prayers are vital. The simple words "Thanks be to God" can be as effective as participating in elaborate rituals.

Whereas prayer is important in the strengthening of our spiritual belief survival mechanism, it should not be an end in itself. It should be connected with something or someone. It should be the vehicle that connects us with the spiritual.

Strategy #2: Develop a Belief in the Spiritual

Belief in divine power or a higher consciousness is a major strategy for strengthening the spiritual belief survival mechanism. Virtually everyone has the need to believe in the spiritual, regardless of whether they deny it. Such belief does not necessitate a super-religious approach to life. It means simply that we need to accept that somewhere, "out there" or within us, resides a power higher than ourselves.

As with prayer, belief in the spiritual may evoke specific images and feelings within us. Like our ancient forebears, we may see God in a cool forest, in the towering mountain range, or in the blazing sunset or the rushing river. The important point is that wonderful feeling of connection with something greater than ourselves: the spiritual aspect of life.

When doing research for this book, I asked hundreds of clients to tell me, at random, what was important to them. With uncanny consistency the responses were surprisingly similar and usually expressed in one or two words: God; happiness; faith; my kids; the Bible; my family; my church; and my home. Periodically, someone would mention career or educational goals, marriage, their country, world peace, and ridding the world of hunger, but this was exceptional. Invariably, the most frequently given responses included happiness, family, and something connected to their belief in a divine power. Even when family or children was mentioned first, spiritual belief, and specifically belief in God, ran a close second.

Gradually, I realized the important role spiritual convictions played in sustaining the four basic life elements when the lives of people with whom I had worked closely were torn apart by tragedy. Despite the fact that they had sustained incomprehensible losses, they were somehow able to carry on—in work, family, play, and social functions. Initially I thought they were merely "denying reality," but it soon became apparent that the courage they displayed resulted from belief in a divine power, not from denial. That belief, in turn, sustained the four basic elements of their lives. It is doubtful that any of them had conscious awareness of this, as illustrated in the following brief case vignettes.

Maureen. She was, in the vernacular, "poor white trash." She conceived of herself as a poet, a country singer, a sage authority on human nature, and, above all, a devoted mother. In reality, she was none of these. Her life could easily be summed up as a colossal failure. Although everything she was bespoke her irreverent nature, she believed herself a highly religious person, her lies and underlying rage notwithstanding.

If you were to meet her, you could surely never forget her. One day she came in to see me and announced that her oldest son had just drowned. Although her eyes were filled with grief, there was a dispassionate resolve in her steady voice. Her composure never wavered. As I groped for something to say she began to comfort me . . . ." Now, now Paul . . . Not to fret. Timmy is with the Lord now. I'm sad, yes. But God will take care of him . . . *and me.*" That was it. "God?" I silently questioned her use of the term. "Maureen talking about God?" *Yes!* She was invoking God now because, deep within, that was her sustaining force. In her moment of despair, she would survive. Her spiritual belief survival mechanism was at work!

Patti. A forty-year-old mother of five children sat in my office pouring out her heart. Her oldest son was in prison for rape. The second-oldest son was on parole for check forging. Two younger daughters were in treatment facilities, one for prostitution and the other for drug abuse. The youngest son was in a foster home.

"How do you keep going?" I asked. Matter-of-factly she responded: "I look at it this way. Every day you get one day older. You get *spiritual.* You have to laugh or else you go crazy. You have to have a sense of *humor. You think positive.* You give yourself praise constantly . . . no one else does."

By relying on her spiritual belief and play survival mechanisms, this woman was able to survive. How else could she have done it? How could any of us have made it? She did not prosper, but she *did* survive. I firmly believe that without these mechanisms going for her, especially her spiritual belief survival mechanism, Patti would probably be spending her last days inside a state mental institution. And who knows, maybe some day, if she learns more about survival, she may prosper as well!

Many similar accounts of survival could be given. In each case the individuals involved maintained strong belief in a divine power even though they were not necessarily religious persons in the conventional sense. The common thread that bound them together was a conviction that strengthened their spiritual belief survival mechanism.

When I asked these individuals about the way they survived their losses, I discovered that *not one* of them mentioned any of the survival mechanisms as mechanisms—that is, they did not *consciously* identify spirituality or play or work as something they deliberately used to sustain themselves in times of trial. Nor did any of them mention the four basic life elements as being something they consciously wished to strengthen. They merely stated that God or the Lord had helped them through their problems. When I listened carefully, however, I could hear self-esteem, meaning, strength, and control as the underlying reasons for their survival.

Strategy #3: Take Time to Meditate

A great deal has been written on the subject of meditation. As a spiritual survival strategy it is centuries old. Not until the arrival of Maharishi Mahesh Yogi, a Hindu monk, in San Francisco in 1959, however, did meditation gain the kind of popularity it has today. The Maharishi literally transformed Western thinking to accept the power of meditation. Hundreds of thousands of individuals in the United States now practice some form of meditation on a daily basis. Millions do so worldwide.

A brief presentation of meditation should be helpful to those readers who are unfamiliar with the wonderful benefits available through this medium. Readers who *are* familiar and who may currently practice meditation may be further helped by this brief overview.

To meditate means simply to go into oneself in a positive, optimistic way by which the mind is freed of stress and anxiety and by which its fears, worries, and apprehensions are put aside for a specified period of time. When this occurs, the body's natural healing properties are activated and permitted free reign as the meditator acquires a perspective such as never dreamed possible.

I recall a colleague-friend of mine telling me he had taken a course in transcendental meditation, developed by Maharishi Yogi, to cure himself of his stressful feelings and worries. When he was half-way through the program I happened to run into him one day in a shopping mall. I asked him how the meditation was working out. He told me he was more stressed out than ever! He said that learning how to sit, how to breathe, what *not* to think about, and how to relax his muscles during meditation had confused and frustrated him. I have known others who have done extremely well in transcendental meditation, so perhaps my friend had made a "job" out of meditating. This is clearly how *not* to do it!

Meditation should be a very simple, uncomplicated procedure. In truth, it is closely aligned to prayer in its basic nature and the results it produces. A person reciting "The Lord's Prayer" over and over in a meditative posture may release the same healing powers as someone chanting a mantra. If we know how to pray, we will know how to meditate, and vice versa.

Four basic steps will help you begin proper meditation:

1. Locating a quiet environment.
2. Deciding on an object on which to focus your attention.
3. Maintaining a passive attitude.
4. Maintaining a comfortable position.

Relaxation and proper breathing also play an important role in successful meditation. To attain these, you need to review some of the popular references on meditation. By following these steps carefully, you should not only reap excellent results, after awhile you should find the procedure becoming second nature. Great thought and effort should not be required to achieve significant reduction of stress and anxiety. Self-discipline and consistency, however, are necessary. One good source for learning more about the meditation strategy is Dr. Herbert Benson's *the Relaxation Response*. Benson demystifies the entire meditative process to the point where virtually anyone can master it.

Strategy #4: Attend a House of Worship

I will never forget the day. It was a freezing Sunday morning in January 1962 at a small Pentecostal church in Southern Ohio. I was visiting my family in the area, and we decided to attend worship services together. I was sitting, along with other members of my family, among parishioners. During the sermon, a man in his mid-forties stood up and began, in a joyful manner, to shout: "Hallelujah, hallelujah . . . Praise the Lord . . . Hallelujah!" It was evident he was moved to express himself in this way because of what he was feeling at that moment. The minister suspended his sermon and allowed time for the man to continue his expression of obvious jubilation, which lasted several minutes. The congregation, too, seemed to accept what was occurring. When he finished speaking, the worshiper sat down, and the service resumed as if nothing unusual had happened.

But something *did* happen on that cold Sunday morning of which I was unaware at the time, something very important! The spiritual belief survival mechanism was being strengthened, in front of me, and for people I had previously written off as "a bunch of kooks." Indeed, their behavior seemed bizarre to me at the time, but its ultimate purpose was clearly in tune with what that man expressing himself in the sanctuary perceived he needed in order to *survive*.

We live in the era of the "electronic church." Nearly six million viewers tune in each Sunday morning to watch their favorite evangelist or television pastor. Although there are literally hundreds of religiously-oriented television and radio broadcasters, their basic message is always the same: "What I have to say will enable you to survive and prosper." Indeed, a similar weekly message is delivered in our churches and synagogues as well. The degree to which people can accept this message determines the degree to which they will strengthen their spiritual belief survival mechanism and, hence, their four basic life elements.

It is important to emphasize again my basic premise that each of us has, already deep within us, a spiritual belief survival mechanism needing enhancement. Though we may deny that such a mechanism exists, it resides there nevertheless. The extent to which we accept this and consciously undertake to develop it, along with the other survival mechanisms, will ultimately determine our level of personal happiness and prosperity. Happiness, again, is defined as promoting the four basic life elements to their highest levels.

Survival Strategy #5: Read Inspirational Works

Billy Graham is one of the most recognizable figures in the world today. I remember seeing him for the first time when he was just beginning his trek to legendary status. It was under a tent in the Los Angeles winter of 1949, when I was twelve years old.

That year Graham viewed Los Angeles, the "City of Angels," as the city of sinners. He was there to save souls— to do battle with Satan. His major weapons were the Bible and his undaunted belief in God. I can still see him standing there on that wooden platform, sandy blond hair flying, the open Bible draped across his palm, exclaiming, "The Bible says . . . !"

Experiences like listening to Billy Graham and attending the Hungarian Baptist Church introduced me to what would become a major strategy for enhancing my own spiritual belief survival mechanism: reading the

Bible. This book has, for nearly four thousand years, provided hope and comfort, security and balm, to countless millions of people. For them it is an emotional insurance policy.

But the Bible is not the only vehicle to religious thought. From Judaism's Torah to the sacred *Vedas* of the Hindus, from the Buddhist *Law of Karma* to Taoism's *Tao Te Ching* and the *Koran* of Mohammed, the world's major religions have produced writings that have served a fundamental purpose: to give huddled humanity a sense of security and comfort. These works have given direction to many in times of confusion and self-doubt, hope when the human spirit failed. They have provided structure and purpose to rich and poor alike and have given meaning to nations about to crumble as well as those large and powerful.

Through these works, again and again, we hear words of great power, comfort, and assurance . . . *survival. All* great philosophers, teachers, mystics, and healers whose writings can be categorized as spiritual can enhance the spiritual belief survival mechanism. You are therefore encouraged to explore the thinking of writers such as Ralph Waldo Emerson, Henry David Thoreau, Emily Dickinson, Lao-tzu, George Santayana, and Kahlil Gibran. You will find in them, as many have, comfort and a source of spiritual renewal.

We must understand the powerful role spirituality plays in our lives. Enhancement of the spiritual strengthens us beyond what we can imagine. Studying the writings of the great philosophers and mystics and putting these thoughts into practice are effective means of strengthening our spiritual belief survival mechanism. As Emerson said: "Excite the soul and the weather and the town and your condition in the world all disappear; the world itself loses its solidity, nothing remains but the soul and the Divine Presence in which it lives."[9]

Basic Life Elements Affected by
the Spiritual Belief Survival Mechanism

First, personal control;
second, inner strength;
third, life meaning;
and fourth, self-image.

NOTES

1. "Joseph Campbell and the Power of Myth," WNED/PBS, Buffalo, March 15, 1990.

2. M. Scott Peck, *The Road Less Traveled: A New Psychology of Love, Traditional Values and Spiritual Growth* (New York: Touchstone, 1978), pp. 197-208, 210-221.

3. Viktor E. Frankl, *The Unconscious God: Psychotherapy and Theology* (New York: Simon and Schuster, 1975), p. 25.

4. *Ibid.*, pp. 61-68.

5. Luke 15:24, *The Holy Bible: Revised Standard Version* (New York: Thomas Nelson & Sons, 1952), p. 88.

6. *Webster's Third New International Dictionary: Unabridged* (Springfield: G & C Merriam, 1969), p. 816.

7. Herbert Benson, *the Relaxation Response* (New York: Avon Books, 1975), pp. 23-27, 66-74.

8. Ivan Boszormenyi-Nagy and James L. Framo, eds., *Intensive Family Therapy: Theoretical and Practical Aspects* (New York: Harper & Row, 1965); Murray Bowen, *Family Therapy in Clinical Practice* (New York: Jason Aronson, 1978), pp. 6-7; Merle A. Fossum and Marilyn J. Mason, *Facing Shame: Families In Recovery* (New York: W.W. Norton, 1986), p. 8; Michael E. Kerr and Murray Bowen, *Family Evaluation: An Approach Based on Bowen Theory* (New York: W.W. Norton, 1988), pp. 61, 112-133, 177, 233; James F. Masterson, *The Narcissistic and Borderline Disorders: An Integrated Developmental Approach* (New York: Brunner/Mazel, 1981), pp. 46-48; Masterson, *The Search For The Real Self: Unmasking the Personality Disorders of Our Age* (New York: The Free Press, 1988), pp. 51-74; Salvador Minuchin and Braulio Montalvo, et al., *Families of the Slums: An Exploration of Their Structure and Treatment* (New York: Basic Books, 1967); Virginia Satir, *Peoplemaking* (Palo Alto: Science and Behavior Books, 1972), pp. 26-27, 225-227, 230-240; Carl Whitaker, *Midnight Musings of a Family Therapist* (New York: W.W. Norton, 1989), pp. 83, 180-181.

9. Ralph Waldo Emerson, "The Divinity School Address," in *Selections from Ralph Waldo Emerson*, Stephen E. Whicher, ed. (Boston: Houghton Mifflin, 1957), p. 99.

SURVIVAL MECHANISM INVENTORY # 9
SPIRITUAL BELIEF

Inventory Statements	Rating Check Appropriate Box					
	SA 5	A 4	U 3	D 2	SD 1	Score
1. My parents instilled within me a strong sense of spirituality during my formative years.						
2. I believe some kind of spiritual thought is important to my survival.						
3. I do not *have* to attend formal religious services to be a spiritual person.						
4. I have had a least one emotionally moving experience that I can call spiritual.						
5. My idea of God is something or someone that need not be completely understood to be accepted.						
6. I can sometimes be very happy alone, in the quietness of my own thoughts and feelings.						
7. When I am frightened I find myself leaning on spiritual concepts.						
8. I accept the fact that I am not the center of the universe but only a part of it.						
9. Because of my spiritual convictions, dying no longer frightens me.						
10. To be strong spiritually means I must seek a higher power.						

Key   SM Strength Quotient =

SA - Strongly Approve   **10 - 24** Weak
A   - Approve   **25 - 34** Average
U   - Undecided   **35 - 50** Strong
D   - Disapprove
SD - Strongly Disapprove

13

Survival Mechanism #10: Positive Mental Attitude

Things are in their essence what we choose to make them. A thing is according to the mode in which one looks at it. "Where others," says Blake, "see but the dawn coming over the hill, I see the sons of God shouting for joy."

—*Oscar Wilde*

WHILE I WAS COMPLETING the research on positive mental attitude, this tenth and final survival mechanism, the thought occurred to me that a positive mental attitude is the fountainhead for all of the other nine mechanisms. Without such an attitude we would have no hope, and without hope, what is life? Of course, as we know, all the survival mechanisms are interdependent. So, despite its lofty status among the mechanisms, the mechanism of positive mental attitude, to be optimally effective, does rely on the others.

In the mountainous quantity of self-help literature, perhaps no other single concept has received more attention than the concept of positive mental attitude. Yet none offers a clear, succinct definition of the term. Here is what

I believe can serve as a universal definition: *a positive mental attitude is a state of mind that projects an individual's "seeking spirit" and unrelenting quest for an optimistic outcome to life's experiences, whatever they may be and whenever they may arise.*

To possess a positive mental attitude means simply to be optimistic rather than pessimistic. It means to have a future orientation—a "seeking spirit." Having such an attitude requires that we shed any arrogance we might possess. If we want to enhance the positive mental attitude survival mechanism but see an obstacle, such as arrogance, in our path, we need only add love. Love never fails to change poison into medicine, hurt into healing.

Perhaps more than anything else, to possess a positive mental attitude requires that you *want* to have one. Without a burning desire, a passion, most of us fall short of having a truly positive attitude no matter how many books on the subject we read. The reason for this is the heavy concentration of negativity that permeates most of our lives on a continuing basis.

Over the years I have concluded that the amount of negativity in the world far outweighs its positive counterpart. For this reason those of us seeking a positive mental attitude, in order to neutralize that negativity and hence obtain our life goals, must understand the functioning of four specific patterns: the *feeling pattern*, the *thinking pattern*, the *speaking pattern*, and the *doing pattern*. These four distinct patterns emerge quite clearly when we consider positive as against negative attitudes and their impact on the four basic life elements. I will review each pattern separately and then discuss how they interact to enhance the survival mechanism of positive mental attitude.

The Feeling Pattern

The origin of our feeling or emotional self lies in the part of the brain that neurophysiologists call the *limbic system*, or "old brain." Lying deep within the cerebrum, the limbic system is, in many ways, the "controller of the controller." As such, it dictates to our *neocortex,* or "new brain," what is right, wrong, good, or bad, as a result of its perception of our survival needs. As brain researcher Paul MacLean states, "A throwback to mice, rabbits and cats, the limbic system is hooked on survival, the preservation of the self and the species . . . ."[1]

From a survival mechanism perspective, we must understand at least some of the basic tenets underlying the limbic system and the way it generates our emotional or feeling life. When we read, for example, of a grisly mass murder, or hear news reports of the way an airliner with hundreds of people was shot down because of an incompetent military directive, we can safely assume that the limbic system was somehow involved in such atrocities.

Being a part of our ancient, reptilian past, the limbic system is vastly different from our thinking system, that larger portion of our brain evolving about forty thousand years ago inside the skull of Cro-Magnon humans. Our limbic system was there long before the dawn of civilization, there with the mammal-like reptiles that are our distant kin, calling to us from 250 million years ago.

Each time we hear of tragedy or are involved in it ourselves, our limbic system is also involved. This connection is a normal part of our *flight-fight-survival instinct* and will probably be with us yet another 250 million years—that is, unless we blow ourselves up first.

Our limbic system interacts profoundly with our thinking system. The interaction can be so intense that, in many cases where anxiety and emotional flooding are extreme, our feelings force their way into our thinking to such an extent that we may be uncertain where feelings leave off and thinking begins. Sometimes we *think* we're thinking, but we are feeling. At other times, when our feelings have chronically intruded on our thinking, we may *feel* that we're feeling, but in truth we are thinking! The degree to which we are able to differentiate our thinking and feeling systems will determine the extent of our maturity and, hence, our personal happiness.

The Thinking Pattern

The *thinking pattern* represents our "state of mind" most of the time. It is the sum total of what we think about, either consciously or unconsciously, as we go about the task of daily living. This pattern also includes our hopes, dreams, fears, and expectations. Whenever we consciously or unconsciously *expect* something, either good or bad, to happen, it generally does happen. Our expectations have an uncanny way of never letting us down!

A negative-thinking father told me recently that he expected his teenage son to be arrested, so I was unsurprised when not long thereafter I read in the local newspaper of the son's arrest. The boy had been pushing drugs for quite some time. Long before his criminal career got under way, however, his father told me he believed that the son was "born under an unlucky star." As this case and countless others like it prove, the *thinking pattern* in essence means *visualizing* what we want (expect) in life. If we don't want it, we had better not visualize it.

To be a positive person means moving from less successful to more successful thinking patterns. Our thoughts create our reality, be it good or bad. As the old saying goes, "A man becomes what he thinks." And, sadly, very often what we *don't* think dictates what we will never become. When we marvel at the grand achievements of others, we frequently see the image of what we could have done . . . what we could have been. These images, these ghosts of our alienated past, return in all their grandeur to haunt us.

Changing the thought process begins in the imagination. Whatever mental image you hold is what you will ultimately possess. If you hold fast to a mental image of past failures, you will undoubtedly continue to fail in the future. Dwelling on the negative past keeps reinforcing the negative processes. It keeps you stuck in a negative pattern. To get unstuck requires changing your mental image.

The Speaking Pattern

"Beware, beware!" warned the Hindu mystic. "What goes forth from you will come back to you."[2] And the words that go forth from us, or those that come to us from others, will undoubtedly create a lasting impression. "Words," states Wilferd A. Peterson, "can lift us into heaven or lower us into hell."[3]

The *speaking pattern* represents, quite literally, the way in which we speak. It is what, where, when, how, why, and to *whom* we say the things we say. The spoken (and sometimes unspoken) word is a powerful force. Its power is not limited to what we say, or think about saying, in public. What we say, or think about saying, in private can be even more potent.

The interesting point regarding speaking patterns is the subtle way in which they become addictive. Speaking habits can, in fact, become so addictive that they literally transform the way we think. This point has been reinforced to me time and again as I listen to the litany of negative words sounded by clients whose lives are not working. Most of them have spoken negative words for so long that for them to change the habit is a monumental task.

Nevertheless, I try to encourage clients to change their negative speaking patterns into more positive ones. If they say, "Life is no damn good" or "People are rotten" or "My kids are lazy good-for-nothings," I attempt to redirect their speech toward the use of fewer negatives in describing their life condition. This process enables them to acquire an altered life perspective. In psychotherapy we call this "reframing." Instead of "Life is no damn good," for example, perhaps they can say, "Sometimes life has obstacles we need to overcome." Instead of "People are rotten," they can perhaps reframe by saying, "Sometimes people are disappointing, but that's what helps us learn and grow."

Despite my efforts, however, unless rigorous, continuing reinforcement is afforded, I find that most negative clients revert to their original speaking pattern. Words and their use are habit-forming. If you doubt the tenacity of old, established speech patterns, try this little experiment. Decide to say nothing negative for thirty days. No matter what happens, no negative! If you should slip after the eighth day, go back to day one and start over. If you slip again, repeat the process. This exercise, I believe, will impart new meaning to the time-worn expression, "To err is human . . . ."

The *speaking pattern,* then, means verbalizing either audibly or silently, consciously or unconsciously, whatever it is you want or expect in life. More on this later.

The Doing Pattern

While studying *prosperous* survivors over the years, I have noticed that, for them to maintain their survival skills, they have forged a positive attitude toward life. To have a positive attitude means doing something about the things that you *can* do something about. It means acceptance of the time-honored "Serenity Prayer" of Alcoholics Anonymous, which says, "God grant me the serenity to accept the things I cannot change, courage to change the things I can, and wisdom to know the difference." A negative attitude represents trying to do something about something you cannot possibly do anything about, something that is clearly out of your control.

The *doing pattern* means *materializing* or *actualizing* what you ardently desire in life. It means adopting a positive attitude and "going for it." As noted earlier, doing means *action.*

Several years ago I worked with a young mother of four children. Although she struggled to be both devoted mother and wife, two of her children were in trouble with the law, and her husband, having embezzled company funds, was also in deep legal difficulty. The harder she tried to correct the situation, the worse it seemed to get.

One day she decided she would do something for *herself.* She started by joining a health spa. It wasn't long before she met someone who introduced her to an employer who wanted to hire her as a secretary for his firm. Eventually she advanced to a point where the company paid her way through a two-year college program in bookkeeping. After several more years she returned to school and received her Bachelor's degree in business. Today she is a successful career woman in a large company.

On her march to freedom, this woman also realized she was caught in a destructive marital relationship, so she divorced her husband, eventually remarried, and today owns a new life. Her life is new because her feelings are new. Her feelings are new because her thoughts are new. Her thoughts are new because her words are new. And her words are new because her actions are new. She found a way to put the four patterns together, and it worked!

Mutual Interdependence among the Four Patterns

Feeling, thinking, speaking, and doing are mutually interdependent functions of the three-pound miracle inside our heads: our brain.

"All he had to do was open his mouth, and I could tell where his head was" is a commonly heard expression. It reflects the intuitive way in which most of us connect a person's speech with his or her way of thinking. The question, "What can you expect from someone like him?" signals the way we equate action with thinking, personality, or attitude. When someone says to you, "What in the world were you thinking about when you said that?" that person correctly assumed that your thoughts precipitated your words. And when we hear the expression, "What you say is what you get," we presuppose the opposite—that our *words* will result in certain consequences or actions. And, of course, when we ask the family teenager to take out the trash and are greeted with the response, "I don't *feel* like it!" we realize anew that doing something and the way we *feel* about doing it can be vastly different.

The important point to remember is that the four patterns—feeling, thinking, speaking, and doing—are closely linked. Activating any one pattern precipitates a response in any or all of the others, although not necessarily in the normal sequence of feeling, thinking, speaking, and doing.

If we feel it, therefore, we're likely to do it. And if we do it, we're likely to feel it . . . again. If we feel it again, we're probably going to think it again—and so forth. Soon the four patterns become one—*feelingthinkingspeakingdoing.*

As the four patterns become firmly ingrained in our overall mental functioning, we develop a "mind-set" or world view. This becomes our "philosophy of life," our perception of ourselves and our reality. Our mind-set, in fact, *becomes* our reality. It represents the emotional, mental, and spiritual caldron from which evolves our most significant human quality: our *attitude.*

Attitude Isn't Everything . . . It's the Only Thing!

Your attitude and actions can and *will* affect people in remarkable ways . . . and when you least expect it. This principle is illustrated by the story of the man sleeping during the Sunday morning sermon. When the preacher shouted out, "Who in the congregation wants to go to hell?" the man jumped to his feet. Observing that he and the preacher were the only two people standing, the man exclaimed, "Preacher, I don't know what we're voting on, but you and I seem to be the only ones for it!"

The moral to this story, of course, is that some people will make decisions that affect their entire lives as the sole result of what *you* do. And what you do is invariably tied to your attitude toward life.

When we stop to think about it, life is really not very complicated. Dr. Nathan Ackerman, one of the founding fathers of family therapy, said, "Life is a little bit of laughing, a little bit of crying, and a little bit of loving in between."[4] I would like to paraphrase Ackerman's quote by saying that life is a little bit of success and a little bit of failure and a *whole lot of searching* in between. Whether we get more success or more failure depends on our searching ability. Frequently, we search in desolate regions when, as Russell Conwell has assured us, "acres of diamonds" await us in our own back yards.[5]

To be successful means searching in the right place for our treasure. It also means *consciously choosing* to claim that treasure when it is found. The fact that human beings make choices is already well established. What most of us fail to realize, however, is that the kind of choices we make is also within our conscious control. And the actual choices we ultimately make are determined by the attitude we maintain toward life. That attitude, in turn, is rooted in our self-image. If our self-image is high, we choose successful enterprises. If low, we choose failure.

Self-image and attitude are closely linked concepts. When our self-image is right, our attitude will be right as well. We frequently hear people speak about so-and-so being successful or that such-and-such an enterprise was a "rip-roaring success." In truth, *any kind* of success is always measured from the point of view of one's attitude. If we think we are successful, then we are. If we think we're not, then we're not, even if we are!

It doesn't really matter what hardships life happens to send your way. When your attitude is properly developed, you run through the hurts. Besides, with a positive mental attitude we learn to welcome the hurts and the failures, since *all* success is, in the final analysis, based upon failure. Indeed, we are at our best when we are engaged in the struggle for victory. When we stop struggling, we're finished—dead. We have to have something to aim for. As I review my own life, I find that the years I have labored the hardest, in retrospect, are those in which I take my greatest joy.

I am forever amazed at how fearful people are of struggle. In reality, obstacles are positive forces in our lives— there to test us, to help us grow. We need to maintain the attitude that we will overcome whatever comes along. If we look at obstacles as representing *something we need in order to learn*, then there is a reason for them. This brings us back to the perception survival mechanism and the fact that the way we see a thing is often more important than what we see.

Make no mistake about it: you and I are a product of our thoughts. Pick up any self-help book dealing with personality or emotional development and you will be impressed, again and again, with the importance thinking plays in our lives. Unfortunately, what we think about the vast majority of the time is negative. Negativity is the top-selling item in this country. It is a commodity undoubtedly here to stay. If you question this, just pick up any local newspaper and check out the headlines. Then go to your local public library and take a look at the headlines of any newspaper from twenty years ago. See any similarities?

Attitude is the only thing! It is the glue that holds everything together—your world and mine. We have become so accustomed to living in a negative society that people have stopped *wanting* to believe anything positive. Just eavesdrop on any casual conversation. Even when someone remarks about how fine the weather has been, someone else will be sure to point out that rain is predicted. Incredibly, being positive is a threat to most people. The fault, however, is not theirs entirely. They have been programmed all their lives to think negatively.

Paradoxically, we are attracted to positive people and repelled by negative ones. We realize, even if unconsciously, that there is something special about positive individuals. They make us feel good about ourselves and our circumstances. They brighten our day, if only for a little while.

Negative persons, on the other hand, are basically trouble-makers. Their greatest satisfaction in life is running around stirring things up and making such statements as, "You can't, it won't work, that's wrong, why don't you quit? give it up!" and "Stop trying." Of course, one of life's greatest pleasures is accomplishing what the negative person says is impossible.

I like to compare a negative-thinking person to a garbage truck filled with slimy, smelly garbage. Now, imagine this maggot-ridden garbage truck pulling up to your beautiful, carpeted living room (which, in this case, is your mind!) and dumping its entire wretched load smack onto your living room floor! How long do you think you would tolerate that? About as long as it would take for you to call the police, right? Well, that is about how long you should tolerate a negative person filling up your mind with his or her pessimistic ideas.

The entire concept of the positive mental attitude survival mechanism is predicated on the notion that we become what we *think* we will become. It is rooted in the idea that we believe, as fact, what we have been told all our lives up to this present moment. The basic premise behind this mechanism is essentially two-fold: first, the brain is like a computer, and second, the brain can be programmed.

I will expand on the programming concept in just a moment, but first it is important that I say a few words about personal responsibility. Despite the fact that we are who we are because of previous life circumstances and programming, we cannot abdicate the role we ourselves play in our life's outcome, good or bad. Each of us is, in the final analysis, responsible for his or her own personal destiny.

Thus, if we are depressed, angry, guilty, frustrated, or disappointed with life, we must remember that, with rare exceptions, we *choose* these emotions and other life circumstances. No matter how forcefully we may argue to the contrary, no one "causes" us to feel a certain way or "causes" things to happen to us. Rather than wasting our energies arguing the futile notion that forces and people act *on* us, we need to accept the fact that our destinies lie within our personal control. The key is to develop the inner resolve and strength to control our emotions and thereby control ourselves and our futures.

Programming: Beware the Negatroids!

Dr. Robert Schuller accurately warns us about "the most dangerous and destructive force on earth—the Negative Thinking Expert."[6] Such individuals run around uncontrolled, chirping wildly about how great they are and how much they know. More important, they are forever broadcasting fear and pessimism. Their booming voices carry forth a message of failure and discouragement virtually everywhere they go. They love to hear themselves shout out the obscenities of despair, defeat, and failure. Their gospel is negative thinking, their scripture is the morning headlines and the eleven o'clock news.

What makes these individuals so dangerous is that they usually come equipped with credentials a mile long. Their degrees, years of training, and so-called "vast experience" are used as weapons to lure unsuspecting throngs of would-be followers. I call these negative-thinking experts *Negatroids*. They come from the land of cynicism. They believe only in what has the capacity to fail, and their major victory is converting an idealist into a skeptic.

If you are not on guard against Negatroids, you are almost certain to become their victim. You see, individuals such as I am describing are much like the sea. We can either choose to sail through them without letting any water in, or we can open the hatch and sink. Once again, the choice is ours.

Essentially, we must learn to listen *selectively* to what the Negatroid says. Studies have shown that approximately thirty percent of all the information that comes into our brain through our five senses is from "out there"— the environment, and about ninety-nine percent of that information is negative. The remaining seventy percent of the information we receive comes from our stored or repressed memories, sensations, impressions, images, and feelings, all of which are carefully housed within the depths of our unconscious. Of course, before the unconscious became unconscious, it was conscious. If our previous calculations are correct, we can say with fair certainty that most of that seventy percent is also negative! Considering these rather startling statistics, it is easy to understand why the phrase "We are our own worst enemy" is so apropos for most of us.

In order to counteract these negative forces produced by negative people and situations, it is imperative that we destroy not only the negativity already within us but also whatever is constantly being pumped in from the outside. If we fail to do this, our positive mental attitude survival mechanism will languish and eventually die. And with it, of course, will go the basic life elements. To best achieve resistance to negative forces (Negatroids), it is essential that we learn to program the brain effectively. As with most things, however, programming the brain is easier said than done!

To program the brain effectively against negativity requires that we first accept certain universal concepts. Perhaps foremost is that we accept the reality that "one's attitude *does* determine one's altitude"—that attitude *does* make a difference, that it is more important even than fact.

Unfortunately, it is difficult for most people to grasp the importance of attitude in living a happy, productive life. Although the fulfillment of our hopes and dreams is in large measure a result of the attitude we maintain in daily living, few of us give much attention to the development of this attitude, which is our most precious commodity. We do, however, without so much as a second thought, devote enormous time, energy, and personal resources to the enhancement of our knowledge and to the acquisition of "things."

Although I am certainly one hundred percent in favor of people's increasing their knowledge or purchasing a home or new car, I believe the flow of our life energies is frequently misdirected when technology (knowledge) and possessions take precedence over the enhancement of attitudes.

People may give lip service to the importance of attitude, voicing such statements as "stay positive," "get an attitude adjustment," or "be careful, what you say is what you get," but in reality, most of us live our lives quite differently. Instead of devoting time and energy toward developing our attitudes, we spend that time and effort toward less enduring pursuits. The end result of our faulty prioritizing is that our attitudes, instead of becoming more positive and resilient, begin to languish and, in many instances, turn negative and ultimately self-destructive.

Let us examine, for instance, what happens to us as we go through our life cycle. We spend anywhere from twelve to sixteen years of our lives obtaining a formal education (some of us a little less, others a little more) and anywhere from forty to fifty years working, either for ourselves or for someone else. Throughout our entire formal education or work careers, few of us will take one course, seminar, or workshop on how to acquire, develop, and maintain a positive mental attitude. Probably, most of us will die without having heard even one speaker give a five-minute lecture on the subject of positive mental attitude.

Fewer than five percent of us will have read one positive-thinking book or listened to one inspirational tape. And yet countless millions among us will have routinely gone to bed with the sirens, screams, and psychic maiming of the eleven o'clock news still ringing in our ears. Is it any wonder that we live in a negative world?

Still, some individuals deny the effects of such continuing emotional bombardment. They have become so emotionally numbed that, even in the midst of the most chilling carnage, they have become immune to the suffering of their fellow humans.

The Pike Experiment

One of the most famous stories in the annals of scientific literature illustrating the power of programming—in this case, negative programming—is the so-called Pike Experiment. Several years ago a group of scientists placed a large Northern pike in a tank filled with minnows. Now if you know anything about the Northern pike, you know this fish has huge, razor-sharp teeth and a voracious appetite. It is so vicious when feeding that it has been called the "freshwater barracuda."

The Northern pike used in this experiment swam about freely, devouring every minnow in sight. Then, in a second phase of the experiment, the scientists placed a clear Plexiglas barrier in the middle of the tank. The pike was on one side of the barrier and the minnows on the other.

At first the pike seemed content to watch as the minnows swam about on their side of the tank. Soon, however, it decided it was time for a snack. WHAM! Its pointed snout smashed into the invisible barrier. WHAM! WHAM! WHAM! Again and again the pike tried desperately to reach the delectable morsels. But all its efforts were in vain.

Soon the great fish grew weary and defeated. It settled down at the bottom corner of the tank and seemed to stare out at the world with angry indignation. At this point, the scientists performed phase three of the experiment: they removed the barrier. The minnows almost immediately started swimming around the entire area of the tank.

They swam under and around the pike. They bumped into its long toothy snout and nibbled at its huge dorsal fin. Nothing happened! All the pike seemed capable of doing was to brood and glare helplessly at its captors. After a while the scientists poked and prodded the pike themselves in an attempt to get it to move. Day in and day out they introduced new methods to encourage the great fish to eat—to *survive*. All was in vain.

One day, a researcher came to check on the pike's condition. He found the giant fish floating on its back, dead of starvation! Programmed to believe it could never again capture its food, this fierce predator had given up the struggle for life.

Psychologists call this kind of experiment "aversive conditioning." The name we choose to give it, however, is unimportant. The fact remains that many of us are exactly like that pike. We have been so beaten and battered by life that we no longer feel up to the task of living, let alone prospering. The irony, of course, is that even as we complain and are ready to quit, countless opportunities arise literally under our noses, awaiting our discovery. But alas, like the pike, we choose to starve to death in a sea of plenty.

Where, then, does *positive* programming fit in? Surely, if a bunch of scientists can program a fish to starve itself to death, human beings can program themselves to succeed in life. I think the average person is smarter than the average fish!

To program ourselves positively we must be willing to accept one basic and unchanging principle: WE ARE WHAT WE CHOOSE TO BE. No matter how we may struggle against this principle, it remains steadfast. You see, the brain works like a garden—what we plant will grow. If we choose to plant the seeds of success and happiness, our lives will be radiantly successful and happy. If we choose to sow the seeds of failure and despair, we will reap the fruits of failure and despair. Even though we may resist accepting the idea, the choice is ours to make.

Why is it that so many of us make the wrong choices in life? It seems that no matter how hard we try or how noble our intentions, we continue to fail. The answer to this perplexing question can be summed up in one word: *change.*

We are so fearful of changing who we are to what we could be that we avoid change at all costs. Many of us, of course, camouflage this avoidance with elaborate smoke screens to confuse ourselves and others. Some of the biggest failures think their lives are perfectly acceptable, and they have everyone, *especially themselves,* convinced of this. In their denial, these failures have carefully learned how to be comfortable with their misery. But when the dust clears, there they stand, like that proverbial "Rock of Gibraltar." Unfortunately, their foundation is shifting sand.

How Can We Change Ourselves?

It is *wanting* to change and *choosing* to change that actually produces change. There is an enormous discrepancy between what we *think* we are doing and what we actually do or what we *say* we do and what we actually do.

Many clients of mine honestly believe they are changing—or trying to change. In truth, vast numbers of them are engaging in a charade. They may superficially "try," but their private fears keep them locked into old patterns. Many times they will confess their desire to change, they will speak the words, but no change comes because they take no action. Their words fall, empty, and like dry leaves are quickly blown away. Instead of belief and courage they have doubt and fear; instead of action, stagnation.

Every now and then one of them will actually take the first honest step they have ever taken towards maturity. They *speak* change, then they *believe* change is possible, and then they put that belief into *action*. The magic combination of speaking, believing (thinking), and action is what produces results!

People don't and won't change because their negative self-image will not allow them to. Life has so beaten them down that choosing anything but failure is foreign to them. Despite protests to the contrary, once a person gets accustomed to and comfortable with losing, it tends to become a habit. Any semblance of self-esteem they may have had is gone.

Genuine self-esteem comes from learning healthy self-love, not the narcissistic love promoted by Hollywood and the daytime "soaps." You have to say *and believe*, "I deserve the best *in spite* of my past." But saying it is not enough. You have to go out there with conviction and a consistent effort and *do* the things that produce the changes you desire. That is what produces the foundation for a positive mental attitude and good self-image and, with it, the *inner* change necessary for personal growth.

Real change means getting out of our "Comfort Zone," as James Newman calls it,[7] and daring to accept, in a responsible way, all the challenges life offers us. It means getting off the easy chair and into the trenches. Perhaps this entire concept can best be summarized in D. H. Lawrence's great poem, "Vitality:"[8]

VITALITY

Alas, my poor young men,
do you lack vitality?

Has the shell grown too heavy for the tortoise?
Does he just squirm?

Is the frame of things too heavy
for poor young wretched men?
Do they jazz and jump and wriggle
and rush about in machines
and listen to bodiless noises
and cling to their thin young women
as to the last straw

just in desperation,
because their spirit can't move?
Because their hope is pinned down by the system
and can't even flutter?

Well, well, if it is so it is so;
but remember, the undaunted gods
give vitality still to the dauntless.

And sometimes they give it as love,
ah love, sweet love, nòt so easy!
But sometimes they give it as lightning.

And it's no good wailing for love
if they only offer you lightning.
And it's no good mooning for sloppy ease
when they're holding out the thunderbolt
for you to take.

You might as well take the lightning
for once, and feel it go through you.
You might as well accept the thunderbolt
and prepare for storms.

You'll not get vitality any other way.

Positive Mental Attitude Survival Mechanism Strategies

Strategy #1: Associate with the Winners!

Attitudes, positive or negative, are contagious. Acceptance of this one principle will carry you far toward achieving your goals in life. If you're hanging around negative individuals, disassociate yourself from them . . . *fast!* What they have may be catching. You will find it takes much less energy to be around positive people, and the rewards are far greater.

Another expression I have for this strategy is the "steer clear of what you fear" strategy. We should hold a genuine fear of the *Negatroids* who may find their way into our lives and make a strong effort to "steer clear" of them. If we don't, their message of gloom and doom will become our lasting legacy. Instead of victory in our lives, we will inherit their mantle of defeat.

To strengthen your positive mental attitude, go out of your way to associate with positive individuals who will allow you, by their very presence, to feed your mind with life-sustaining nourishment. Instead of pulling you down, they will uplift you. Instead of holding you back, they will urge you forward.

A few years ago I was involved in a business enterprise with several people who were among the most positive, upbeat folks I have ever been privileged to know. They thought, spoke, and acted as if each day were a gold mine just waiting to be discovered. I benefited from their presence in my life, not only financially but, more important, in my personal growth. Perhaps the most valued lesson I learned from them is that the difference between a winner and loser in life is whether you get up after you've been knocked down.

Their credo was to live each day by the "Golden Rule." They believed that when you give yourself away in the service of others, it will come back to you tenfold. I have attempted to follow that philosophy and found that, the more I have been able to give, the more I have received— frequently out of proportion to what I have given!

I cite this example to illustrate the importance of our associations. If we are to develop the positive mental attitude survival mechanism, it is crucial that we keep our associations—whether friendships, business dealings, or casual social relations—positive and that we "steer clear" of the Negatroids.

Franklin D. Roosevelt put the matter correctly in his famous declaration that "The only thing we have to fear is fear itself." I would, however, like to humbly amend his immortal words by adding "and Negatroids." Other than a charging lion, I honestly believe that Negatroids are the only real threat to a positive-thinking person. Negatroids are dream stealers who will *always* want to steal your dream simply because they don't have a dream of their own. It is always the association with non-dreamers that holds us back from improving our lives.

This contention is borne out by current research. A few years ago Drs. Samuel Yochelson and Stanton E. Samenow studied the criminal personality in a comprehensive way. Among other things, they wanted to determine the degree to which criminals bonded together for mutual support and collaboration. They found conclusive evidence that, not only did "crooks run with crooks," but once a criminal way of life became firmly established, rehabilitative efforts could do little to change it.[9] Such studies prove irrefutably that when you run with winners you become a winner, and if you choose to run with losers you will inevitably become a loser yourself.

One of my absolutely favorite wild creatures is the American bald eagle. It is befitting that this glorious creature is our national symbol. With a wingspread of from six to seven feet, its magnificent white head and tail framing its powerful body, this monarch of the skies soars for miles from the Gulf of Mexico north to the Arctic. You will rarely find the bald eagle or any of its cousins flying in a flock, because unlike chickens, eagles are loners. The only ones able to keep up with them are other eagles.

When you decide with whom you will choose to associate, ask yourself this question: "Would I like to fly with the eagles, or would I rather scratch with the chickens?"

During the years I have practiced as a therapist, I have dealt with thousands of hurting people. For years it remained a mystery to me why so many of them chose failure over success. It eventually dawned on me that they chose failure simply because their self-images dictated that they do so. And the single most important reason they could not elevate the self-image was their associations. They were so afraid of who they *could* become that they chose to cling to losers who insured their failure and galvanized their low self-esteem.

When seeking out associations, be sure to look for people whose views of life are at least as affirmative as your own. Their thought processes, hopes, dreams, goals, principles, attitudes, and life-views should be at or above the same positive level. If you feel your own level of self-view is low, stay away from anyone whom you perceive to be at or near the same level of negativity! Reach beyond yourself and go with the more mature, positive individual.

Any person whose level of positive mental attitude is lower than yours will tend to pull you down to his or her level. You will rarely, if ever, pull him or her up. The clearest evidence of this occurs when a spouse-to-be thinks he or she will change the alcoholic fiance. Such marriage partners realize only years later, all too tragically, that "I'm stuck with an alcoholic who refuses to change."

Strategy #2: Programming the Mind

To develop the positive mental attitude survival mechanism to its fullest, we must learn to program the greatest computer known to man: the human brain. If we could only realize what a marvel of engineering our brains are, we would treat them with the dignity and awe they deserve.

An article in *Time* magazine summarized the brain eloquently: "the brain is the master control, the guiding genius behind all of man's actions .... Everything that man has ever been, everything he will ever be, is the product of his brain."[10]

The average brain weighs only about three pounds. It contains, however, between ten billion and one hundred billion neurons—the brain's information transmitters. Each of these neurons "transacts business" with neighboring neurons at lightning speed. While a sophisticated high-tech computer can store and recall some one hundred billion bits of information, the capacity of the brain seems infinite. It is a warehouse with the capacity to store trillions of bits of information that can theoretically be recalled at any time. Within a split second it can process countless sensations, thoughts, feelings, ideas, and reactions.

As further reported in *Time,* scientific studies have documented conclusively that "some of the brain's chemical reactions take as little as one-millionth of a second. As many as one hundred thousand neurons may be involved in transmitting the information that results in as simple an action as stepping back to avoid being struck by an oncoming car."[11] With this knowledge, it is easy to understand how people's lives can "pass before them" when threatened with catastrophe!

When compared to a man-made computer, the human brain is so superior that the most advanced computer, even those still being developed, cannot begin to measure up. If we could imagine a computer that could contain the same number of bits as the average human brain, it would be a hundred stories tall and cover the state of Texas. Even then, it would be only a second-rate imitation. No computer, no matter how sophisticated, can begin to compare with the three-pound miracle.

Programming the brain is a three-step process. These three steps are the result of three distinct but mutually interdependent systems or mental processes that we need to be aware of when we set about the task of programming our brains.

First of all, like computers our brains have an *input system.* This is the system into which information is fed—basically, our five senses. To program the brain positively, therefore, we must see, hear, touch, feel, and smell positive things. If we choose (as many of us do) to program the brain negatively, all we have to do is reverse this process.

Second, our brains have a *throughput system*. This is the system that actually processes the information that the input system allows in. It is the conscious and unconscious part of our mind that assimilates, rejects, partializes, synthesizes, and integrates information into some kind of meaningful whole. The throughput system enables us to absorb information from both within and without so that we don't psychologically and emotionally regurgitate it the minute it hits us.

Third, our brains possess an *output system*. This refers to what comes out of our mouths and other overt and covert actions we use that reflect what the other two systems have already processed. It is, ultimately, the "finished product."

Now, a very interesting phenomenon occurs as the words and/or actions of the output system issue forth. These very words and actions, even as they are being spoken and performed, return once again to our input systems! The entire cycle, positive or negative, is then reinforced as the process is repeated again and again. When we view the matter this way, we find it easy to understand how bad habits become established, because, once we are locked into negative patterns of feeling, thinking, speaking, and doing, it becomes almost impossible to change them—even *with* positive thinking! The best solution is not to get into the negative habit patterns in the first place.

To program the brain effectively with positive thoughts and emotions we need to feed it the right information. In the next two sections, you will read about the strategies that I consider to be the most important for programming the brain positively. But remember, *you* must do the programming. Because the brain never sleeps, unless we consciously and actively determine to program it positively it will automatically receive the negative inputs from the media, from Negatroids, and from life events that continuously bombard all of us, and it will recycle those negative inputs perpetually, thus locking us into a permanent negative pattern.

Strategy #3: Watch What You Say to Stay Out of Harm's Way!

When we stop to think about it, it is an astonishing phenomenon that from time immemorial, virtually everything that has ever happened (or will happen) was *spoken* into existence. Clinical observations tend to support the notion that "What you say is what you get." Indeed, words, mere words, are the most powerful force in the universe because they come from thoughts. And thoughts and ideas represent power. As we have discovered, when we have an idea and then speak it, the next logical step is for the idea to be transformed into action. When we consider that seventy percent of what we say is said to *ourselves*, it behooves us to say the *right* things, since those words will become actions. Those actions will in turn result in a pattern of life.

The strategy of speaking positively is highly important in strengthening the positive mental attitude survival mechanism. What makes it so is the fact that most people suffering from depression, guilt, fear, worry, and other debilitating emotions are generally negative-thinking and *negative-speaking* individuals. As a result, their positive mental attitude survival mechanism is woefully inadequate for sustaining the four basic life elements.

Such people, as a result, lack adequate *inner strength*. Clearly, they perceive themselves and their circumstances to be out of *control* most of the time. They lack the level of sufficient *self-esteem* to carry them through life's inevitable pitfalls. And, despite the frenzy of their daily activities, their lives are devoid of *meaning* and purpose. The central theme of this book is that without these four basic life elements to sustain us, we cannot achieve personal happiness.

OH, MY ACHING HEAD! Frequently, deficiencies in the strategy of speaking positively manifest themselves as psychosomatic disorders. One of my clients, a handsome, intelligent man in his late thirties named Bob, is a classic illustration of this phenomenon. Bob suffers from migraine headaches. He's had them for the past fifteen years. Despite visits to some of the country's leading medical experts, he continues to go through hell. Not only does he suffer the actual physical distress of the headaches, he is also clinically depressed over not being able to find a cure for the problem. When I see Bob I usually greet him with the question, "How are things going, Bob?" And without fail he responds with, "Oh, fair to middlin'—not too good, not too bad."

Each time I get that response I think of one of my favorite expressions, one that describes the condition of "average": best of the worst and worst of the best. What a way for a man or woman to go through life!

Several times I have discussed Bob's self-image with him. Recently I asked him, "Bob, how do you ever expect to get better when you keep programming yourself to stay sick?" His answer both astonished and saddened me. With an "I give up" shrug he said, "Well, Paul, I don't really mind the headaches that much any more. In fact, they're kind of comforting—almost like a friend. Actually, if I ever got rid of them now, I honestly don't know what I'd do. They're like an old pair of shoes: they bother me, but somehow I just can't bring myself to part with them."

I couldn't believe my ears. He was not only lying to himself, he actually *believed* his own lies! How sad that so many of us persist doggedly in this kind of circular mental programming. It is so vitally important to accept, as scientific fact, that *what we say is what we get*, to realize that we can't have it if we don't say it. And if we don't want it, if we say it we're going to get it! It is therefore necessary that we start . . . *RIGHT NOW*, saying the *right* things—positive things—in order to strengthen the positive mental attitude survival mechanism and, with it, the four basic life elements.

Remember that your attitude is most important when you are *alone* with your thoughts and feelings. These quiet moments are the breeding ground of self-doubt and fear. What do you say to yourself during these unprotected moments? What kinds of self-statements do you make without even realizing it? Do you catch yourself saying such words as *try, can't,* or *quit?* To develop the positive mental attitude survival mechanism you must eliminate these and similar words from your vocabulary.

As I point out below in a section on visualization, our minds think in terms of mental images. When we want to program it positively, therefore, we must speak (and think) in positive, descriptive phrases. Depending on our wishes, for example, we should practice making such statements as, "I can feel the warm ocean lapping gently at my feet as I'm walking along with my beloved on Waikiki Beach"; or "I can see that extra money from my raise going toward the log cabin in the mountains we've dreamed about for so long"; or "I can see the white blood cells chewing up and grinding to pieces every cancer cell in my body"; or "It is so wonderful to feel the pain of my depression lifting like a dark cloud from my mind."

Strategy #4: Visualize Your Way to Personal Happiness

Much has been written about the subject of imagery and visualization. Over the past fifteen years, giant strides have been made in research and therapy demonstrating beyond doubt that what we see in the mind's eye will affect the outcome of our lives.

Fears, anger, guilt, worries, insomnia, backaches, headaches, depression, lack of self-confidence, bad habits, and a host of other useless human maladies can be traced to the way we mentally "see" or visualize things. These same negative emotions and physical problems can also be dramatically eliminated or alleviated simply by learning to *see* ourselves and our circumstances more optimistically.

Researchers have demonstrated that our imaginations can pattern certain nerve impulses in the brain—positive or negative—that, if uninterrupted, can become habitual. So we reinforce habits, good or bad, by *mentally practicing* them in a persistent way.

If, for example, we are chronic procrastinators, all we need do to maintain this habit is to visualize ourselves in this role and to speak it into existence. If we wish to break this habit, we need to see ourselves as efficient and organized. But this change will come only through deliberate and systematic practice.

Research has shown that positive, protracted imagery has a powerful effect on the autonomic nervous system. By continuous practice and repetition, we can program our autonomic nervous system to literally believe *anything*—positive or negative. By continuously visualizing yourself as an expert golfer, for instance, you will become one. Or if you persist in seeing yourself as a "failure of the fairway," you will achieve that end also.

When you are sad or depressed, you need to rid yourself of the image of loss that is causing the sad and depressed feelings. If you feel anxious or fearful, you need to rid yourself of whatever threat is producing the fear.

Hope for any of these problems comes from gaining personal *objectivity* and *control*. Here again, we see the four basic life elements coming into play. If we can learn to detach ourselves from our fears and depression, for example, and to do something about them *before* they gain a stranglehold on us, then we achieve a measure of control over these monsters.

To enhance the positive mental attitude survival mechanism we must learn to systematically and deliberately *force* negative images out of our minds by refusing to participate in negative thinking. Instead of seeing ourselves as fearful, we need to see ourselves as courageous. Rather than holding onto thoughts of depression, we need to imagine ourselves joyously running barefoot on the beach. Instead of entertaining a self-image of defeat, we should imagine ourselves, in vivid detail and living color, as successful human beings.

The more successful we become at visualizing, the

more likely we are to achieve our dreams and goals. If we desire a successful marriage, instead of simply yearning for the day when that wish becomes a reality we should see that day as already here—*now*. The more effectively we maintain images of personal control, the more likely we will possess our heart's desire. Albert Einstein said, "Imagination is more important than knowledge." Don't worry about learning all kinds of elaborate techniques or theories. Learning to use mental imagery and visualization is simple. Your own personal motivation is the most important ingredient toward its mastery.

HOW TO VISUALIZE To properly visualize what you want, all you need to do is follow these five steps:

1. Accept the fact that you possess a powerful force . . . *your imagination,* and that you are going to use it successfully to visualize what you want.
2. Set aside a couple of times each day when you can be alone with your thoughts and feelings.
3. Locate a comfortable chair in which to sit. Avoid lying down, because you should not fall asleep. Deliberately let go of muscle tensions. *RELAX.*
4. Take in a deep breath and let it out slowly. Wait a few seconds and repeat. Do this for two or three minutes, or until you feel a sense of calm and serenity—just as you do when meditating. Meditation and visualization are parallel pursuits except that meditation is the more passive art while visualization, as the fifth step indicates, requires a more conscious effort.
5. Vividly and carefully imagine, *in exquisite detail,* precisely what you want. Do not focus on what you *don't* want; that's negative. See yourself, instead, as actually acquiring the thing in life that really matters to you. Vividly picture events, feelings, thoughts as occurring in the manner you would like to see them occur in reality. If, for example, you have concerns regarding illness, death of a loved one, a career change, or relation-

ship problems, see yourself mastering the situation. Hear the actual words you will say.
Experience the thoughts, feelings, and sensations
you are likely to have. Picture yourself actually
going through whatever actions you are likely to
go through . . . and doing it successfully! What
does the ad say? "Master the possibilities."

This exercise will force you to consciously and deliberately focus on images that will ultimately forge a
thought process clearer and more distinct than the one
you may currently possess. It prepares you more effectively
for the future.

That's it! If you follow this game plan, your positive
mental attitude survival mechanism will be profoundly
strengthened. Your four basic life elements will increase
and be sustained, and you will be a happier and more
prosperous person.

*Strategy #5: Read the Right Books, Listen to the Right
Tapes, Attend the Right Seminars*

THE BOOKS Twelve years have passed since I first
picked up and read Napoleon Hill's legendary book, *Think
and Grow Rich.*[12] I remember poring over every word in
that classic as its timeless truths spoke to me. I didn't
consciously realize it then, but I was strengthening my
positive mental attitude survival mechanism. I needed
what that book had to say . . . right then! My mental attitude was at low tide, and Hill's magic words were breathing new life into my weary spirit.

From *Think and Grow Rich* I moved on to another
classic, Dr. David J. Schwartz's *The Magic of Thinking
Big.*[13] To this day I can recall his words hitting me like a
Mack truck: "How you think determines how you act. How
you act in turn determines how others react to you."

Such a simple truth—and yet how elusive it had been
to me. I read and reread that line probably a hundred times.
I kept thinking that if such a simple and yet profound truth

could elude me, then surely countless tens of thousands and perhaps millions of other people who had never even picked up a positive-thinking book were also unaware of it. I could not help feeling that much of the frustration, bitterness, and resentment in the world could be eliminated if Schwartz's simple axiom were followed in practice.

Soon I began a serious study of the positive-thinking writers. These included Robert Schuller, Og Mandino, Napoleon Hill, Maxwell Maltz, Dale Carnegie, Norman Vincent Peale,[14] and a host of others. They all seemed to have one basic message: *how and what you think determines the way your life will turn out.* If you think positively, hopefully, optimistically, your life will be a success—by whatever standards you measure success. If you think negatively, despairingly, your life is sure to fail. Period!

I kept reading. After a while, I noticed a curious phenomenon occurring. I was becoming more and more optimistic with each passing day. Although this occurrence might not seem noteworthy, in truth it was. What made it almost heroic was the fact that I continued to work in an extremely negative environment without its having much lasting impact on me! This phenomenon is so important that I need to explain its effect on both clients and colleagues.

SO WHAT'S NEW AT THE ZOO? I have practiced marital and family therapy for seventeen years. Before that I was employed as a social worker with a child welfare agency, an inner-city settlement house, and the Big Brother organization. This amounts to twenty-four years of direct, hands-on work with people who are hurting.

During this time I observed the human spirit both triumph and crumble. Sadly, the vast majority of clients I have seen in treatment have failed. For years, convinced that improper training and general ineptitude somehow ill-prepared me to save the human race, I blamed myself for this phenomenon.

After long, anguishing years, however, I gradually realized that my so-called failures were not unique. Moreover, I discovered that my colleagues were not having much better luck! And upon close scrutiny of the scientific literature, I found that study after study bore out the dismal failure record of most forms of psychotherapeutic treatments.

I began to ask myself: why? Why, with all the training, experience, and ongoing self-study was the community of mental health practitioners rendered virtually helpless to accomplish the task for which they had been so carefully prepared?

The answer came. It did not, however, come with a resounding, "AHA! The fault lies here!" No. Instead, it was more subtle, much more elusive. While searching for an answer, I spoke with many of my colleagues and colleague-friends. I also interviewed dozens of professionals from several mental health-related disciplines. I questioned countless clients and friends of clients, client family members, and a host of others who were part of the client support network. I approached this task cautiously and meticulously, the way one would approach a research project.

At first I asked the obvious questions. I then went on to more sophisticated, detailed questions designed to give me insight into the issue of failure. What I found, from clients and professionals alike, was confirmation that the *overwhelming majority of clients were continuing to fail, despite the best available clinical help.* If clients were depressed, they continued to be depressed. If children were in trouble with the law, they continued to be in trouble with the law. If young men and women were chronically unemployed, they continued to be unemployed. If people were alcoholic or drug-dependent, they remained so. And so forth. It made no difference what the symptoms were, the list of failures was endless and chronic.

Whenever possible, I attempted to interview clients in their homes. I found this setting to be a more low-key, relaxed atmosphere in which to discuss important life issues. More important, it gave me the opportunity to observe people as they *really are*, on their home turf. One of my observations, the one that, as it turned out later, proved to be among the most important, was that most clients had *no books in their homes!* This excludes, of course, such books as telephone directories, cookbooks, or other utilitarian books necessary for the performance of routine tasks.

Also noteworthy was that, even in clients' homes where some books were evident, I could find no books advocating positive thinking. In those homes where books were present, the vast majority were of the murder mystery, romance, or suspense/novel variety.

Whenever I asked clients if they had ever read anything by Norman Vincent Peale, Og Mandino, or some of the other positive-thinking authors, the answer was predictably negative. Not only had they never read any of these classic works, most had never even heard of them or their authors.

I always suggested that the clients "pick up a copy of . . . " and here I would recommend a specific book to fit their needs . . . at a local bookstore and begin to apply its contents to their lives. I recommended that they *purchase* a paperback edition rather than checking out a copy at the library. I did this purposely to encourage clients to underline important sections and commit them to memory.

The predictable response was indifference, or a limp "I'll have to try that sometime." This answer was common even among clients whose lives were in the worst turmoil imaginable. The moment I heard the word "try," I *knew* they would never do it. A few clients purchased a book, took it home, and then never picked it up again. Even fewer purchased it, *actually read it,* but then relegated it permanently to some dusty corner.

There were, however, a handful of clients—perhaps one in a hundred—genuinely interested in my suggestion and motivated enough to follow the idea through. They thanked me, went out (many that very day!) to purchase the book and, like starvation victims, literally devoured every word in it.

When I went back to see those individuals, perhaps a week or two later, they were excited and eager to talk with me about the contents of the book and, more important, about application of its lessons to their personal lives. These same people were also receptive to any other positive-thinking books and related materials I might recommend to them. In fact, several of them asked me such questions as: "Has Norman Vincent Peale written other books besides *The Power of Positive Thinking?*"

The overwhelming majority of those clients who became "positively addicted" to reading the self-help, positive-thinking books improved their lives significantly. They strengthened their positive mental attitude survival mechanism, benefiting the four basic life elements as a result. Understandably, the basic element that seemed to be most dramatically affected was *self-esteem.*

Therapists I interviewed had only a slightly better track record when it came to reading positive-thinking books. Most of them thought such books were "pure hype," superficial, or not "scholarly" enough to merit their attention. Interestingly, these same therapists readily devoured mystery novels, sometimes one a week, claiming such reading was "relaxing" and "therapeutic."

Most of the mystery and suspense thrillers therapists read were loaded with negative story lines. None of these therapists, however, believed that such negative programming had any effect whatever on their own attitudes and the possible negative messages they might subsequently convey to their clients. Moreover, these same therapists thought nothing of the fact that many of their clients were routinely engaged in reading negatively-oriented books and magazines. They made no connection between clients' reading matter and their mental state.

The so-called "professional reading" that therapists did also invariably had negative content. Such topics as drug and alcohol addiction, child sexual abuse and maltreatment, rape, incest, wife-battering, schizophrenia, depression, child-murder, and a host of other such topics were common fare. As with their inability to connect client reading habits with client attitudes, neither did the therapists seem able to equate their own reading habits with attitudinal difficulties they were experiencing. Add to this the negative input from television, movies, and the daily newspapers, and it seems little wonder that the "blind were leading the blind"!

Lest I be accused of overstating my case, I am eager to admit that many outstanding films and television programs are being produced. And we are fortunate to have many responsible journalists, novelists, and nonfiction writers who consistently offer us top-notch reading matter.

The mental health field, however, by definition, is a negative one. As such, those of us who work in it invariably and *voluntarily* subject ourselves to continuous bombardment from innumerable negative sources. As a result, we are programmed to expect negativity on a daily basis. It is not an exaggeration to say that, with rare exception, we *seek* negativity. Thus, even when we have the opportunity to choose the positive, hopeful, and optimistic, we invariably go with the negative out of habit. We are, paradoxically, predisposed to the negative over the positive even as we urge our clients to improve their lives by thinking positively!

This "double bind" undoubtedly creates enormous inner conflict for most therapists. To counter this, they seek out escapes in their reading and viewing matter. Those escapes are, however, ultimately negative and serve to cyclically reinforce the very dilemma of negative thinking from which therapists so desperately seek sanctuary. Although most therapists I interviewed were well-intentioned, well-trained, and *apparently* positive, the majority of them had been so completely negatively programmed (most without their conscious awareness) over the years that their helping qualities had been severely eroded.

I remain convinced that both the professionals and the clients I have studied would have fared much better had they been involved in an active, ongoing program of reading positively-oriented materials.

THE TAPES Today, opportunities for programming the brain to think optimistically are virtually limitless. Audio and video cassette tapes offer anything from a "pep talk" to entire programs on how to improve one's life. Granted, many of these programs are nothing more than "pep talks," but even so they serve the vital purpose of enhancing our positive mental attitude survival mechanism.

In addition to many excellent commercial films available, television, too, despite some exceptions, can provide both entertaining and educational programs of high quality. The self-improvement literature, both books and tapes, is so vast that we are foolish not to take advantage of the wealth of positive programming it provides.

Don't forget the huge selection of *musical* tapes available. Some of these, of course, are produced by known commercial artists, both instrumental and vocal. Others, however, while not featuring commercially known musicians, can prove highly valuable to enhancing your positive mental attitude survival mechanism. Some religious artists have produced tapes of "praise" music that, for many, provide meditative results facilitating positive mental programming.

Several firms offer *subliminal* tapes. These tapes normally carry "silent" messages of positive affirmations. Through elaborate technology, the listener hears only soothing music or waves breaking gently. Consciously unheard are powerful, positive affirmations dealing with everything from weight-loss to the enhancement of self-esteem. The messages are designed to penetrate the listener's unconscious mind through the caressing music and the relaxation it promotes. As one listens, defenses are lowered, and the unconscious is freed to absorb the affirmations.

WORKSHOPS AND SEMINARS Should you ever be afforded the opportunity of attending a workshop or seminar on positive mental attitudes, I strongly encourage you to take advantage of it. I have attended many of these. The atmosphere is usually so positive and upbeat that, if I should be feeling a little blue, they never fail to lift my spirits. Larger functions normally feature major speakers of the stature of Robert Schuller, Denis Waitley, or Leo Buscaglia. Such speakers are usually so inspirational that one's spirit and attitude cannot help being energized.

240

Workshops dealing with everything from self-image improvement to enhanced interpersonal relations are conducted from coast to coast. Needless to say, the *quality* of these functions is only as good as the leaders conducting them. Countless charlatans are out there making a fortune on P.T. Barnum's astute observation: "A sucker is born every minute." There are, however, many highly qualified leaders who routinely give workshops or seminars around the country, usually in major metropolitan centers. Some gear their presentations to professional audiences while others are more lay oriented. Some presenters are so skilled that their appeal is universal.

Watch and listen for ads on television and radio to know when key speakers may be coming to your area. Your local newspaper will probably carry an advertisement when an important seminar or workshop is being held locally or regionally. Public libraries, colleges, and universities frequently post notices for important seminars and lectures. Registration at one of these will undoubtedly land you on a mailing list so that you'll be notified of others to come.

Unfortunately, most of the better seminars charge a fee, and from one to two hundred dollars a day is not uncommon. Despite the cost, however, most people who attend these sessions find the money well spent. The benefits gained from a well conceived, well run seminar on achieving improved self-esteem can last a lifetime.

Formula for an Improved Positive Mental Attitude

Below is a partial list of activities that, if done on a consistent basis, will significantly help increase your positive mental attitude survival mechanism.

1. Each night, spend at least a half-hour reading a positive book, magazine, or similar piece of literature. I suggest reading at night because that is when the content of what you read is more likely to be absorbed by your unconscious mind.

Although literally hundreds of books are available, there are certain "classics" I like to recommend. They include *The Magic of Thinking Big* by David J. Schwartz, *Think and Grow Rich* by Napoleon Hill, *See You at the Top* by Zig Ziglar,*[15] *How to Win Friends and Influence People* by Dale Carnegie, *The Power of Positive Thinking* by Norman Vincent Peale, and *Move Ahead with Possibility Thinking* by Dr. Robert Schuller.

2. Pick out specific words, phrases, or sentences from positive mental attitude books (or think of your own statements) and print or type them on three inch by five inch cards. Carry a set of these affirmation cards in your pocket or purse. Read these affirmations at least six or eight times daily—if possible, speaking them out loud. This habit will reinforce the positive messages you want your unconscious mind to record.

Remember, if you do a thing twenty times it becomes a habit. If you do it a hundred times, it becomes a way of life.

3. Invest in a quality cassette tape player. Begin to build a library of positive mental attitude audio cassette tapes that you can play when you're driving or riding or walking to and from work. For additional programming, purchase a video cassette recorder and start regularly viewing positive mental attitude videocassette tapes instead of the latest sitcoms. Considering the enduring nature of your investment, both audio and video tapes are priced fairly reasonably. Each time you play a tape you increase the strength of your positive mental attitude survival mechanism. Many of the same people whose books I recommend have also produced both audio and video pro-

---

*I once suggested this book to a colleague. His response was, "I don't like the title. If I ever write a book, I'm going to call it 'See You in the Middle.'" Do you think he needed to read Ziglar's book?

grams. Write to the book publishers for the address where an author's tapes can be purchased. Or check with your local bookseller or public library. Booksellers in particular can usually provide you with assistance on such matters as titles,·costs, and shipping time. Some of the larger booksellers frequently keep such audio and video tapes in stock themselves.

4. Attend functions where a positive mental attitude speaker is appearing. You may have no farther to go than your local church or temple. Guest speakers frequently appear at college campuses or public auditoriums. Big-name speakers like Zig Ziglar and Og Mandino are often booked into large music halls in major metropolitan areas by agents who advertise their appearances in advance.

As with all the survival mechanisms, it is crucial that you *do something* if you are to strengthen your positive mental attitude survival mechanism. I have absolute and unwavering confidence that if you do what I have suggested in these five strategies, your positive mental attitude survival mechanism will strengthen significantly. Moreover, you will experience a joy in your life that until now you may have thought was reserved for a chosen few.

Basic Life Elements Affected by the Positive Mental Attitude Survival Mechanism

First, self-image;
second, inner strength;
third, personal control;
and fourth, life meaning.

NOTES

1. Quoted in Judith Hooper and Dick Teresi, *The Three-Pound Universe* (New York: Macmillan Publishing Company, 1986), p. 43.

2. Quoted in Wilferd A. Peterson, *The New Book of the Art of Living* (New York: Simon and Schuster, 1963), p. 54.

3. *Ibid.*

4. Quoted by James L. Framo, in a lecture October 14, 1971, at Symposium on Family Psychotherapy, Georgetown University, Washington, D.C.

5. Russell Conwell, *Acres of Diamonds* (Old Tappan, New Jersey: Spire Books, 1960), pp. 9-10.

6. Robert H. Schuller, *Success Is Never Ending; Failure Is Never Final* (Nashville: Thomas Nelson Publishers, 1988), p. 69.

7. James W. Newman, *Release Your Brakes!* (New York: Warner Books, 1977), pp. 161-170.

8. Vivian de Sola Pinto and Warren Roberts, eds., *The Complete Poems of D.H. Lawrence* (New York: Penguin Books, 1971), pp. 558-559.

9. Samuel Yochelson and Stanton E. Samenow, *The Criminal Personality*, 3 Vols. (New York: Jason Aronson, 1986).

10. Peter Stoler, "Exploring the Frontiers of the Mind," *Time*, January 14, 1974, p. 50.

11. *Ibid.* p. 55.

12. Napoleon Hill, *Think and Grow Rich* (Greenwich: Fawcett Publications, 1960).

13. David J. Schwartz, *The Magic of Thinking Big* (New York: Cornerstone Library, 1965).

14. Dale Carnegie, *How To Win Friends and Influence People* (New York: Simon and Schuster, 1937); Maxwell Maltz, *Psycho-Cybernetics* (New York: Pocket Books, 1960); Og Mandino, *The Greatest Salesman In The World* (New York: Bantam Books, 1968); Mandino, *The Greatest Miracle In The World* (Bantam Books, 1975); Norman Vincent Peale, *The Power of Positive Thinking* (Old Tappan, New Jersey: Spire Books, 1956).

15. Zig Ziglar, *See You At The Top* (Gretna, Louisiana: Pelican Publishing Company, 1978).

SURVIVAL MECHANISM INVENTORY # 10
POSITIVE MENTAL ATTITUDE

Inventory Statements	Rating *Check Appropriate Box*					
	SA 5	A 4	U 3	D 2	SD 1	Score
1. *Most* of the time I see myself as a happy, optimistic person.						
2. As a rule, positive, optimistic people live longer, happier, and more prosperous lives.						
3. My parents have (or had) a tendency to "see the cup as half full rather than half empty."						
4. I believe the brain never sleeps, that it is programmed continuously.						
5. It is untrue that people with a positive mental attitude are usually "pollyannaish."						
6. I can remember, as a child, being taught by my parents to "think positive."						
7. I believe that whatever we speak, good or bad, will ultimately come to pass.						
8. If you have a positive mental attitude, you are less likely to have chronic serious life problems.						
9. Sometimes it is difficult to stay positive in a negative world.						
10. In the long run, it takes more energy to be negative than to be positive.						

SM Strength Quotient =

Key

SA - Strongly Approve
A - Approve
U - Undecided
D - Disapprove
SD - Strongly Disapprove

10 - 24 Weak
25 - 34 Average
35 - 50 Strong

Conclusion

ON A BEAUTIFUL FALL DAY a few years ago, while driving along the rim of the picturesque Allegheny Mountains, I witnessed a scene that has remained etched in my memory. Upon approaching a bend in the road, my eye caught what appeared to be a glow coming from the forest. Searching the source more intently, I noticed that the glow was nothing more than the bright morning sunlight bouncing off a cluster of birch trees. I slowed my car and, for a brief moment, remained transfixed. "Sunlight shining on ordinary, leafless birch trees," I thought, "has made the ordinary transcendent." As I moved into the shadows, however, the angle of light changed, and the trees no longer radiated the sun's light as they had just moments before. Once again, they melted into the forest and were gone.

When we change, *really change*, we stand on the threshold between light and darkness . . . between life and death. On the one hand, the forces of our destructive past pull us backward, and on the other, the positive forces pull us forward to the future. This is decision time. We must either let go of the past and move on or else allow ourselves to return to it and the life of sameness that caused our original misery and shame.

Frequently, as we march through life, we lose sight of our early visions and goals. The struggle to survive saps us of the crisp energies that in our formative years were so plentiful. The survival mechanisms can, however, redeem much of what was lost if we but learn how to use them effectively in daily living. Indeed, they represent a road map to the personal happiness and prosperity we all seek, their beauty resting in simplicity and accessibility to all.

To me, life poses one simple, fundamental question: When we come to the end of it, will our music still sing within us? The answer to this question, I feel, rests with our capacity to discover and strengthen those survival mechanisms that live within each of us. Someone once wisely said that knowledge is something we acquire from our own experience, whereas *wisdom* is what we have learned *plus* what others can teach us. Truly, if we could have the courage and honesty to look at our world and the universe of our own mind and enter our own darkest fears, then, I believe, wisdom would come.

Imagine yourself now lying upon some deserted beach overlooking the endless expanse of a great ocean. You are eighty years old. You're reflecting on a past life—*your* life. Not another soul is present as, in the silence, you contemplate the long stretch of years. Were they productive? Were they eventful? Most of all, were they happy? No answer comes save the echo of the life you have lived. No rush of insight other than your now time-worn memories. Think of yourself upon that beach and dare, just once more, to dream.

Bibliography

Benson, Herbert. *The Relaxation Response.* New York: Avon Books, 1975.

Berne, Eric. *What Do You Say After You Say Hello?* New York: Grove Press, 1972.

Boszormenyi-Nagy, Ivan, and James L. Framo, eds. *Intensive Family Therapy.* New York: Harper & Row, 1965.

Bowen, Murray. *Family Therapy in Clinical Practice.* New York: Jason Aronson, 1978.

Bristol, Claude M. *The Magic of Believing.* New York: Pocket Books, 1948.

Carnegie, Dale. *How to Stop Worrying and Start Living.* New York: Simon and Schuster, 1975.

———. *How to Win Friends and Influence People.* New York: Simon and Schuster, 1937.

Cousins, Norman. *Anatomy of an Illness as Perceived by the Patient.* New York: W.W. Norton, 1979.

Ellis, Albert, and Robert A. Harper. *A New Guide to Rational Living.* North Hollywood: Wilshire Book Co., 1975.

Erikson, Erik H. *Identity: Youth and Crisis.* New York: W.W. Norton, 1968.

Frankl, Viktor E. *Man's Search for Meaning: An Introduction to Logotherapy.* Boston: Beacon Press, 1962.

———. *The Unconscious God.* Translated by Phil Flayderman and F. Toby Weiss. New York: Simon and Schuster, 1975.

Freud, Anna. *The Ego and the Mechanisms of Defense.* Revised edition. New York: International Universities Press, 1966.

Freud, Sigmund. *A General Introduction to Psychoanalysis.* New York: Washington Square Press, 1935.

Gardner, John W. *Self-Renewal: The Individual and the Innovative Society.* New York: Harper Colophon, 1964.

Giblin, Les. *How to Have Confidence and Power in Dealing with People.* New York: The Benjamin Co., 1956.

Glasser, William. *Positive Addiction.* New York: Harper & Row, 1976.

———. *Reality Therapy.* New York: Perennial Library, 1975.

———. *Stations of the Mind.* New York: Harper & Row, 1981.

———. *Take Effective Control of Your Life.* New York: Harper & Row, 1984.

Goldstein, William N. *An Introduction to the Borderline Conditions.* Northvale, New Jersey: Jason Aronson, 1985.

Gorney, Roderic. *The Human Agenda.* New York: Bantam Books, 1972.

Hill, Napoleon. *Think and Grow Rich.* Revised edition. Greenwich: Fawcett Publications, 1960.

Hooper, Judith, and Dick Teresi. *The Three-Pound Universe.* New York: Macmillan Publishing Co., 1986.

Jampolsky, Gerald G. *Love is Letting Go of Fear.* New York: Bantam Books, 1979.

Kerr, Michael E. and Murray Bowen. *Family Evaluation.* New York: W.W. Norton, 1988.

Kroll, Jerome. *The Challenge of the Borderline Patient.* New York: W.W. Norton, 1988.

LeShan, Lawrence. *How to Meditate.* New York: Bantam Books, 1974.

Maltz, Maxwell. *Psycho-Cybernetics.* New York: Pocket Books, 1960.

Mandino, Og. *The Greatest Miracle in the World.* New York: Bantam Books, 1975.

———. *The Greatest Salesman in the World.* New York: Bantam Books, 1968.

———. *The Greatest Secret in the World.* New York: Bantam Books, 1972.

Maslow, Abraham H. *The Farther Reaches of Human Nature.* New York: Penguin Books, 1971.

Masterson, James F. *The Narcissistic and Borderline Disorders.* New York: Brunner/Mazel, 1981.

———. *The Search for the Real Self.* New York: The Free Press, 1988.

McGinnis, Alan L. *The Friendship Factor.* Minneapolis: Augsburg Publishing House, 1979.

Moody, Raymond A., Jr. *Laugh After Laugh: The Healing Power of Humor.* Jacksonville: Headwaters Press, 1978.

Newman, James W. *Release Your Brakes!* New York: Warner Books, 1977.

Peale, Norman V. *The Power of Positive Thinking.* Old Tappan, New Jersey: Spire Books, 1956.

Peck, M. Scott. *The Road Less Traveled.* New York: Touchstone, 1978.

Pelletier, Kenneth R. *Mind As Healer, Mind As Slayer: A Holistic Approach to Preventing Stress Disorders.* San Francisco: Delacorte Press, 1977.

Satir, Virginia. *Peoplemaking.* Palo Alto: Science and Behavior Books, 1972.

Schuller, Robert H. *Move Ahead with Possibility Thinking.* Old Tappan, New Jersey: Spire Books, 1967.

————. *Peace of Mind Through Possibility Thinking.* Garden City: Doubleday & Co., 1977.

————. *Success is Never Ending; Failure is Never Final.* Nashville: Thomas Nelson Publishers, 1988.

————. *The Be-Happy Attitudes.* Waco: Word Books, 1985.

Schwartz, David J. *The Magic of Thinking Big.* New York: Cornerstone Library, 1965.

Selye, Hans. *Stress Without Distress.* New York: New American Library, 1974.

Siegel, Bernie S. *Love, Medicine & Miracles.* New York: Perennial Library, 1986.

Strecker, Edward A., and Kenneth E. Appel. *Discovering Ourselves.* 3rd. edition. New York: The Macmillan Co., 1958.

Viscott, David. *Risking.* New York: Simon and Schuster, 1977.

Waitley, Denis. *Seeds of Greatness: The Ten Best-Kept Secrets of Total Success.* Old Tappan, New Jersey: Fleming H. Revell, 1983.

————. *The Psychology of Winning.* New York: Berkley Books, 1979.

Ziglar, Zig. *See You at the Top.* Gretna, Louisiana: Pelican Publishing Co., 1978.